$1000 Billion A Day

John Roberts is a freelance financial journalist.

JOHN ROBERTS

$1000 BILLION A DAY

Inside the Foreign Exchange Markets

HarperCollins*Publishers*

HarperCollins*Publishers*
77–85 Fulham Palace Road,
Hammersmith, London W6 8JB

A Paperback Original 1995
1 3 5 7 9 8 6 4 2

Copyright © John Roberts 1995

The Author asserts the moral right to
be identified as the author of this work

A catalogue record for this book
is available from the British Library

ISBN 0 00 638340 8

Set in Meridien by
Rowland Phototypesetting Limited
Bury St Edmunds, Suffolk

Printed in Great Britain by
HarperCollinsManufacturing Glasgow

To Alexander

Contents

Preface

Most of us are aware that exchange rates – particularly the value of the pound against other currencies – affect us. Usually the impact is adverse through the need to raise interest rates, or inability to lower them because of what is happening to sterling. Very few people realize that dealing on the foreign exchange markets is many times the value of international trade. Most of it is speculation.

When the television news, reporting yet another sterling crisis, shows shirt-sleeved yobs screaming down two telephones at once, selling the pound short (while others shout at them to sell more), what is going on? This book tells who moves the currency markets, how they do it and why.

1

MARKETS RULE. OKAY (?)

'Lower here!' he shouts.

The speaker, Andre Katz, is thirty-one. He is a dealer in what he calls 'cable'. He talks all day long of being 'paid £10', being 'given $20', but on an average day he alone reckons to turn over $1.8 billion. That's about £250 billion a year and more than the annual sales of Britain's thirty-five largest companies combined. When he says £10 or $20 he's counting in millions. 'Cable' is the £:$ exchange rate.

Andre Katz is chief foreign exchange trader in Barclays' dealing room near the Tower of London. He shouts 'Lower here' to let those around him, dealers in other currencies, know the pound has eased significantly against the dollar. A few feet behind him sits Guy Hurley, one of the bank's small team of proprietary traders, buying currencies he hopes to sell at a higher exchange rate in a few days or weeks or, perhaps, selling first in the hope of buying them later at a lower rate. You could call him a currency speculator.

At the end of the day it is Guy's job – he's not sure why – to give the Visa credit card group's American headquarters the exchange rates London was quoting at the close of business. It will use those to charge in Deutschmarks the German paying with her card during a shopping trip to Paris and to convert the dollars spent by a British holidaymaker in Florida into sterling. This is what you might call bona fide foreign exchange: actual trade. It is a small part of trading in the world's dealing rooms.

The Bank for International Settlements, based in Basle, is in many ways the central bank of central banks. The Bank of England and its counterparts in most developed countries often treat the BIS as they would like their own commercial banks to behave towards them. It asked the Bank of England and central banks in twenty-five other countries to scrutinize all foreign-exchange dealing by banks, other dealers and brokers throughout April 1992. The BIS report, published almost a year later, said that this 'appears to have been a fairly calm month in the exchange markets . . . most dealers reporting . . . that activity was either below normal or normal.'

Once double-counting had been eliminated (because both sides of a transaction will report it) the BIS estimated that dealing on the world's foreign exchange markets in April 1992 amounted to $880 billion a day. This is more than twenty times the level of world trade. Direct investment – companies building factories and the like overseas – and portfolio investment by insurance companies, unit trusts and others buying foreign shares together is equivalent to between 10 and 15 per cent of foreign-exchange dealing. Thus no more than one fifth of foreign-exchange business is for trade and investment. The other four fifths is made up of the dealings of banks and other financial operators between themselves. They are trying to use money to make more money.

This phenomenon is growing. The BIS conducts such surveys every three years and this was the third. Between April 1989 and April 1992 global turnover in foreign exchange grew 42 per cent, several times faster than world trade and investment. Today foreign exchange dealing is reliably but unofficially estimated to exceed $1000 billion a day.

Speculators can make profits (and play a useful role) when they are an appropriate part of a market. A seller of corn, cocoa, copper or shares who finds there is not a big buyer around just when she needs to sell might be glad of the speculator who has no use for the commodity and buys only in the hope of profit when a buyer does turn up. But in the foreign exchange markets where four fifths of the dealing is without underlying purpose, speculation is close to becoming a zero-sum game: the total profits made by dealers can't be significantly different from the total losses.

Two factors could give the speculators a positive result overall:

- profits made at the expense of international traders and investors. It is notable that one of the fastest-growing activities in recent years has been corporate treasury; companies have been setting up their own treasury departments – some as large as the banks' own dealing rooms – so as to manage for themselves the interest rate and currency risks they previously entrusted to their bankers.
- intervention by the world's central banks trying to hold currencies at particular exchange rates. A central bank, such as the Bank of England, will hold the government's foreign exchange reserves. This 'kitty' of gold, foreign currencies and the right to draw from the International Monetary Fund can be used to cover the need to pay for imports if there is any hiccup in exports or, more usually, to help towards covering any trade deficit.

The central bank may, however, use the reserves to support an exchange rate. The Bank of England might sell some of the dollars and Deutschmarks in its reserves to buy sterling in the foreign exchange market. It will hope to tip the balance of supply and demand in the market so that the extra buying lifts the pound while extra selling lowers the dollar and Deutschmark so that the exchange rate between sterling and those currencies rises.

In the face of that soaring activity on foreign exchange markets, this central bank intervention is losing effectiveness. More than 140 countries belong to the International Monetary Fund. Between them they can muster total reserves equivalent to about $1 trillion ($1,000,000,000,000).

Looks a lot, doesn't it? It is equivalent to just twenty-four hours' foreign-exchange dealing – puny.

That's because, of course, the central banks' ability to influence exchange rates is not dependent on their matching the sum total of foreign exchange dealing. They need only to tip the balance. If you've got a kilo on each side of the scales an extra gramme on one side might tip them but, on the other hand, if you're adding the odd gramme to scales with a tonne on each side, the practical effect may be negligible.

That the central banks' power to move markets is weakening became evident in the episode the BIS described as 'the most significant events in the international monetary system since the breakdown of the Bretton Woods arrangements. (That was 20 years ago, when the non-communist world stopped pegging currencies to the dollar and let them float.)

The storm which led to the virtual breakdown of Europe's exchange rate mechanism, vitiating the painstakingly negotiated Maastricht Treaty, was not confined to Europe alone. Having already driven the US dollar to a record low against the Deutschmark it engulfed also the Australian and Canadian currencies, eventually forcing the Bank of Canada to exacerbate recession by raising interest rates.

Europe was the epicentre. The first wave swept away the entire foreign exchange reserves of Finland, drained 46 per cent of Norway's foreign currency holdings in just two days and Sweden – despite raising interest rates to 500 per cent – suffered an outflow of $26 billion in just six days. This is equivalent to that entire nation's economic output for forty days and is 11 per cent of GDP.

In the midst of all this, the twelve finance ministers of the European Community jointly pronounced that changing exchange rates in the monetary system 'would not be the appropriate response to the current tensions in the Exchange Rate Mechanism'. Within three weeks, rates had been changed and both sterling and – despite earlier devaluation – the Italian lira had been forced out of the ERM.

Sterling fell despite overnight interest rates being raised to 100 per cent a year and bank base rates – the benchmark for most deposit and overdraft rates – being jacked up from 10 per cent to – for a few hours – 15 per cent.

Intervention on a massive scale by Europe's central banks proved unavailing. The Bank of England later estimated that in June–September inclusive the volume of official intervention had been more than $160 billion – $40 billion a month. The

Bank of Italy said that in the last seven months of the year central banks had used $200 billion, half in the month of September alone. Thus even after the pound and Lira had been driven from the ERM, intervention was still more than $10 billion a month.

The amount of foreign currency used was equivalent to $588 for every man, woman and child in Europe. More significantly, the high interest rates imposed in a vain endeavour to hold exchange rates deepened the recession which was enveloping mainland Europe, aggravating unemployment.

All this was not enough to beat the markets.

'Dealers do talk and think in somewhat militaristic terms,' comments Stephen Bell, chief economist at the City investment bank Morgan Grenfell. 'They talk of having a go at a currency and trying to knock out a central bank.

'Because they need to end each day without heavy open commitments – they prefer to end all-square – they are like fighter pilots; they must return to base after each day's sortie. The proprietary traders at the banks are the long-distance bombers and can hold positions.

'In the case of sterling, the fighters saw that the bombers had knocked out the opposition defences.' Currency reserves, where not exhausted, were severely depleted.

At the forefront of Britain's defence of sterling was Terry Smeeton, chief manager of the foreign exchange division at the Bank of England. From a shared windowless office adjoining the dealing room – and often also from their homes throughout the night – he and his deputy, David Ingram, fought a rearguard action, intervening to support sterling by tactical buying on the currency markets, deploying the reserves judiciously.

'It's certainly something which concerns you round the clock,' he told me. 'Talking specifically about the pressures leading up to sterling's departure from the ERM: really it was four to six weeks before then that the pressures started to build and we started building our defences in return.

'It was a very stressful period for everybody and it was a big commitment to try and ensure that the objective we'd been given at that time was fulfilled.'

Had they managed to hold the line, they might have been lauded as heroes. Instead, there was the morale-sapping effect of constant retreat, one long-extended working day after another for week after week. Tiredness becomes cumulative.

'It was something which David and I and one or two others took home with us each evening. We look after sterling not just when we're here in the office, but at home and throughout the night (and quite a lot of movement occurred at times throughout the night). So it was a very stressful business and we were pretty committed to it.'

When, eventually, they left late in the evening they would leave instructions with an appropriate dealer in whichever foreign exchange markets were open, to call them if the pound fell below a certain exchange rate.

'It feels pretty bad at 1.30 in the morning when some dealer in Hong Kong rings up and says it's come through the level you wish to be woken at,' acknowledged Terry Smeeton ruefully.

'It's a battle – I think that's the right word in relation to that operation – when not everything is effective immediately. You have various tactics you employ, various fall-backs where you intend to dig in. You make a stand here and maybe make an advance from there, thanks to what may happen when something fortuitously turns up.

'It certainly wasn't clear – during, for instance, August 1992 when we heavily engaged in the defence of sterling – it was by no means clear that we were going to lose the day at that stage.'

Defeat brought widespread dismay. 'Once we'd come out of the ERM, people became generally gloomier in the UK economy and establishment generally,' notes Roger Bootle, chief economist at Midland Bank.

'You can see that in surveys of consumer confidence and what business actually did; they sacked people hand over fist.'

This proved the wrong response. With the pound no longer pegged to the Deutschmark, interest rates could come down sharply and, in time, demand and economic activity began, unequivocally if sluggishly, to revive.

Even at the Bank of England the inevitability of devaluation is now accepted. The government could not lower interest rates within the ERM because those were effectively pegged to being no lower than rates on the anchor currency, the Deutschmark. The markets perceived – rightly – that either sterling would have to be depreciated within the ERM or – as actually happened – it would have to suspend its membership altogether and use that room for manoeuvre to reduce interest rates.

It was a one-way bet. In neither circumstance was sterling going to appreciate against the Deutschmark. The Bank could not then save the pound.

The markets have been proved right in that case, at least. The devaluation forced on sterling was justified by the country's economic dilemma.

The UK had a balance of trade deficit, showing that demand for goods was greater than national output and the excess demand had to be met from abroad. The classic response would normally be to cool demand by raising interest rates (thereby changing the relative attractiveness of saving rather than spending). But unemployment was also high, showing that the nation had considerable unused capacity at the same time. If demand was greater than output and yet there was unused capacity, the problem must be that the capacity was selling its output at the wrong price – that is, at an overvalued exchange rate.

The BIS 63rd annual report, covering that turbulent period in the foreign exchange markets, concludes: 'Only three narrow-band ERM currencies avoided either a devaluation or a switch to a floating-rate regime. The three were the French franc, the Danish krona and the Belgian franc.

'A combination of sound fundamentals and clear commitments on the part of the authorities concerned was successful in eventually convincing the markets that attacks against these currencies were bound to fail – and they did.'

This was the BIS reporting for the year to the end of March

1993. It was published three months later, in June. Within two months – over the weekend as July turned into August – it was proved wrong. The French franc succumbed to attack and the ERM became inefficacious. The bands within which member currencies became free to move – 15 per cent either side of the central rate – are so wide as to be meaningless.

But were the markets justified by economic facts this time?

The people who sold sterling in 1992 had seen that recession in Britain made it necessary to have interest rates lower than the level at which the pound could hold its value in the ERM. When sterling was forced out of the ERM, sure enough it settled at a lower value against the Deutschmark and interest rates were cut.

But what of the French franc?

'With the pound the markets were essentially right,' concludes Roger Bootle, expressing the view of a consensus of economists. 'With the fall of the franc I don't think you can jump to that conclusion necessarily. The French have not slashed interest rates – they don't believe it would have much impact on their recession – and the franc later returned to about where it had been before the attack began.

'Accordingly, you could argue that the exchange markets forced a development with regard to the franc which was not justified by the economic fundamentals.'

Regardless of economic justification, interest rates or the billions thrown into intervention, the markets marched on.

Even before that final assault on the ERM, the BIS writes in its annual report of the earlier currency storm, 'as one currency after another fell, so did the competitive position of others worsen, thus increasing the risk that one or other of them would become the object of the next speculative attack.'

Stephen Bell recalls, 'With the ERM they were like a conquering army: go in and hit one currency, make their profits and then use their increased resources to attack the next victim.'

We have seen the near-destruction of the system agreed in the Maastricht Treaty. If they have not destroyed them, the currency markets have severely damaged the arrangements painstakingly negotiated on behalf of 340 million people by their democratically elected representatives. Yet there was no great public outcry against what the markets had done. In Britain, even the opposition, sceptical about the workings of markets, directed its fire at the government for its unrealism rather than at the destructiveness of dealings which thwarted the wishes of the people. Notable about public reaction, first to the fall of sterling and the lira from the ERM, and then to the incapacitation of that system, was the political acceptance of such developments as an ineluctable fact of life: rather like the weather. Even in countries unquestioningly committed to closer economic integration and the development of a single currency, there was not widespread anger. Scapegoats were more likely to be politicians than members of the financial community. Why this unquestioning acceptance of market rule? It is because markets usually reflect the decisions of thousands or even millions of people going about their daily lives. Not so, however, the foreign exchange markets.

The speculators are not only banks. Many are household names and the leading lights of British industry. A company buying supplies from abroad or selling its goods overseas faces the risk that a change in exchange rates could inflate its costs or depress its income. The treasurer's role is to ensure the business is protected against such risks, by using the currency markets. With the range of complex financial instruments on offer, it may be possible not just to secure insurance against risk but also ensure a profit from the transactions if all goes particularly well. It is a small insidious process to move from protecting the company through use of the markets to speculating on the markets. Treasurers following the market day to day may stray beyond the actual currency needs of their companies and try to win extra profit – kudos in the boardroom – by betting on the market trend. They then rank among the speculators who seem sometimes to make currencies move in a particular direction for no apparent reason.

Today, capital flows – investors moving their money around

the world – are a bigger factor in the international economy than trade. Multinational companies invest about $150 billion a year outside their home countries.

'Undoubtedly the potential volumes are massive,' notes David Ingram at the Bank of England. 'One of the reasons for that is that a number of the big international investors now manage very large portfolios: insurance funds, pension funds, unit trusts etc.. They do now look at the structure of their portfolios. They may be invested in ten different currencies and they may decide that because of trends – economic trends or whatever – that there is an economic risk associated with a particular currency or group of currencies. They will start hedging that risk out of their portfolio.

'Of course, as soon as those funds start to move then you can sense that other market participants will decide to do the same thing and the volumes will start to rise. In that case these will be genuine hedging transactions protecting the value of their portfolios. And it's at that stage that the speculative element comes into the market because they see a momentum there which may move an exchange rate.'

A dealer, a trader or speculator in any market might sell something they think is overvalued. In most developed markets it is possible to 'sell short' – that is, sell something you don't already hold. That is feasible in developed markets where it is possible either to borrow what you are selling or to agree to delay in honouring the sale. Just as they will hope to buy cheap and sell dear, some operators might hope to sell dear first and buy cheap later. Key is the belief that the market price is wrong: out of touch with reality.

Foreign exchange markets may have gone one step further. Instead of selling – or selling short – currencies they believe to be overvalued, are operators in this market selling heavily in the belief that the sheer weight of their money can force events from which they can profit – a fall in the currency?

At the Bank of England, foreign exchange chief Terry Smee-ton believes it. 'That tendency has grown in recent times,' he told me. 'There has been – there remains – pressure on treasury managers to continue to deliver good returns. That means that at times, when there is not a lot of business going on, it may be that an institution or a group of their customers may perceive that there is something to be gained by targeting a particular currency.

'This seems to have been more evident since sterling came out of the ERM, when we had the pressures on the weaker ERM currencies themselves during the summer of 1993.

'So I think there is a tendency now to expect the treasury area to generate good returns and thus a need on the part of some of the people driving these things to find something which may move: where if pressure is applied they may get a result in terms of profitable movement. That is, I'd say, something that's become more prevalent recently than it was five years ago or in the mid-eighties.'

How do they manage it? Andre Katz, after years of watching and listening second-by-second for small subtle shifts in the £:$ market, believes it may emerge spontaneously as so many traders seize on what appears an opportunity. 'Once a movement starts rolling you tell other people and they tell their customers. Perhaps their customers need to get out of their positions in the opposite direction [for example, if the dollar starts to fall and they've been backing it to rise they'll quickly sell]. It adds weight. More and more people jump on the bandwagon.

'The exchange rate can be moved right against economic fundamentals for a month or so, then three or four months down the road it will probably come back into line with the fundamentals.' For a moment, the weight of funds behind a particular idea in the market, sometimes behind a fad, can drive an exchange rate far from what trades flows, relative competitiveness, price comparisons or interest rate differentials suggest it should be. In time, reality reasserts itself.

The foreign exchange market has developed on such an enormous scale, backed by speed of communications, that change can happen with unexpected speed. 'Technology has transformed parts of the forex market,' says Dr Jim O'Neill, chief currency economist at Swiss Bank Corporation. 'With all these damn screens all over the world, people can act on things that they're very uninformed about, just like that.' He snaps his fingers.

'Right now you have people in New Zealand talking about the Italian political situation. So something hits the wires about [Italian premier] Berlusconi and someone says "I want to sell lire". And it's so easy with the modern communications.'

This, he thinks, rather than deliberate collusion, might explain market aberrations. 'There's been a slight migration towards exaggerated opinions which could give the appearance of people ganging up and trying to attack currencies but usually the market is so big that those people will be wrong because when the masses start acting on something it's too late.'

In these markets some say that what matters is not reality at all – not economic fundamentals or flows of funds – but how people react to it. Pointing to the lack of apparent rhyme or reason in many exchange rate movements, they argue that it is a question of psychology. A currency may be overvalued but, if enough people – for whatever illogical reason – keep buying, it will become even more overvalued. What matters when it comes down to buying and selling a currency is not so much what its value ought to be but what the sum total of human decision has made it. Moreover, these 'chartists' – or technical analysts – assert that a chart of the exchange rate will show how people have been behaving towards the currency, how attitudes have been changing. They claim there are certain regular patterns of behaviour which enable the analyst sometimes to predict the next move.

Bank dealers speculating, corporate treasurers hedging themselves against risk or trying to snatch extraordinary profits by anticipating events, international investors switching their funds, perhaps in the hope of thereby causing events: these broke the system by which Europe was moving towards a single currency.

The European Exchange Rate Mechanism fell apart in all but name over the weekend of 31 July to 1 August 1993. That followed two days of turmoil – and unprecedented market intervention by central banks – as on Thursday 29 July the council of the Bundesbank, Germany's central bank, decided only to tinker with interest rates, disregarding market pressures which had been building.

At first, on the Thursday itself, it was not clear which other currencies would come under attack alongside the French franc. Several were to do so, among them the Spanish peseta, despite its having been devalued already three times in a year.

As Europe's markets closed for that day, the afternoon sun streaking between the trees of the Paseo del Prado and filtering through a yellow awning above the window to suffuse his office with an almost ghostly light, Manuel Conthe, director general of the Spanish Treasury, reflected on the fate of the currency for which he cared.

'Sometimes speculators play a useful role and sometimes they tend to play a destructive role,' he told me. 'They were obviously beneficial when they forced the first and second devaluations of the peseta, which was very clearly overvalued. They made money also with the lira and pound, so they played a useful role because they forced currencies to come down to reality.

'But now I think the speculation which is going on has nothing to do with fundamentals or reality and of course speculators can make money even when they are harmful for the financial community and for economic relations among countries.

'They don't care, for instance, about whether the existing French franc to Deutschmark parity is justified or not. The only thing they want is for the French franc to be devalued because that way they make money.

'Sometimes I feel that the ethical standards in the foreign exchange markets are not very high. I recognize that sometimes governments are wrong and speculators are right and they play a useful role. Sometimes authorities are right and speculators wrong and sometimes the speculators need to be taught a lesson and be forced to take losses.

'I think in the case of the peseta we are on pretty safe ground: three depreciations and now in the lower part of its

ERM band so that the potential for a recovery is now so great that I see more risk for a speculator that the peseta might gain value rather than depreciate further.' He was proved right, within weeks the peseta had climbed 16 per cent.

'The big debate going on in the market and among the regulators – sparked by the ERM turmoil and the way that some of these New York leveraged funds are growing dramatically – is could it be that on certain days, if three or four of them do speak together and reach the same conclusion and so collude and put on enormous speculative or investment bets, could it be that they could force something?' wonders Jim O'Neill of Swiss Bank Corporation.

'I think I'd admit that they possibly could. But it would have to happen, they would have to be successful, very quickly.

'Let's suppose they all talk on the phone and agree the Portuguese escudo looks a bit vulnerable: "Why don't we sell half a billion dollars each and see what happens?"'

The suspicion must be that the foreign exchange markets have become different in character from other markets. Elsewhere speculators make or lose money anticipating what major bona fide users of the market will do and how the market will react to changes in underlying circumstances. They may add useful liquidity to the market and they take risks. Failure of a crop, failure of a company, may be risks others are anxious to avoid, risks they can pass on by selling to or buying from the speculator.

But in the foreign exchange markets the speculator seems to be driving events: governments intervening through the central banks are unable to resist the pressure regardless of whether it is justified. This may be why the volume of currency trading is apparently five times that needed for the purposes of moving goods and capital around the world. Speculators thus decide exchange rates – the rates at which trade is done – determining competitiveness.

One factor which may help them wield such power is the ability to 'leverage' transactions. A company or individual investor may borrow most of the funds they are using. Borrowing is only the simplest method. There are more sophis-

ticated facilities available which allow some to trade ten or
more times the money they commit.

London not only is the largest single centre for international
currency dealing but, according to the BIS survey, also increased its global share of trading from 25 per cent to nearly
30 per cent between 1989 and 1992. More of the currency
trading involving the dollar is in London than in New York.
London trades the Deutschmark more than twice as much as
Germany. Is it entirely a coincidence that London plays also a
leading role – second only to the whole USA – in the markets
for derivatives?

This is a market about which many worry, sometimes at
great length, but with little understanding because it quickly
becomes arcane and incomprehensibly technical. It can be,
and often is, an inherently risky market.

Derivatives are contracts based not on the underlying investment but on its price, so that instead of buying or selling an
actual share or currency, you buy the right, perhaps even a
commitment, to buy or sell.

Derivatives can be a form of insurance, to cover against the
risk of an adverse movement in the underlying price. And just
as an insurance premium is a small proportion of the value of
the risk covered, likewise the buyer of a derivative may cover
a large amount of currency risk for a small initial outlay.
Whether her outlay may increase depends on the type of
derivative she buys: a futures contract or an option, for
instance.

With a futures contract the buyer may pay perhaps only 10
per cent margin – downpayment – and when she eventually
sells, receive or pay the difference between buying and selling
prices. An option gives its holder the right to buy or sell for a
certain period. They don't have to do either and can just sell
the option again for a profit or loss. No one may ever use the
option – for instance if it is the right to buy at a particular price
which is higher than you would have to pay in the market –
but in that case when the option reaches the end of its validity
time it expires worthless and all the money paid for it is lost.

These are just the simplest of the instruments available in the currency markets. The survey by the Bank for International Settlements found that trading in currency options alone had more than doubled in three years. One characteristic of derivatives is that they enable the investor to separate his risks. A German investor in UK government stocks – gilts – faces two risks: the danger that the gilt itself will fall in price, probably because of a general rise in interest rates, and the risk that the pound will fall in value against the Deutschmark. But he can use an option or other derivative to cover – hedge – either of these specific risks.

'The traditional investor has a lot more instruments at his disposal and may decide, for instance, that gilts are fine but he doesn't like the sterling risk so he'll hedge it away,' explains David Ingram.

'The hedge funds have taken this degree of sophistication to another degree. They quite often do not invest in the underlying assets at all but use the derivatives markets to get exposure – or negative exposure, whichever they wish to obtain – against a particular currency without actually committing vast amounts of funds. They're essentially using derivative instruments to obtain such exposure in a highly geared way.'

These hedge funds, in other words, do not tie up capital buying shares, gilts, or even currencies. Instead they use derivatives to ride on the movements in prices of those investments and so may get perhaps 100 per cent gain from a 10 per cent movement in the underlying price. They do, however, risk losing their entire investment through a 10 per cent adverse move.

It is not only on recognized stock markets that investors and speculators are buying and trading these sometimes exotic financial instruments. Most currency exchange options are bespoke; rather than buying an option traded on an exchange the investor or speculator may find it better to buy an option drawn up to meet their specific needs. Banks sell these 'over the counter' – OTC – and will proffer them via trading screens.

The investor buying a currency option traded on an exchange can sell it on that exchange at any time during its period of validity. Whoever grants the option – the writer – can also buy on the exchange whatever they need to cover their risk. The risk can be considerable: the writer who grants someone the right to buy at a specified price could find the price has doubled, trebled or soared through the roof. A bank selling a bespoke option OTC faces a risk which is only theoretically quantifiable. It may or may not have offset that risk in some way. As a result, we don't know today how big a risk the banks are taking in the foreign exchange markets.

Richard Allen manages the banking supervision division at the Bank of England. I asked what was the biggest problem he faced. 'Looking from the systemic point of view, it's knowing just how big the market is,' he told me. 'We don't have a real idea of how big the OTC market is and we don't have a clear idea, if one aggregated all the risks, what they would come out to.

'One of the difficulties is that if you've got a group of banks doing a lot of business with customers that in a sense the risks are hedging themselves out: there are end-users and there are banks as intermediaries between them.

'If they're in some way trading for their own account without really having much regard to end-users at all, then they could be stacking up risks which don't really have a home of their own to go to when things go wrong.'

Banks trade heavily in the foreign exchange markets and may be taking on risks through options and the like. But at least in the UK the Bank of England imposes rules designed to ensure that no bank trading out of London takes on unlimited risks.

There are no such controls or restraints on the big speculators in the foreign exchange markets. The traders, investors and speculators who seem to be in the driving seat, thwarting the will of governments on occasion, are free to operate on almost any scale. They are limited only by the resources they command, they can borrow or can achieve by leverage of ever more ingenious financial instruments.

These speculators are not necessarily strange, obscure entities based in exotic locations. Allied-Lyons, the brewery and food group, admitted in early 1991 that it faced losses of perhaps £150 million from foreign exchange speculation. In the currency options market, it had committed itself to selling dollars at a given price (in terms of other currencies) but the dollar unexpectedly rose, pushing up the price at which it had to buy dollars to meet the commitment.

At the very beginning of 1994 the German metals, mining and engineering group, Metallgesellschaft, said it had incurred losses of probably more than DM2 billion, wiping out its entire share capital. While the futures contracts it had been trading in New York were for oil, German companies had sometimes used such contracts as an indirect means of taking a position in currency markets.

No one knows how much are the total risks such speculators are taking. When his Quantum Fund group made a profit of $1 billion out of sterling's fall from the ERM, New York investment guru George Soros admitted he had 'bet' $10 billion on it. This was the size of the funds he committed. How much else might others commit?

Apart from the power they may thus have to dictate events – such as the enforced loosening of the ERM when the French franc was soundly valued – what if one or several should default?

'Central banks are tending to look not only at the individual institutions but also at the system as a whole and worrying about whether there are linkages between markets which can become mutually destabilizing: once one bit falls down the whole thing collapses on itself like a pack of cards,' Richard Allen at the Bank of England told me.

'I don't think we know enough yet really, in terms of the statistics of these derivatives, to judge what the real implications are systemically.'

In the Barclays dealing room proprietary trader, Guy Hurley, trying to make money for the bank out of the movement of currencies, warns, 'The important thing in doing this is to remember that no one has a clue what's going on. No one is that good. This market humiliates us all on a regular basis, whether it's George Soros or me.

'You're having to express two opinions at once. It's not a simple liking or dislike, as with a share at a particular price. Here you have to say not only "like sterling" but also "I hate the dollar". It's a double-edged sword.'

Dealer Andre Katz, meanwhile, has found that two deals in the last forty seconds have left him holding £10 million he doesn't want. 'Cable has moved ten points against me and that's $10,000.

'I don't want to lose my profit for a silly position really. You sometimes get £20 or £30 positions but today's not the day really. Just try and nick a point here, nick a point there.'

A 'point' or 'pip' is 0.01 of a per cent.

'The markets are totally different from what they were six or seven years ago when you'd get a move of 3 cents or 4 cents in the £:$. Now you're trying to get a couple of pips each time.

'The average age of dealers has gone up because banks are looking for more mature people and people who've experienced quite a lot already. Banks are looking for someone who can make three or four thousand pounds a day. And the bank's making £800,000 out of that one person a year.'

2

DERIVATIVES

Funny Money - More Bang to the Buck

> . . . the market volume which affects prices can
> be dramatically increased by the use of derivative
> products, such as options, with no major
> investment of capital. Price movements triggered
> by derivative markets can therefore spread very
> rapidly and reinforce the relevant price swings
> in the spot markets.
>
> Deutsche Bundesbank monthly report, October 1993

From the Bundesbank's technocrats to the prating Congressmen on Capitol Hill, they're all worrying today about derivatives. These financial instruments − so called because they derive their value from some underlying instrument and have no intrinsic value of their own − are cause of concern because they might:

- Distort the markets, giving punters such as George Soros market firepower wholly disproportionate to their real resources.

They also pose:

- Systemic risk. This is the danger that if one big player loses heavily enough his default might cause losses which others cannot meet, triggering a domino effect.

So unquestioning is the acceptance of market forces today, so widespread the belief that 'you can't buck the markets', that concern with the possibility of speculators dictating events with harmful economic effects has become secondary to the fear that banks and others, by engaging in arcane activities they do not fully understand, may incur losses on such a scale as to bring down the whole financial system.

To Congressmen such as Henry Gonzalez, chairman of the House of Representatives banking committee, the auguries cannot be good: look at the hundreds of billions of dollars American banks lost in loans to the Third World, particularly Latin America; and look at the hundreds of billions cost to taxpayers of bailing out savings and loan companies when, through mismanagement and fraud, shoals of these 'thrifts' – the US equivalent of building societies – went into default.

Aggravating fears about derivatives have been their complexity and the complicated mathematical formulae which characterize them. As Jonathan Fiechter, acting director of the Office of Thrift Supervision, remarked to the House banking committee hearing in October 1993: 'The world of derivatives is new and unfamiliar to many institutions. The language is arcane; the technical foundation that underlies financial derivatives is complex, and the techniques that are used to measure and monitor derivative exposures are very sophisticated.'

Procter & Gamble lost $102 million on what is called a 'diff swap'. In essence, it was gambling not on the differential between German and US interest rates but on how quickly those interest rates would converge.

A few days after P&G had owned up to this loss, the somewhat smaller Air Products company confessed to having lost $60 million. The granddaddy of them all, however, was the Japanese company Kashima Oil. Getting derivatives wrong cost it $1,500 million.

Fortunately, Kashima and the companies which own it had deep enough pockets to cover this loss. What if they hadn't? The banks on the other side of the deals Kashima did would have built a whole edifice of transactions to cover themselves. Those hedging transactions might engender a whole range of obligations which, had Kashima defaulted, some banks might have been unable to honour; their failure in turn might fatally affect the creditors of those banks. That's systemic risk. Kashima and others will not just be dealing with their own countries' banks. This business is truly international, a default can come from anywhere. Compounding the fears is the concentration of this business: seven banks do between them 90 per cent of all derivatives business in the USA.

What should be done about it? As Congressman James Leach, another House banking committee member, expressed it: 'We have an enormous political science dilemma: What happens when we have a problem which is beyond the sophistication of Congress and other political entities?'

The reflex action in Congress, in accord with the instincts of politicians worldwide, is to legislate. Working, generally, from the premise that 'if we don't understand what you're doing we'll stop you doing it', the General Accounting Office, the investigative arm of Congress, published a lengthy report pointing out that many of the important players in the derivatives markets are outside the financial sector and so beyond the supervision of regulators who oversee banks, stockbrokers and the like.

The GAO suggested that all users of derivatives should be subject to regulation, preferably by the Securities & Exchange Commission. The first problem it faced was the response from SEC chairman Arthur Levitt, who replied that he did not want greater supervisory powers and saw no need of them. In that view he enjoyed the support of Federal Reserve Board chairman, Alan Greenspan.

The Bank for International Settlements likewise has argued against direct controls on the use of derivatives but supports Mr Greenspan and others in suggesting they should be closely monitored. The keyword, as in all markets, is 'transparency'. Cases such as Kashima and Procter & Gamble would surely not have happened if more people had been able to see what was going on.

Less disinterestedly, the Securities Industry Association, the American Bankers' Association, the International Swap & Derivatives Association and similar trade bodies argued that decisions about whether to take on such risks were a matter for the people facing them, the risk of default was something a counterparty could and should consider and regulating derivatives heavily would raise the cost or reduce the availability of what, for many industrial enterprises, is insurance without which they dare not embark on international trade. They omitted to mention that the amount of derivatives business in foreign exchange dealing alone is many times the level of international trade.

This funny money is big business. The notional value of trading in futures – just one type of derivative – is some $140,000 billion a year, equivalent to half of all foreign exchange business. The value of all derivatives outstanding at any moment is probably around $16,000 billion. Such figures are, to a healthy being, incomprehensible. US banks alone are engaged in some $7,000 billion of swaps – another derivative – which is some 10 per cent more than America's entire gross domestic product.

Trade in derivatives is growing fast, particularly now outside the USA, and it has some prestige patrons. The Bank of England uses futures in its management of the UK's currency reserves; the Bank of Italy uses options; and the Bank for International Settlements itself – the central banks' central bank – is one of the heaviest users of swaps and other derivatives. The International Swaps & Derivatives Association reckons that while swaps worldwide grew sixfold in the five years to the end of 1992, yen-denominated swaps grew tenfold. The Bank for International Settlements found that, of all segments of the foreign exchange markets, options turnover grew the fastest, more than doubling in the three years between its 1989 and 1992 surveys.

The simplest variation on a spot foreign exchange transaction – and not a derivative at all – is a:

FORWARD contract. This is an agreement to buy or sell a given amount of currency at an agreed rate on a particular date. A forward is no dearer than ordinary spot market trade. An exporter who knows she is to receive a specified quantity of French francs in six months' time can remove all uncertainty about how much in sterling that will be worth by selling the francs for sterling six months forward. But the deal is irrevocable. She is safeguarded if the franc falls against the pound but, as she has sold those francs at a fixed rate, will lose the potential gain from the franc rising against sterling.

In some cases, that risk can be as important as the risk of loss from an adverse movement.

FUTURES contracts are forward agreements standardized into generic forms so that they can be bought or sold on an organized exchange. The initial outlay is not the nominal value of the contract but a proportion, known as the margin, usually 10 per cent but possibly higher. As the movement of exchange rates changes the value of the futures contract, the buyer will either face a margin call and have to top up the margin to reflect the increase in his liability or the value of the contract will rise to show a profit. When the futures contract is due for delivery, settlement is in effect the difference between the exchange rate on the contract and the current spot exchange rate, with no need to go through the cumbersome process of exchanging the underlying currencies.

Because a futures contract is a traded security the holder can sell it to take his profits or limit his losses at any time during its life. With only 10 per cent margin as the initial downpayment and the value of the contract dependent on the whole of the underlying contract, a 10 per cent rise in the contract produces a 100 per cent gain in the capital outlay but likewise a 10 per cent fall wipes out the investment.

By this simple means a currency speculator can get $10 million of currency exposure for every $1 million he bets. That's what in English is termed 'gearing', in American 'leverage'.

SWAPS are agreements on the lines of 'I'll pay for you, if you'll pay for me.' Someone who has a liability to make regular payments, for instance, in D-marks but has an income in dollars will swap with someone who has exactly the opposite problem. Often it is a question of a borrower finding it cheaper to raise money in one currency and swap than to raise funds directly in the currency he wants.

Ms Jessica Einhorn, treasurer of the World Bank, raised $3.6

billion worth of borrowing in currencies the bank didn't want and then swapped them. 'It allows us to use the world's capital markets to diversify our borrowings into a pool of currencies and to lock in our borrowing at lower cost,' she explained. It saved an estimated 0.4 per cent a year on interest rates.

Except for the shortest-term, currency swaps are rarely what market vernacular terms 'plain vanilla'. Banks and other traders in currencies don't, after all, actually want truckloads of folding paper. If they are taking any other than the shortest-term view of a currency, they will need to invest in something which pays interest. Interest rate swaps – 'you pay my floating rate interest and I'll pay your fixed interest' – become integral with currency swaps.

OPTIONS have become the fastest-growing derivative in the currency markets, growing at perhaps 35 per cent a year. An option is the right – but not the obligation – to enter into a transaction. Even within the top management of banks, according to authoritative reports, the implications of that are not fully appreciated.

A call option is the right to buy, a put option the right to sell, one currency for another at an agreed rate. (This means, of course, that a call option to buy D-marks for dollars is equally a put option to sell dollars for D-marks.)

This can be used as insurance since the price you pay for the option is akin to an insurance premium and the first advantage is that you immediately know and limit your outlay. Next, you exercise your option only if it suits you to do so. If you have an option to buy at one exchange rate and the currency falls to a lower rate, you simply abandon the option. In that case the money you paid for the option is gone. Just as you do not go back to the insurance company and demand a refund because you have made no claims on your household insurance, so the seller – known as the 'writer' – of the option pockets the premium you paid them.

Let's consider in more detail for a moment what happens. Let's say the exchange rate is £1:$1.50. The right to use that exchange rate at any time in the next three months is valuable whether:

- you fear that the dollars you're due to be paid during that period will fall in value
- fear the pound will fall against the dollar and inflate the cost of a bill you'll be paying in dollars
- believe that the dollar will rise (and the pound fall) so you will be able to sell dollars at $1.50 to the £1 and at the same time buy dollars at only, let's say, $1.47 to the £1
- think that sterling will rise so you'll be able to sell pounds at $1.55, having bought them at only $1.50.

Depending on which way you need to cover your liability or want to speculate, you will buy an option either to buy pounds at $1.50 each or to sell at that rate. You might pay perhaps two pence (three cents) on every pound you have the right to buy or sell.

If the exchange rate doesn't move throughout the three months then your option – which has been just the right to engage in a transaction during that period – expires worthless. You've lost your tuppence (three cents) in the pound.

If you were expecting or fearing a rise in sterling against the dollar – and had therefore bought the right to buy sterling at $1.50 so that you would then sell those pounds at more than $1.50 each – you need the pound to rise to $1.53 just to recoup the cost of your option. (In fact you'd need a slightly larger rise to cover your brokerage fees and other transaction costs, but we're keeping it simple.) On the other hand, if at some time during that three months the exchange rate had moved to $1.65, that would be a 10 per cent rise in the sterling exchange rate but for every 3 cents you had paid you would have secured the right to buy at $1.50 and now sell at $1.65, making 15 cents on every 3 cents you had laid out: a profit of 400 per cent (15c–3c cost = 12c = 4 x 3c cost) And that from a 10 per cent movement in the exchange rate.

If you had got it wrong and sterling fell against the dollar then you have limited your losses to the two pence in the pound you paid for the option. You don't do a thing. An option gives you the right to buy or sell, it does not give you an obligation.

That's only the simplest form. Options are quoted and traded. When the exchange rate is at £1:$1.50 you could buy an option to sell sterling at $1.55. This option is described as being 'in the money' and the price of the option will reflect the instant profit you could make from buying £1 at the current exchange rate of $1.50 and using your option to sell at $1.55.

Then there's the option to sell sterling at $1.45. As you can sell sterling at $1.50 in the market at the moment, that option is 'out of the money' and consequently cheaper.

But look at the option to buy sterling at $1.55. That is 'out of the money', too. What's the value of being able to buy £1 for $1.55 when you can already buy at $1.50 at the current exchange rate? Because that option would not be profitable to use right now it might be priced at perhaps one penny (1.5 cents) on the pound. You don't break even until the exchange rate has moved to $1.5650 ($1.55 at which you have the right to buy sterling plus the 1.5 cents cost of your option).

But look at what can happen. If the exchange rate climbs 10 per cent from $1.50 at present to $1.65 then you exercise your option to buy sterling at $1.55 and immediately sell at $1.65, making 10 cents on every 1.5 cents you paid for your option, a profit of 8.5 cents on every 1.5 cents, which is 567 per cent profit from the 10 per cent movement in the exchange rate, compared with 400 per cent profit from the option at $1.50.

Moreover, if you got it wrong, your loss – again limited to what you paid for the option – is only 1.5 cents on every £1 you covered instead of 3 cents. Your risk is therefore smaller and, in the example I have given, your return greater, but the option at $1.50 became profitable to use on a smaller exchange rate movement.

The price at which the option can be exercised compared with the current exchange rate is one factor affecting its value. Another is how long it has to run before it expires.

The value of an option depends on several variables, giving rise to a gamut of theoretical mathematical models. Most important are the volatility of the currency itself – the bigger the risk of an adverse movement, the more you'll pay to insure against it – and how long it is valid. This gives rise to an alphabet of factors relating to an option:

Delta: the rate at which the price of an option changes in response to a move in the price of an underlying. If an option's delta is 0.5 a $2 move in the underlying will produce a $1 move in the option.

Gamma: the rate at which the delta moves up or down in response to changes in the price of the underlying.

Rho: the rate at which the price of an option changes in response to a given move in interest rates.

Theta: the rate at which the price of an option changes because of the passage of time, otherwise known as 'time decay'.

Vega: The rate at which the price of an option changes because of a change in the volatility of the underlying.

If you find some of those concepts a little challenging then perhaps you'd rather not think too hard about what's involved with an option on a swap not of currencies themselves but of a currency futures contract: think of Procter & Gamble's 'diff swap'.

Options serve a useful purpose of enabling a corporate treasurer, for example, to secure the right to buy a currency – and so eliminate the risk of exchange rate movements – in case it is needed. They can also give you gearing with a vengeance.

That factor can make options attractive to currency speculators. The Bundesbank suspects this is often behind the use of such derivatives, noting in its October 1993 monthly report, '. . . the instruments may also be used for speculative purposes, which is obviously being done on a major scale, for the buoyant global growth of derivatives can no longer be ascribed mainly to a pent-up demand for hedging foreign exchange, interest rate and other exposures'. As they enable currency speculators to have impact on the foreign exchange markets many times their capital outlay, do options and other financial derivatives give them undue market influence and mean they cause disorderly – wild even – markets?

'Derivatives markets are being used because they're a

cheaper way of undertaking certain risk profiles in these markets than dealing through cash or futures markets direct,' notes currency economist Dr Brendan Brown, head of research at Mitsubishi Finance. 'If the derivatives markets were not there the same people would be taking the same positions but maybe in a slightly costlier way.

'But that doesn't mean there would be more volatility. If anything the opposite is true because you have much more liquidity.'

The extra currency trading which options promote adds liquidity to the markets – more deals being done increasing the ability of the market to absorb any one deal – and so reduces the volatility of exchange rates. And don't forget that the option has reduced volatility in other respects elsewhere, just as an insurance policy reduces the volatility of your personal fortunes. Moreover, because the seller of an option shoulders a risk, they will take protective action which will incidentally tend to stabilize the market.

Dr Jim O'Neill, chief currency economist at Swiss Bank Corporation, avers, 'using an option as a protective tool reduces the volatility for anyone that uses it. Buying a put or a call for a corporation clearly reduces their potential volatility in their earnings stream. It's an insurance premium.

'You tend to have periods of stability added to by the options because people are writing protective strategies either side. But then when something really significant happens to get you out, the existence of all those options adds to the volatility because it requires an underlying cash transaction.'

But Trevor Cass, with a quarter of a century's firsthand experience of trading and managing dealers in Barclays' currency dealing room, suspects that options distort liquidity. He says: 'It all comes down to reasonableness: a reasonable chance of getting a reasonable price in a reasonable amount in [i.e. covering] a reasonable space of time. Then I think you've got liquidity.

'What happens with leveraged transactions is that sometimes there are periods when one of these measures becomes unreasonable. That to my mind would say it damages liquidity

'I don't know if you can look at an option the same way as a spot transaction. If you buy a currency someone else has sold it. So there's the balance. Is the option sold the mirror image of an option bought, however? I suspect not.

'The seller of the option takes a risk which is not the mirror image of the buyer of the option. So leveraged transactions may add volume but distort liquidity.'

The impact of derivatives on the foreign exchange markets particularly taxed the mind of the Bundesbank when its efforts to hold the ERM together in July 1993 proved eventually unavailing. In Frankfurt they were initially puzzled how so much central bank intervention was not enough to see off the speculators.

The Bundesbank's monthly report in October of that year reflected: 'One cannot definitely say to what extent derivative transactions have been a factor in the recent turbulence in the exchange markets. There is a clear linkage, through arbitraging, between currency options and currency futures, on the one hand, and traditional forward exchange transactions on the other.

'However, as long as the volume transacted in the traditional foreign exchange markets exceeds that traded in the futures and options markets, these markets are unlikely to cause any lasting disruption. If the futures and options markets continue to grow, this situation might well change and raise the question of how far the autonomous creation processes . . . should be restrained after all.'

The same report noted that derivatives do not show up in the banks' published accounts. They are 'off balance-sheet' but for Germany's banks came to the equivalent of 90 per cent of the amount showing on the balance sheets. Aggregating all the banks filters the true picture. In terms of the business of the 827 banks which engage in such activities, the share increases to no less than 113 per cent.

In other words, the banks engaged in derivatives did more than twice as much business as they disclosed in the very document outsiders rely on to judge a bank's creditworthiness and whether it is adequately capitalized or overtrading. That undisclosed business was in derivatives, the riskiness of which is difficult to quantify. Almost half the off balance-sheet volume related to foreign currencies and over the previous thirty months such activities had soared from DM1,800 billion to DM3 trillion. Currency options almost trebled to over 10 per cent of all off balance-sheet foreign exchange transactions.

'Almost all of the activities of some institutions with highly specialized business consist of off balance-sheet operations. This illustrates the degree to which the informative value of balance sheets as a guide to the overall business of banks has been reduced,' mourns the Bundesbank.

The situation is similar in America. Bankers Trust, now one of the USA's largest banks, has more derivatives credit risks off balance-sheet than loans to customers on balance-sheet. The banks monitored by the Federal Reserve Board held $7,000 billion of derivatives in early 1993. JP Morgan, customarily revered as the paradigm of banking prudence, disclosed that in 1992 more than half of its profits came from derivatives. Another US giant, Chemical Bank, revealed that 30 per cent of its revenues for the first nine months of 1993 had come from derivatives. It carries on its books $2,500 billion of derivatives contracts. When the investment bank Salomon Bros teetered on the brink as a result of its scandalous misbehaviour in the US Treasury bond markets, it was carrying on its books more than $600 billion of derivative contracts.

This means that no one has an accurate picture of what is going on. In the USA, for instance, traded options come under the tutelage of the Commodity Futures Trading Commission, which at the behest of Congress undertook a study of financial derivatives. 'Data generally are available only for broad categories of derivative products and market participants,' was the complaint. Exchanges complain that because they were more closely regulated and bore more onerous reporting rules, they lose out competitively to OTC swaps which, because they are not traded in any market, escape supervision.

The banks are taking big risks. Do they know what they are up to?

When a corporate treasurer uses an option to shed a contingent risk, someone else is taking it on. Howard Flight, joint managing director of fund management group Guinness Flight, comments: 'Ultimately the whole thing can't net off, somebody's got exposure somewhere and the danger is that bank dealing rooms don't really have the ability to manage the situation.'

The leverage which an option works for the speculator who buys an option works equally on the provider of that option. At the outset they cannot know whether the currency rate will move in the direction which makes you exercise the option. If they do not hold the currency you have the right to buy, or a matching option or other derivative to cover the risk – if, in the colourful jargon of the financial markets, they are 'writing naked' – they can catch a very nasty cold indeed. They receive only the premium you pay to buy the option, a small proportion of its underlying effect. Theoretically at least, the losses from writing – selling – options without cover are infinite.

They grow not only in volume but also in variety and complexity. That carries hazards of its own. Bank of England associate director Ian Plenderleith warns: 'The very fact of the rapid growth in scale and variety brings new risks, actual or potential, in derivatives. Rapid growth in itself involves risks for the participating institutions, since even where the instruments are not completely new to the market, they are probably new and unfamiliar to some of the people involved with them.' Moreover, innovation in this area is relentless. In competing for the business of clients an investment bank will strive ever to improve the financial products it offers. It recruits mathematicians who devote weeks and months to devising ever more intricate formulae to cover ever-growing numbers of variables and contingencies.

Cautions Brian Quinn, head of supervision at the Bank of England: 'Expertise in derivatives trading is limited. If the demand for this new source of profit should expand faster than the supply of people capable of doing the business there can only be trouble ahead. Derivatives trading is for grown-ups.'

Are the banks grown-ups? They are writing the currency options and taking the risk. More than half of all currency options are those which banks sell over the counter to their customers. The customers want these OTC options because standardized traded options do not fit perfectly the risks they are covering. But that means that the banks cannot perfectly 'lay off' through the traded options markets the risks they accept in tailoring options to customer needs.

'The constant fear is that derivatives business is growing so much and that the risk management side of it is so badly understood by the players, that it could lead to a crash,' warns Jim O'Neill of SBC. 'This is the most widely discussed aspect and probably the least understood and that's because it's so complicated.

'It could well be that, if a less well-capitalized bank that hasn't got very sophisticated risk management technology consistent with its activity had a very large exposure at a time of a very large shock to the economic and financial system, then it would not be out of the bounds of possibility that a less well-capitalized bank might have problems.'

But how real is the risk of a bank miscalculating? According to James Wrangham, treasurer of Courtaulds, 'For quite a long time you could get enormous variations on a relatively straightforward swap or currency option from whichever bank you went to. And that means essentially that one or more of the banks was mispricing it and therefore dealing in instruments where they had not really worked out what the economic effect of their pricing was.

'I think the latest report of the Group of Thirty is quite a good attempt at focusing on how a bank should manage that and the sort of prudential things a bank should do to make sure it isn't either taking much more counterparty risk than it thinks or mismanaging its pricing of its portfolio.'

The Group of Thirty, a Washington-based think-tank dominated by international bankers, set out detailed guidelines on how to manage the risks involved. It said that senior managers of firms that deal in derivatives should know and sanction what their derivatives teams were arranging. Seems obvious?

A survey by Price Waterhouse found that almost one third didn't.

The Group of Thirty also recommended that derivatives positions should be revalued daily to reflect the day's market changes. Given that a small movement in the underlying market can have a leveraged effect on an option and therefore the bank's exposure, that may seem equally obvious. But more than half the banks did not 'mark to market' in this way and among those that did methods of doing so varied widely.

Dealers should run stress simulations to determine how their portfolios would perform in a worse-case scenario, said the report. Whether any supervisor would be able to understand the simulation well enough to judge its validity is another matter.

Soon after publication of that report, in September 1993, the IMF published a study which revealed that there are many transactions which the senior managers of banks and securities houses do not fully understand. The growth of derivatives trading could have created unknown risks for banks, the danger of which is not confined to the banks involved: 'Participation in derivatives markets can cause firms to become connected through complicated transactions which are not easily understood,' warned the IMF.

Firms can also become involved directly. Federal Reserve Board chairman Alan Greenspan cautioned in late 1992: 'A significant number of participants in the market for financial derivatives are unregulated non-bank financial institutions and increasingly even non-financial institutions. A failure by one of these institutions to perform on its contractual obligations could impose serious losses on customers and could result in serious systemic problems.'*

'Systemic risk' is what keeps central bankers awake at night, gives them nightmares, or both. As the Bundesbank expressed it in its October 1993 encyclical: 'The growing use of derivative instruments in strategies covering many markets has

---

* Speech to Federation of Bankers Associations of Japan, 14 October 1992.

reinforced the integration of the financial markets and hence increased their vulnerability. In the event of the failure of a major market player or serious market disruptions, one cannot be sure whether hedging or replacement contracts will still be available in the derivative markets. Once the spot markets, too, are no longer sufficiently liquid, this may trigger chain reactions and jeopardize the financial system as a whole.'

The danger of spot markets not being liquid enough could arise if derivatives continued to grow at their recent hectic pace. What the markets fear – the nightmare scenario for any central banker – is one or two major banks or other institutions defaulting and by so doing bringing down others, whose failure in turn affects more; what Sir Jasper Hollom, then Deputy Governor of the Bank of England, once described to a Commons committee as the 'widening circle of collapse' experienced in the 1930s.

At the Bank, Richard Allen, manager of banking supervision, told me, 'central banks are tending to look not only at the individual institutions but also at the systems and worrying about whether there are linkages between markets which can become mutually destabilizing, such that once one bit falls down the whole thing collapses on itself like a pack of cards.

'I don't think we know enough really, in terms of the statistics of these derivatives, to know yet what the real systemic implications are, but we're working on this as a matter of priority.

'My personal view is that derivatives can be risky if they're used by the wrong people – just as guns if they're used by the wrong people are dangerous – but they can do a lot of good as well, in that they can be used for risk reduction and do not necessarily lead to ever-increasing amounts of risk.'

It is the *sine qua non* of currency markets that they are international. This not only means that any systemic collapse would likewise be global but also heightens the risk of such an event.

When Federal Reserve chairman Alan Greenspan came to London in February 1994 to speak at the Bankers Club banquet marking the tercentenary of the Bank of England, he devoted much of what might have appropriately been a ceremonial and celebratory speech to a jeremiad on such dangers.

'Internationally active banks create the potential for systemic risk,' he warned. 'Disruptions or difficulties at one of these institutions could well have a significant impact on a wide range of other financial institutions and through them on the economy.

'This potential for systemic risk arises from the nature of internationally active banks. These banks are generally large. They fund themselves in international money markets, including London, where creditors are relatively quick to restrict funding to banks thought to be in trouble, and where the problems of one bank can easily affect funding to other banks from the same country.'

The international character of currency trading enhances the possibility of a mishap in derivatives triggering a systemic collapse. Rules vary between countries. Every bank prudently limits its counterparty risk: the maximum it will allow to be outstanding from any other bank. But against that it will usually offset what its owes that bank and look at the net amount. Often – but not always – that will be enshrined in what is called a 'novation clause' which simply means that the two counterparties agree to offset mutual claims and liabilities. As the Bundesbank observed, 'The extent to which, apart from what are known as novation clauses (which are everywhere recognized as being enforceable) other set-off agreements will actually hold up in court if one party is wound up, is unclear as far as German or international insolvency law is concerned.'

A Swiss bank may write – sell – DM:Yen options to a Swedish bank on a huge scale, creating an exposure of tens, perhaps hundreds, of millions of dollars. It is relaxed because against that it shows gains on the $:DM options it had bought from the same counterparty and likewise relaxed about the Swedish bank's ability to honour the deal. The two claims will be simply offset.

Without a novation clause, if the Swedish bank were to fail, the Swiss counterpart would find itself required to meet its gross liability on the options it had sold that bank but might rank only as a creditor – eventually receiving only partial repayment – in respect of the profits it has on the options it bought from that bank.

Novation clauses may give false comfort when they apply to options and some other derivatives because these instruments are so new that they do not have equal recognition in laws around the world. A bank in one country might find itself liable under its own laws for the full exposure of the options it wrote for a bank elsewhere but, under the laws of the country in which that bank wrote options, only entitled to offset what it paid for the options it bought, not their full value.

It gets worse. A Copenhagen bank buys from a Parisian bank an option giving the right to buy francs for D-marks. The French then buy from a Frankfurt bank an option to sell D-marks for dollars, from a New York bank they buy an option to buy sterling for dollars and from a London bank the right to sell sterling for francs. But all those options incur transactions costs so at various exchange rates the French bankers have also sold options on the $:DM, on £:$ to banks in Spain and Japan. Then they have a swap agreement with an Australian bank.

As the Bundesbank put it: 'The question arises as to the legal enforceability of balances that are generated, particularly in the case of facilities in which a number of countries participate, since a netting procedure must be compatible with all the legal systems involved. The more legal systems are affected, the more difficult it will be to find a satisfactory solution.' The peril is piqued by derivatives business being so concentrated.

One must not lose sight of the fact that currency options and other derivatives are useful to companies engaged in international trade and investment. Launching a new product into an export market, even trying to sell, deliver and get paid promptly for an established product or service is fraught with enough uncertainties. The financial risk of exchange rates can be passed to the banks and other risk-takers – speculators – through derivatives. The system can then spread the risk so that it has no great impact on any single entity.

This procedure holds out the promise of engendering financial stability. 'The mere spreading of the risks among several other market participants may have a stabilizing effect on the financial system,' the Bundesbank accepted. But seven banks are responsible for 90 per cent of all exposure to OTC derivatives in the USA. Six banks do 90 per cent of London's foreign exchange derivatives turnover. Swiss Bank Corporation claims to have one quarter of the currency options market. 'To the extent that business in individual derivative products is confined to a few institutions acting as market makers, the viability of the market segment concerned could be adversely affected if extreme supply or demand conditions obtained,' notes the Bundesbank. 'In the event of the collapse of a market segment, resultant disruptions might also spill over to neighbouring market segments – in particular to the spot market.

'A broadening of the markets for derivative products is therefore in the interests of the overall stabilization of the markets. But the more new products are tailored to the specific needs of market players, the narrower the individual market will be.'

Let's not be alarmist. Leave that to the central bankers such as Alan Greenspan and the Bundesbank. Some take comfort from the agonies of worry about derivatives shown by those responsible for preventing mishaps in the banking and financial system. 'I regard the agonising as immensely healthy,' says Howard Flight, joint managing director of fund management group Guinness Flight. 'Prevention is better than cure and the mere fact authorities around the world are taking stock is a very healthy sign. I think the probability is that there won't be any serious accidents.'

Jim O'Neill agrees. 'I would imagine that central banks are doing more work on that than on anything else right now because it is a potential problem. I work on the basis that so long as central banks worry about something all the time then it's going to be okay. So I like the fact that central banks worry so much.'

What, apart from such commendable worrying, are the central banks doing, however? The Bank of England has introduced a regime where the more a bank can show it knows what it is doing, the more risk – still within limits – it will be allowed to take. 'I don't have any problems with new instruments *per se*,' banking supervision manager Richard Allen told me. 'There are bound to be areas where you might want to start drawing lines or thinking quite carefully about the nature of underlying risks that the bank is running.'

If a bank writes options, what it reports to Threadneedle Street depends on whether it has been granted expert status. There are two levels of reporting for currency options. When they begin writing options all banks must report on a deliberately restrictive basis because Richard Allen's team recognize that the risks of options can, for the uninitiated, be quite large. Moreover, the guidelines by which Threadneedle Street limits banks' total foreign exchange exposure are so designed that a bank will more quickly get to its limits by writing options. But a sophisticated bank can claim that it has the expertise to handle greater risk. The Bank of England team will visit the bank's offices and go through everything, no holds barred. 'We'll go through the business plan,' Richard Allen told me. 'Why are they doing it? What's the strategy? What do they hope to be trading? Are they trading volatility or underlying currency movement? What currencies they're using, what maturities, what types of options, because we're hearing more and more about exotic, structured, options. We'll look at the systems and controls in place and the internal limit structure that they have. And we're quite hands-on in looking at those.'

If the bank is then granted expert status it need report only on its unhedged delta exposure. That, the Bank of England recognizes, is by no means the whole story, hence the emphasis on ensuring that there are adequate reliable systems in place.

Derivatives grew largely because currency risk grew when currency rates became more volatile. The risk is there whether you have derivatives or banish them. An instrument may enable you to handle and control risk, but if you mishandle the instrument the risk may grow worse.

Paradoxically, whereas the foreign exchange market has no physical marketplace and is all by telephone and screen trading, the trading in the even more intangible and esoteric derivatives takes place largely in specific buildings. They have physical presence. And how.

These are the pits. Literally. In Chicago, London and elsewhere around the world a broker telephones your order directly to an order desk adjacent to the trading pits on the exchange floor. The message then passes by messenger – 'runner' – or hand signal to a broker in the trading pit. In that jostling, heaving maelstrom of brightly blazered bodies all trying to shove their way in, all shouting their bids and offers in what looks like hopeless incomprehensible chaos, the deal is done. This is rather inadequately called 'open outcry' and means that the second every bid and offer reaches the floor it gets equal chance in the market as of that instant. Meanwhile all bids, offers and trades are relayed within seconds to price reporters at computer workstations overlooking the floor and, through quote vendors, are instantaneously disseminated worldwide.

The biggest of these marketplaces are the Chicago Board of Trade, founded in 1848, and the Chicago Mercantile Exchange, which set up in competition in 1874. They still trade farm product futures by open outcry in the pits as they did at the outset. Financial futures started in the 1970s.

The two Chicago markets cooperated in developing jointly with Reuters the Globex screen trading system. The idea was for users worldwide to move on to a screen-based system when open outcry trading ended. To date, this has not been a success, partly because of reluctance by many potential customers to take risk when the underlying market is closed. The development has not been helped, either, by petty jealousies. The Chicagoans would not let the London International Financial Futures Exchange (LIFFE) trade on Globex its highly successful German government bond (bunds) futures contract. So LIFFE didn't join Globex. Other futures exchanges were deterred by suspicions about the system's management control being under the influence of the two US markets. The Chicago Board of Trade decided to withdraw from Globex.

The US futures markets, notwithstanding that they have continued to increase their trading volumes, have been losing global market share. American futures exchanges raised their turnover by 20 per cent in 1992, Europe's rose 66 per cent. (But Japan's fell for two consecutive years). More than half of all futures trading is now outside America.

In Europe, the big success has been LIFFE which, started only in 1982 – more than a century after its American rivals – is already the world's third largest derivatives exchange. LIFFE, which now incorporates the London Traded Options Market has faced challenges from French rival MATIF – which was the only other exchange to join up with Globex – and the German screen-based system Deutsche Terminborse (DTB). To date, LIFFE has won. Despite determined and united efforts by all the German banks there is still a greater volume of German government bonds traded on LIFFE than on the DTB.

MATIF and DTB – one an open outcry, the other a screen market – have joined forces to rival London but MATIF chairman Gerard Pfauwadel admitted to me that – unlike London – it has been unsuccessful in launching futures contracts in currencies other than its own. 'We were not able to develop liquidity in these and I think the main reason is that we were in competition with London,' he told me. 'It is also clear that London is, for the secondary market, a more developed place for exotic products than we are in Paris.'

The Franco-German duo harbour, however, a longer-term plan to lead other European futures exchanges – there were more than twenty at the last count – in ganging up against LIFFE. 'For this link between MATIF and DTB, once we have constituted the hard core – the Franco-German hard core – the idea is to try and provide an access to the other European exchanges. So they will have the possibility to list their products and in that case it will not be necessary – because we will have this cross-exchange access mechanism – to list on the Franco-German platform other European products, which constitutes a kind of aggression to other European exchanges.

'It is exactly the contrary of the strategy of London, which is trying to launch any type of European product and to build liquidity whatever happens in the domestic field.'

* * *

Business activity tends to gravitate towards financial centres, so there has been considerable rivalry in establishing them. Around the world – in Hong Kong, Singapore, Copenhagen, New York, Zurich, Frankfurt, Sydney, Paris and Tokyo – the value of being an international financial centre (and consequently the nerve centre for myriad other business and quasi-political activities) has been recognized.

London has not just taken the lead and kept it, despite the declining role of sterling, it has even managed to increase its lead. The Bank for International Settlements survey of foreign exchange activity in April 1992, conducted through the central banks of twenty-six countries, reported:

'The United Kingdom is a case apart. It is the single largest centre for foreign exchange trading. In 1992 it accounted for 27 per cent of net turnover, up from 25 per cent in 1989 . . .

'The amount of foreign currency business conducted out of London is so great that domestic currency transactions account for less than a quarter of total trading there. In fact, foreign currency trading is so substantial that a larger share of trading in both US dollars (26 per cent) and Deutschmarks (27 per cent) takes place in the United Kingdom than in either the United States (18 per cent) or Germany (10 per cent) respectively.

'In addition over 40 per cent of all reported deals involving the ecu have one counterparty located in the United Kingdom. This centre is also the second most important site, after their domestic markets, for the trading of Swiss francs, Australian dollars and French francs.'

Why is this so?

In part, it is the luck of geography and of being well-placed between the time zones of East and West. Perhaps, it is in part the residue of empire and an erstwhile Great Power status (though it is hard to associate that with such recent innovations as currency derivatives). Largely, though, it is due to London's international outlook, fostered by a regulatory system which welcomes foreigners. There are more than 350 foreign banks in London, more US banks in the City than in New York. London created and kept the Eurodollar markets conceived out of the loins of the US government's interest equalization tax.

When the Korean Government gave its seven largest securities firms permission to open one full branch each overseas in 1990, all seven headed straight to London. When I asked each why, they separately gave the same answer: Tokyo was nearer and bigger but unwelcoming to foreigners; New York bigger and, while tolerant of foreigners, an inward-looking market; the City was the international financial centre, the place to be.

Because the foreign exchange market itself has no physical marketplace but is all on the telephone and screens, is there any real need for it to be in the City? Could it not as easily – and more cheaply – be in Cheltenham, Crewe or even Cadiz? I challenged Michael Knowles, who as chairman of the broking firm MW Marshall comes as close as anyone to providing the foreign exchange markets themselves with a physical location.

'It is analogous to Silicon Valley or the science parks around universities,' he told me. 'Could we get the same telecommunications network, the right catchment area for staff, the right area for disaster recovery, for example? What of the services provided to keep us in business here and would those same services be provided outside the M25 belt?

'We still need personal direct contact with our customers and customer feedback of the kind they wouldn't give us over the telephone. We've analysed this and believe this is where we should be today.'

Is London's status under threat from European Monetary Union? Competition to be the headquarters city of the European Union's central bank, intended eventually to control Europe's single currency, was intense. Frankfurt won the battle only after bitter in-fighting at the highest levels of international politics. French, German, Dutch and other politicians all believed that wherever the central bank was based, to there would financial activity and the providers of financial services gravitate.

However, whereas the world's largest central bank, the Federal Reserve Board, has its headquarters in Washington, whenever it wants to operate in the markets – to intervene in foreign exchange or to affect interest rates – it has to deal through its member Reserve Bank of New York. That is where the US financial market is centred just as London is – and will probably remain – the locus of international money.

3

HOW WE GOT HERE
After Gold

The belted Earl of Halifax
Confided to Lord Keynes,
'Those Yanks may have the moneybags
But we've got all the brains.'

Currencies have fluctuated violently only since the system of fixed exchange rates, which held good for quarter of this century, broke down in 1971. Will we return to such an arrangement or something similar? Will the rest of the world follow Europe's efforts to establish a single currency? What about gold, which for centuries was the money all the world used?

In July 1944, while war still raged in Europe and the Far East, the representatives of forty-four countries met in the Bretton Woods Hotel, New Hampshire. The United Nations Monetary and Financial Conference agreed to fix exchange rates.

Under the Bretton Woods agreement each government undertook to keep its currency at a fixed exchange rate to the dollar or, if it preferred, in terms of gold. As the dollar was itself pegged to gold – $35 could be converted into one ounce of gold – a country's choice of benchmark made no practical difference. And, of course, fixing the value of every currency against the dollar immediately fixed the cross exchange rate: between, for instance the pound and French franc. (In fact it was not quite so rigid, exchange rates could vary about 1 per cent each way.)

A year before the Bretton Woods meeting the British economist John Maynard Keynes had published proposals for a world organization to stabilize international exchanges and so enlarge international trade. Simultaneously, Harry D. White, US assistant secretary to the Treasury, produced his own separate but similar plan.

A Joint Statement by Experts on these two sets of ideas formed the basis of discussion at Bretton Woods. Out of that sprang:

The World Bank – formally the International Bank for Reconstruction and Development – lending on easy terms to countries which cannot finance their own development.

The International Monetary Fund (IMF) would run the new international monetary system. The new system, the Bretton Woods agreement, fixed exchange rates with the proviso that a country could devalue – fix a new, lower, rate for its currency – if it was persistently running a balance of payments deficit: that is, spending and investing abroad more than it was earning from exports together with what was flowing into the country as investment.

This was the world's first attempt to create and manage money worldwide. It was a deliberate effort to replace gold in the world's money system but – as all other currencies were still pegged indirectly to gold through the dollar – a limited one.

A banknote bears the legend, ' I promise to pay the bearer on demand the sum of . . .'. Paradoxically, the chief cashier at the Bank of England still derives some of the prestige of his office from having his signature on the banknote, even though this promise is made to be dishonoured.

When we were on the gold standard that promise meant what it said: you could take your paper currency to the Bank, demand payment in gold, and get it. People accepted paper currency, which is intrinsically worthless, because it was convertible into gold.

With the whole money supply backed by gold, the level of economic activity was directly affected by how well the country was paying its way in the world. When a country bought from overseas more than it earned abroad, it paid the difference by shipping gold from its reserves. As gold left the country the central bank – the Bank of England – had to reduce the amount of money in circulation by raising interest rates in order to maintain its ability to back all currency with gold. In other words, there was no scope for government deficit financing – the government running up debts to stimulate economic activity.

As the world's largest trader and lender, Britain was keen on global stability and went on the gold standard in 1821. The system worked largely because Britain was willing to let the vast quantities of gold it received swell its money supply and so create spending power which offset deflation in the countries from which gold drained.

The First World War hastened what was already becoming inevitable. Other nations, particularly the USA, were growing in economic might. After 1918 the UK could no longer play the key role in maintaining the gold standard. America and France held 60 per cent of the world's total gold reserves but were not willing to take on the pivotal role in the world monetary system and even acted to prevent inflows of gold into their reserves boosting their money supplies.

One reason, in America's case, was that the dollar itself had only just emerged from a troubled childhood in which the inflationary impact of the now legendary gold rushes had played a part.

By the late 1920s American policymakers were worried about curbing stock market speculation and the French were wary about inflation which had spurted at the beginning of that decade. Even as Wall Street crashed the Federal Reserve Board – the USA's central bank – kept a tight grip on credit, depressing spending. As US imports fell, so Europe's balance of payments deficit grew, draining gold away, so that the money supply and spending power decreased. America can be said to have exported deflation and depression.

Britain, having come off the gold standard during the First World War and, eventually, returned to it, left it again in 1931 and twenty-five other countries followed. The USA stuck to gold until 1933. Germany and Italy stayed with gold but imposed capital controls. The gold bloc – Belgium, France, Holland, Poland and Switzerland – remained tied to gold until

1935–6. Between 1929 and 1936 their industrial output fell by an average of 14 per cent. Germany's and Italy's declined 2 per cent and America 6 per cent. The UK and countries which came out of gold first saw their output rise by 27 per cent.* Incidentally, it is notable that those countries which in 1993 stayed most tenaciously with the ERM were all among those which had stuck to gold, perhaps reflecting ingrained national attitudes and values.

Under the eventual European Monetary Union envisaged in the Maastricht treaty, a single currency and therefore common interest rates throughout the European Union would leave no scope for interest rates and exchange rates to reflect the different impact an external event – widespread drought or a sharp change in oil prices, for instance – would have on different member countries. The real economy – the level of activity – must make the adjustment.

This was one aspect of the old gold standard which Keynes attacked. He argued that it led to unnecessary unemployment. His system would be for countries to run accounts with each other out of a sort of international bank account.

The delegates to Bretton Woods – to which the Earl of Halifax accompanied Keynes – agreed to supplement gold's role in the international monetary system. Keynes had advocated an International Clearing Union and for credit to be automatic for countries in difficulty. The Bretton Woods agreement, based on a modification of Keynes' idea – because the USA feared full implementation would be inflationary – thus gave the dollar a key role in the world financial system so as to create enough international reserves.

Each IMF member country pays an entry fee into a pool of funds which is then available to countries in temporary balance of payments trouble. The fee, or quota, depends on the size of the member country's economy and also decides the size of its vote in IMF deliberations and how much it has the right to borrow from the pool.

* 'Relaxing the External Constraint: Europe in the 1930s', B. Eichengreen, CEPR paper No. 452.

A member country pays its quota a quarter in gold and the rest in its own currency. If it gets into balance of payments difficulties then instead of needing to bring down the shutters on imports it can pump more of its own currency into the IMF and withdraw an equivalent amount of foreign currencies to buttress its reserves. The drawings are normally limited in any one year to a quarter of the country's quota and must not normally accumulate to more than 125 per cent of the quota. The idea of this is to ensure that countries use the system only to tide themselves over temporary balance of payments problems, not to run an increasing deficit.

Given that a country is swapping its own currency for that of others, if there were not this limit then it could be similar to my trying to settle an overdraft by drawing a cheque on the same account and paying it in. It would be worse, as the delinquent country would get others' currencies and debase the whole international financial system by pumping into it increasing amounts of its own fast depreciating currency.

Any country wanting to draw beyond its entitlement needs the consent of the IMF, which may send in a team of inspectors and then attach conditions to the loan: for example, that the government cuts its spending and puts some aspects of the economy in order. (The biggest cut in UK public spending came not, as many suppose, during the Thatcher era but in 1976 when Dennis Healey as Chancellor of the Exchequer had to go cap in hand to the IMF. That was in fact the last time the IMF's resources were used for a developed country and today there's much talk of merging it with the World Bank.)

Half a century after the Bretton Woods meeting and twenty years after the system of fixed exchange rates it created broke down, the dollar has lost much of its importance as the mainstay of international currency reserves around the world.

The role of gold persists. 'The gold standard is the fundamental currency reserve on which we have so far happily not had to fall back,' observed Helmut Schlesinger of the Bundesbank. 'Let it always remain so.' Today, central banks still hold 35,000 tonnes of gold. That is one third of all the world's gold and equivalent to seventeen years' mining production.

If governments invested their gold in government bonds it would earn them more than $20 billion a year in interest. For Switzerland, long noted for its conservative attitude and strong attachment to gold, this loss of potential interest earnings is equivalent to $550 a year for every taxpayer.

Forty per cent of industrial countries' currency reserves are in gold, but it is not a very liquid form of money. Some argue that the central banks' collective holdings are so large that they could not sell enough bullion to reduce its proportion of the reserves significantly without depressing the price they realized and disrupting the market. However, when the need arises a central bank can borrow; gold, for all the efforts to replace and usurp it, remains universally good collateral for loans. The Russian authorities, lacking creditworthiness, began to deposit gold abroad in 1992 to use as security for international loans.

In early 1994, Terry Smeeton, husbanding Britain's reserves at the Bank of England, told a conference in Kalgoorlie that some central bank gold was being used to back a new type of investment, a Euro certificate. He said it would not necessarily result in banks releasing their gold as they could sell or buy certificates throughout the period of their validity. 'The fact that some interest is being earned on central bank gold reserves may enable a reserve manager more easily to keep at bay those within the country who may wish to sell gold.' The Bank of England would not take part in the scheme, he added.

Few countries today, however, even if they held no reserves, would have to close the docks and stop imports of tea, transistors and tractors just because they had not exported enough that month to pay for imports. Most can borrow, first whatever the markets will lend and then, as a last resort, from the IMF.

Today, the main purpose of the reserves is for intervention to support the currency exchange rate. In the last few years central banks have been building their official reserves apart from gold rather unevenly; certainly not at a rate calculated to reflect the burgeoning level of activity on the foreign exchange markets.

Change in Official non-gold Reserves ($bn)

	1989	1990	1991	1992
World	+45.7	+120.2	+49.3	+21.8
Industrialized countries	+30.6	+87.3	−15.7	−26.0

Central banks rely increasingly on their ability to borrow if they need to support their currencies. Not all, of course, can do so and even the most developed countries will prefer to regard borrowing as a second-line defence, keeping a prudent amount of reserves. At the Bank of England, foreign exchange division chief Terry Smeeton's first priority is that they should be secure and readily available: liquid. The return earned on investing them is very much a secondary consideration. Those are the characteristics every central bank looks for in choosing the currencies in which it will hold its reserves: the so-called reserve currencies.

You can always tell a reserve currency: it was the one which rose sharply in a crisis. Central bankers and private sector investors – the Old Lady of Threadneedle Street, the old men of the Pru and BP pension fund, Emily Foggett of Cheam with her widow's mite – are a bit like rabbits. They venture forth ever farther abroad and then, at the first hint of a squall, scurry back to safe haven. Last night's enthusiasm for the Hong Kong dollar or Argentine telephone company shares evaporates faster than morning dew in midsummer. Comfort comes from the security of US government fixed interest bonds. In investment jargon this behaviour is dignified with the term 'retreat to quality'.

Gold, the dollar and the Swiss franc were the world's favourite funk holes. The Swiss franc particularly seems to have lost that role of late. The movement in the price of gold, sometimes sharp in recent years, has been unrelated to crises; and a surge in the dollar today at the outbreak of trouble is modest compared with yesteryear. Central bankers and investors of all kinds have diversified their holdings, no longer trusting in any one currency as an absolute refuge.

Certainly the dollar's role as a reserve currency has declined. It accounted for 80 per cent of the foreign exchange reserves held in the world's central banks in 1976 but only 56 per cent in 1991. The Deutschmark's share has grown over the same period from 7 to 17 per cent and the yen from 1 to 10 per cent. 'Given the greater liquidity of many currencies – which is a by-product of the huge turnover in the foreign exchange market – then we don't really need one currency to have the starring role,' suggests Chris Dillow, economist at Nomura Research Institute's European headquarters in the City.

As the USA's economic hegemony declined and Japan gained relative stature in international trade, politicians and academics alike began to call for the yen to assume the responsibilities of a reserve currency. Yet today the yen accounts for only one tenth of the foreign currency reserves held by central banks around the world. Has the Japanese Government deliberately shirked its responsibility?

'If the Japanese Government were reluctant for the yen to be a reserve currency then it would have been reluctant to see the sharp appreciation of the yen versus the dollar in 1993 despite the fact that the Japanese economy was in no state to sustain an appreciation of that magnitude just then,' says Chris Dillow. 'The Japanese have stood by and let it happen.'

Most central banks have a core percentage in yen. That it is used less than the Deutschmark might simply be a result of geography, suggests Dr Brendan Brown, long regarded as one of Europe's leading currency economists and author of several books on the subject. As a director and head of research at the Japanese group Mitsubishi Finance International, he counters largely US criticism that Japanese restrictions suppress the yen's role as a reserve currency.

'That is simplistic because Japan's geographic situation is less favourable to the yen's developing a larger reserve currency role,' he argues. 'The Deutschmark is Proxy Number One international currency for Europe and most European governments and those outside hold Deutschmarks as their reserve European currency.

'Japan is not in anything like the EC and the Asia Pacific

area is much more dollar-based. That's nothing to do with what Japan's doing but with natural trade flows, the lack of interdependent monetary policies and different stages of development.'

The yen does at least command a larger reserve currency role than Japan's share of world trade, which is less than 7.5 per cent.

'One reason why the concept has declined in importance since 1971 is that it's been seen that countries cannot accept the responsibility of having a reserve currency,' surmises Chris Dillow.

What are the responsibilities and what the advantages of being the host country of a reserve currency?

The first task is to run a current account surplus. The balance of payments is a balance. If a country exports more than it imports so that there is a trade – current account – surplus then, in simple terms, it will have a matching deficit on capital account: investing abroad more than the inflow of foreign investment. It is the money sent abroad for capital investment which is then held by the foreign central bank in its reserves.

'To run the current account surplus that is necessary for the reserve currency then you have to run your economy below the level of capacity – that is, with higher unemployment – than is acceptable for most countries,' notes Chris Dillow.

'Also, of course, there are – as we have seen in Germany – external shocks which can cause you to lose your reserve currency status. In the 1980s you'd have looked at the German current account and unemployment and said that this was a reserve currency, they could carry on with a current account surplus. But now that's no longer the case.

'The same could be true of Japan. People think the trade surplus there is due to structural inadequacies which are going to be addressed.'

Another problem is that with so many foreigners holding large amounts of your currency in their reserves, any loss of confidence will be magnified in its effect by their selling, points out Brendan Brown.

'A lot of investors hold the Deutschmark as a safe store of

value outside Germany. If the Bundesbank took inflationary moves it would get a bigger whammy than if Portugal decided to do that, for instance.

'The advantage of reserve currency status is that a currency popular with the world's investors will tend to have a lower real interest rate (after adjusting for inflation) than other currencies which are seen to have more risk attached. The lower cost of capital benefits your economy as a whole. Your financial sector should gain from your currency being used worldwide. German financial institutions, for instance, are at a relative advantage to their UK rivals because of the Deutschmark being a bigger international currency. Businesses in a reserve currency centre are less exposed to exchange rate risk because their own currency is more acceptable in international trading.'

It was because the dollar could no longer live up to its role as reserve currency – or rather, as the USA failed its responsibilities – that the whole system of fixed exchange rates collapsed.

'The USA did not renege on that obligation because they were duplicitous – although the fact that Richard Nixon was President at the time did not help to dispel that impression – the US economy failed to fulfil that because of fundamental pressures within it,' judges Chris Dillow. 'There is a danger that any other currency that adopts the reserve currency status will be prey to the same pressures.'

What were the pressures which were to destroy the system of fixed exchange rates under which businessmen enjoyed a greater element of predictability in international trade?

The US Government's promise to convert on request every $35 into an ounce of gold, which made central banks willing to use dollars as well as gold bullion as a reserve currency, was backed by the USA having gold stocks equal to three quarters of the world's total gold stock. It also held more than half the world's total official reserves. But the guarantee to keep the dollar convertible put a ceiling of $35 on the official price of gold. It did not allow for inflation pushing up the demand for gold. In time there was upward pressure on the free market price of gold.

In 1961, the central banks of Western Europe and the USA formed the Gold Pool to try and keep the price of gold near the $35 official level. By the mid-1960s, the cost of producing gold was rising and the world's central banks found that the amount of gold they were selling to dampen its market price was greater than the amount of new production they could buy from the mines. After heavy selling of official stocks in 1966–68, they had to yield ground. The governments agreed that their official transactions would still be at a price for gold of $35 an ounce whereas all other business would be at the free market price. There was a two-tier market.

During this time international trade was growing, so the need for official reserves was growing, too. Gold reserves were not growing, so foreign currencies had to play a larger part in the official reserves.

The Bretton Woods agreement was confronted by a credibility problem. You couldn't keep increasing the currency convertible into gold without raising doubts about whether the pledge to convert on demand would be honoured. By 1964 the dollars held in the official reserves of central banks around the rest of the world equalled the USA's gold stock. Four years later the gold stock was enough to cover only two thirds of the dollars in other countries' official reserves. Moreover, rising inflation in America undermined the buying power of those dollars. With the price of gold still fixed in official transactions, central banks had an increasing incentive to convert their foreign exchange reserves into gold. US ambassadors around the world set about arm-twisting, the transatlantic telephone lines burning long and hot with requests, pleadings, cajolings and veiled threats to make central banks hold dollars and not switch to gold.

The crisis came to a head in 1971. President Nixon was in trouble. He faced re-election the next year and the US economy had not been performing well under his tutelage. By July 1971 US economic recovery seemed to be running out of steam, inflation was not firmly licked and unemployment might rise rather than fall. The USA was headed for a $10 billion payments deficit the next year.

A build-up of speculation against the dollar had been gathering force throughout the first seven months of 1971 and ran on into August. In early August a number of countries pressed to convert dollars into other assets, mainly gold.

'Other countries asked us for reserve assets we had not got,' US Treasury Secretary John Connally later recounted. 'We were faced with a run on the bank.' In the second week of August the Deutschmark was 8 per cent – rather than the maximum 1 per cent allowed by Bretton Woods – above its parity with the dollar on the foreign exchange markets, and in the bullion markets gold was $44 an ounce. A central bank could demand from the US Treasury an ounce of gold for $35 and immediately sell for $44. If you were a poor country and did not know how much longer the US Government would honour its promise to support the dollar, what would you do?

In the week which ended – perhaps fittingly – with Friday the 13th of August the outflow from the US reserves was more than $3 billion. The gold in those reserves was already uncomfortably close to the $10 billion regarded as a minimum safety level.

The week had not started well. Over the preceding weekend there had been a furore as a Congressional sub-committee on international exchange and payments said the dollar was overvalued. It urged the IMF to make other countries – especially Japan – revalue.

'If the membership of the Fund fails to confront this issue and does not specify the mechanism through which dollar exchange rates can be promptly restructured,' said the report, 'the US should then promptly consider a unilateral initiative to achieve this same result, perhaps by floating the dollar within specified limits.'

The committee chairman, Senator Henry Reuss, pointed out that with the two-tier gold price the USA could float the dollar temporarily and arrive at a new value without massive disruption.

The response of the US Treasury was to suggest that the sub-committee's limited hearings were not representative of Congressional opinion. (In other words, the Administration had not managed to stuff the hearings with tame witnesses who would toe its policy line.)

The Treasury issued a formal statement, 'No discussions are planned or anticipated with respect to exchange rate realignment at the IMF or elsewhere.' What was considered remarkable at the time was that they bothered to refute or deny the report of a small and obscure committee whose conclusion was not unanimous.

In time, what Reuss had proposed the markets indeed disposed but the execution was to be unmanaged and haphazard. Any opportunity to salvage a perhaps reformed exchange rate system was disregarded for considerations of political convenience. As a leader in the *Financial Times* said that week: 'The chances of the US Administration submitting to this blow to its prestige in a pre-election year is so remote as to be virtually non-existent.' It warned that without currency change pressure for trade restrictions was bound to become overwhelming.

Pressure built swiftly as the week wore on. There were reports that France had converted $470 million into gold. A recent UK repayment to the IMF of £256 million debt arising from sterling's devaluation in 1967 had been in Belgian francs and Netherlands guilders because the IMF already held too many dollars and couldn't take any more.

It was known that on the following Monday morning the USA would have to buy $862 million from the IMF in return for Belgian francs and Netherlands guilders. Their central banks, anxious to avoid the risk to their reserves of dollar devaluation, had exchanged dollars for credit at the IMF on which the exchange rate was guaranteed.

President Nixon broadcast to the American people from Camp David late on the Sunday night. Europe was already in the early hours of Monday morning. He advised beforehand only Dr Henry Kissinger and Secretary of State William Rogers, not Treasury Secretary Connally nor Federal Reserve Board chairman Dr Arthur Burns: a move consistent with political rather than economic manoeuvring. Nixon declared a national emergency.

Convertibility of the dollar into gold or other reserve assets was suspended. There would be a 10 per cent surcharge on all imports except crude oil, petrol and food. Prices, wages and dividends would be frozen for 100 days. Foreign aid was cut 10 per cent. An excise tax levy of 7 per cent on cars repealed. Income tax would be cut. R&D spending was boosted. Federal government spending overall was to be cut $4.7 billion and that meant eliminating one in every twenty jobs in government but measures would be introduced to increase private sector employment sharply. The suspension of the dollar's convertibility – in effect abandoning the Bretton Woods arrangement – Mr Nixon blamed on 'international speculators'.

Most foreign exchange markets and the gold market did not open on the Monday morning. Japan was the exception. By the time Nixon had announced his measures and they had been translated, the Tokyo market was already open and the Bank of Japan took in $700 million at the suddenly obsolete exchange rate. The Tokyo market stayed open. Dealings in the London bullion market did not resume until midweek and whereas Frankfurt, Zurich and New York resumed trading the Bank of England did not allow London's foreign exchange dealers to trade at all that week. President Pompidou of France suggested a two-tier foreign exchange market with commercial transactions at fixed rates. He held that the problem arose from relying on a single reserve currency.

One way out might have been simply to have raised the official price of gold: devalue the dollar – and all currencies pegged to it – in terms of gold. That would have had the effect of raising the value of US gold stocks to match the dollars held in official reserves around the rest of the world. But it would have paid a bonus to those who were generally thought to have played dirty and hoarded gold, together with major producers, Russia and South Africa, while penalizing those who had supported the dollar. It was also seen as likely to fuel speculation about the next adjustment.

In the meantime, during that week, with the foreign exchange markets either in turmoil or closed and politicians' minds wonderfully concentrated by Richard Nixon's declaration of little less than a trade war with a 10 per cent import surcharge, negotiations on how collectively they should respond were fraught. All-night talks by the EEC Six – the UK was not yet a member – broke down at 2.15 a.m. on Friday 20 August. The UK Treasury announced that the £:$ parity would stay at $2.40 as before but 'for the time being dealings will not necessarily be confined within the existing limits'. The $2.40 rate was a bargaining ploy as the UK had no wish and saw no need to revalue. The *de facto* flotation would not be described as such, however, so as to avoid exacerbating tensions within the EEC – particularly between Germany and France. Most European currencies, like sterling, joined the Deutschmark in floating against the dollar. France alone refused and created a two-tier rate. Soon afterwards, before the end of August, the yen also floated.

A few weeks later, the finance ministers and central bank governors of all the IMF and World Bank member countries, together with their retinues of officials, wives, hangers-on, wives' best friends, an inordinate number of bankers and wheeler-dealers with no official excuse – and all of these outnumbered by a legion of journalists – met as usual at that time of year in the Sheraton Park Hotel, Washington DC. The plenary session of the IMF piously called on members to 'collaborate with each other as promptly as possible for a satisfactory realignment of exchange rates within appropriate margins'.

In its long and chequered career of needing to square the realities of the world's economy with the circle of politicians' need for re-election, the IMF has spawned various progeny. The Interim Committee is the policymaking body with real power. At the other end of the spectrum lies the Group of Twenty-four, representing mostly developing countries. The Group of Five and of Seven have less ostensible standing but represent their respective numbers of the world's most developed countries. Then there is the Group of Ten. Founded in 1962 to supplement IMF resources with a General Agreement to Borrow, it has twelve members (finance ministers and central bankers can't count) who have on occasion collectively supplemented the IMF's resources. The G10 ministers were to meet in Rome over the weekend of 22–23 November. US Treasury Secretary Connally, having as chairman issued the invitations, suddenly, on 11 November, postponed the meeting, citing lack of agreement. Their views were too far apart for agreement to be in prospect.

The widest chasm split Europe. Germany and all save France accepted that they should revalue against the dollar. France – whose President Pompidou was personally one of Europe's most ardent bullion bugs – refused to revalue or to float the franc. France hoped to force what it saw as a necessary revaluation of gold, with which both the vaults of the Banque de France and, folklore had it, the cellars of many a French peasant farmer were stuffed.

The USA was now under pressure from the IMF either to convert some of that institution's excess dollars into gold or to make an orthodox drawing from the fund, which by its accounting rules would alleviate the position.

There was also market pressure. By mid-November this is how major currencies had changed over just six months:

Currency	v $	v all major currencies
$	-	−6.9
£	+3.9	−0.6
DM	+9.6	+5.1
Yen	+9.6	+6.9
FF	+0.4	−5.6
Lira	+2.0	−3.3
Sw fr	+9.5	+4.1
Neth gldr	+8.5	+2.3
Belg fr	+7.6	+2.1

As for gold, Senators Reuss and Javits were advocating its dollar price be raised 10 per cent; the official price was now satirically referred to as 'the price at which the USA refuses to sell gold'. Since the Nixon measures the US authorities resisted talk of returning the dollar to gold convertibility.

The G10's ministerial meeting was to be postponed for a

week but on its eve, Friday 29 November, the USA demanded that all other currencies revalue by an average of 11 per cent (the yen by 33 per cent) against the dollar. It would not change the dollar price of gold nor undertake to restore convertibility.

Meanwhile, there had been considerable diplomatic haggling over the trade concessions America could extract in return for discarding its unilateral imposition of the 10 per cent import surcharge. The obdurate on both trade and currency issues was France. President Nixon agreed to meet President Pompidou in mid-December. The meeting, reflecting diplomatic sensitivities that neither should appear supplicant, would be as near midway between their capitals as the Atlantic Ocean allowed: the Azores. So the G10 ministers' November meeting in the Palazzo Corsini agreed to meet again in Washington in mid-December after the two presidents had reached a deal.

The haggling and trade diplomacy over trade concessions continued and agreement emerged that instead of immediately fixing new exchange rates there would first be temporary rates with wide margins.

Nixon and Pompidou met in a small administrative building in Terceira, Azores, on 13 and 14 December. At a press conference in the small, walled garden of the building they announced they had agreed an interlinked trade settlement and dollar devaluation. They did not specify how much other currencies would revalue against the dollar but the principle was established. Exchange rates would also fluctuate in future with wider margins.

President Pompidou had agreed to talks on trade problems between the USA and the EEC. He also agreed to establish an agenda for longer-term negotiations on world trade. President Pompidou hinted that France would not change the official price of gold in French francs.

The G10 meeting in Washington at the end of that week had 'only' to resolve the details. The EEC, Canada and Japan undertook to make further trade concessions to the USA in exchange for formal devaluation of the dollar from $35 to $38 per ounce of gold. Canada would keep its currency floating.

President Nixon personally announced agreement a few minutes after six o'clock on the Saturday evening. These were the new exchange rates for the dollar and how they compared with market rates:

Currency	Par 1 May	Mkt 13 August	Mkt 17 December	New par	Percentage change v 1 May
£	2.4000	2.4196	2.5293	2.6057	- 7.9
Can$	92.5	98.84	100.36 −	−(USc/C$)	
Neth gldr	3.620	3.455	3.276	3.245	−10.4
Belg fr	50.00	49.63	45.55	44.81	−10.4
DM	3.660	3.388	3.259	3.223	−11.9
Lira	625.0	620.5	600.5	581.5	−7.0
FF	5.554	5.513	5.493	5.116	−7.9
Swed kr	5.173	5.156	4.889	4.813	−7.0
Yen	360	357	314	308	−14.4
Sw fr	4.37	4.06	3.88	3.85	−12.0

West German economics minister Professor Karl Schiller described it as 'a fragile building, a fragile work of art'. The new gold price would apply only to IMF transactions.

The Smithsonian Agreement valued each currency as indexed against a 'basket' of other currencies, this being weighted according to the country's amount of trade with each. Even a further 10 per cent devaluation of the dollar didn't hold and within fifteen months – by March 1973 – most had allowed their currencies to float.

The free market price of gold soared to $850 an ounce by January 1980 before relapsing.

The end of the Bretton Woods system left two problems: exchange rates and reserves. The dollar was now less acceptable as a reserve currency. It had lost its most important characteristic: stability backed by convertibility into gold.

As Bretton Woods began to collapse in 1971 Germany led an effort to limit volatility between European currencies. The so-called currency 'snake' started next year. The EEC and Norway agreed to ensure that their currencies varied no more than 2.25 per cent from each other and the whole snake was to fluctuate no more than 4.45 per cent against the dollar. Within a year the peg to the dollar had been untied. France, so often today the arch champion of European monetary union, twice – in 1974 and 1976 – pulled the franc out of the snake which in 1979 metamorphosed into the European Monetary System. In its early years the franc took part in several realignments of the EMS exchange rate mechanism, devaluing against the Deutschmark. In 1971, incidentally, EEC leaders endorsed the Werner Report which called for a single currency by 1980. The dollar crisis overwhelmed that.

They later agreed, at Nyborg, Denmark in 1987, that the ERM needs the full support of member countries' fiscal – tax – policy. Realignments of currencies should be infrequent but changes in central rates kept small to avoid consequent changes in market rates.

Realignments should be less predictable than they had been before 1987. In fact there was not to be another major realignment until 1992. The idea in 1987 was to spot the need early and act before market saw the possibility. They would try to avoid giving the impression that realignments were linked to domestic political events. (This last was perhaps unrealistic but the intention was commendable.) But just as Bretton Woods collapsed largely because of a conflict between the USA's domestic economic and political needs and the requirements imposed by the dollar's reserve currency role, the Exchange Rate Mechanism broke down because of a conflict between Germany's domestic economic problems and the role of the Deutschmark as anchor currency in the ERM.

Some argue that the whole edifice of a single European currency, being built on a fallacy, was bound to fall; that German reunification merely exacerbated the structural deficiencies. Professor Sir Alan Walters – who will never shed the appendage 'Mrs Thatcher's economic adviser' – disputes that a single market needs single currency. 'Today in North America, between Canada and the US, there is a close approximation to the ideal of a common market,' he points out. 'Yet there is no fixed or pegged Canadian dollar to the greenback, nor has anyone suggested that the North America Free Trade

Agreement requires pegged rates or a Namu (North American Monetary Union). Nor does the lack of stability of the Canadian dollar seem to have inhibited economic integration within North America. Canadian—US trade flows are the largest in the world.'

Others claim that the plan approved at Maastricht remains well founded and monetary union can be rebuilt once these temporary strains have been resolved. Certainly, the way in which East and West Germany reintegrated in October 1990 created extraordinary inflationary pressures and these grew even greater than the worst initial fears. First the East German mark, the Ostmark, was worth no more than half a Deutschmark; that was on the basis of the quantity in circulation compared with East Germany's economic output. It makes inadequate allowance for much of that output being both in quality and price uncompetitive internationally.

Instead of the two currencies being fused on the basis of two Ostmark to the Deutschmark, they were merged at 1:1. To increase the amount of money in circulation for the united country very much more than output was inflationary. Reflecting its workers' inferior productivity, East German wage levels had been far below those in West Germany. Making the Ostmark equal in value to the Deutschmark immediately boosted East German workers' spending power. Moreover, as they were now being priced out of work, the cost of supporting them or keeping the factories open with subsidies increased Germany's overall budget deficit. To this inflationary pressure was added the undertaking that East German wage levels would be raised in a few years to West German levels.

The constitutional duty of the Bundesbank is to safeguard the Deutschmark against inflation. The only qualification, drawn in such imprecise terms as to be ineffective, is that the central bank shall act in accord with government economic policy. Faced with fiscal policies which were highly inflationary the Bundesbank could defend the currency only by either raising interest rates or revaluing the Deutschmark within the ERM.

The Bundesbank offered a general realignment of ERM

currencies at the time of German reunification in 1989–90 – before the pound became a full member – and a realignment or hidden revaluation of the Deutschmark could even have been finessed with sterling's entry into the ERM later in 1990. The French rejected the idea both times.

Early that year the Bank of England Quarterly Bulletin suggested that the effect of reunification had been such an economic shock that revaluation of the Deutschmark would be appropriate. A much higher valuation for the Deutschmark would make imported goods cheaper and more competitive, putting downward pressure on prices. It would have also made it harder for exporters to sell overseas, so to remain competitive they would have to curb their costs. That counter-inflationary pressure would have reduced the need to raise German interest rates. Other ERM members would have been spared the tension which arose between the need to keep their interest rates up – so as to maintain their currencies against the Deutschmark – and the damage such interest rates were doing as recession and unemployment deepened.

Though it had the foresight to argue for a Deutschmark revaluation at the time, the Bank of England acknowledges that any revaluation agreed then might well have proved too small because even German experts did not appreciate how severe the fiscal disruption would eventually prove to be. The French authorities in any case rejected both. Ironically, it was the Danes – who had been hosts to that meeting so suffused with good resolution in 1987 – who were to provide the final straw by voting against the Maastricht treaty.

This did not spark immediate and severe tensions within the EMS. Though deepening recession and growing unemployment raised difficult questions about the sustainability of fixed exchange rates within the ERM, the authorities still had enough conviction and credibility with the markets that fixed rates would hold and the underlying economies be forced to converge. There had not been a significant realignment since 1987 – for five years – which was much longer than previously. But first the pound and lira in September 1992 and then the French franc in July 1993 came under pressure.

Market dealers saw that high interest rates to support the pound and lira were in both cases aggravating recession to an extent which would quickly prove politically intolerable. In both cases, also, the recession had already become so severe as to threaten a downward spiral in government finances.

The French franc was statistically good value against the Deutschmark but, by July 1993, the conflict between France's domestic needs for low interest rates to prevent worsening recession and unemployment and the high interest rates needed to sustain the franc against the Deutschmark led to a massive speculative attack and the ERM exploded.

Theoretically, sterling could have come out of the ERM, at least temporarily, as soon as President Mitterand, by calling the French referendum, created what quickly proved a fresh period of uncertainty in the foreign exchange markets. The problem was that John Major had already been so sceptical about the whole Maastricht treaty, negotiating special opt-out clauses for the UK, that such a course would have confirmed the suspicions among many on his own back benchers that his commitment to the European Community was half-baked.

The other option might possibly have been to have raised interest rates but this would have sparked equal political uproar as there was a growing chorus of vociferous demands to cut the high interest rates seen to be so damaging to the economy. The Bank of England itself advised against such a course, believing it might counter-productively raise a distress signal over the pound.

Ecofin – Brussels jargon term for EC finance ministers whenever they congregate – met on Friday 28 August and, although the Bundesbank did not oppose realignment, finance ministers of the other eleven countries ruled against it because they did not want to be seen weakening their efforts against inflation. Once France opposed the others could not have changed their parities without severely damaging their anti-inflation credentials. For most, it was to acquire such credentials that they had anchored to the Deutschmark through the ERM in the first place. The French could not afford to add yet more uncertainty to the outcome of the imminent referendum which was widely cast as a vote of confidence in the government; it would have lost credibility had it wavered from the *franc fort* policy at this stage.

The Bundesbank was now moving interest rates to their highest in Germany since the 1930s. The US Federal Reserve was holding interest rates down to nurture the still fragile economic recovery in America. Investors could borrow in dollars at less than 4 per cent, sell those dollars to buy Deutschmarks and earn more than 8 per cent on their Deutschmark deposit or investment. That steady selling of the dollar and buying of the Deutschmark was, of course, felt in the currency markets. On Tuesday 1 September, the dollar hit an all-time low against the Deutschmark of DM1.3895.

Ecofin met again, this time in Bath, over the following weekend of 5–6 September. Two days earlier the UK had announced arrangements to borrow ECU 10 billion for conversion into sterling. At the Bath meeting, Chancellor Norman Lamont asked Helmut Schlesinger four times to cut interest rates, almost provoking a walk out by the Bundesbank president. Decisions about interest rates are made by the Bundesbank Council, wherein sit representatives from each of the different *lander*, or states. Often their decisions are the result of careful and perhaps almost heated, discussion. Norman Lamont was tactless to ask Dr Schlesinger for something he alone could not deliver. Nevertheless, at the end of the meeting which agreed not to realign ERM currencies, Lamont told the press that Schlesinger had conceded there was no need to raise German interest rates.

The following Thursday Mr Major told the Scottish CBI conference in Glasgow: 'As the Chancellor has made crystal clear, there is going to be no devaluation, no realignment. The soft option, the devaluer's option, the inflationary option, would be a betrayal of our future; and it is not the government's policy.

'We must bite the anti-inflation bullet or accept that we will be forever second-rate in Europe.'

Next day, Friday 11 September, despite the retail price index emerging to show inflation at a five-year low, the pound weakened further. For the lira the pressure had now become intolerable. Over the weekend of 12–13 September EC finance ministers agreed to a 7 per cent devaluation of the lira, within the ERM. Helmut Schlesinger agreed to an unprecedented meeting of the Bundesbank's ruling council at 9 a.m. on Monday morning to consider an interest rate cut.

The Bundesbank, with obvious reluctance, cut its Lombard rate 0.25 per cent to 9.5 per cent and its discount rate by 0.5 per cent to 8.25 per cent. This was a token gesture made with not a little resentment. The discount rate is the interest rate at which the Bundesbank will lend to German banks up to a limit if they are temporarily short of funds. The Lombard rate it imposes if the banks need to borrow more than their facilities and, being a penal rate, is in these circumstances less important.

'There has never been any question of the pound being realigned or devalued,' asserted Chancellor Lamont, 'and at no stage did anybody else suggest that we should move with the Italians.'

Next day, reports began circulating that Bundesbank president Helmut Schlesinger had told the leading German financial newspaper *Handelsblatt* and the *Wall Street Journal* in a joint interview that a more comprehensive change of currency rates within the ERM would have been appropriate and have reduced turbulence on the foreign exchange markets. On Tuesday 15 September the pound fell 3.25 pfennigs to DM2.7800.

Certainly, Schlesinger gave the joint interview to those two newspapers. The Bundesbank has persistently claimed that he was misreported and that his remarks, taken out of context, gained a different meaning to that intended. Both newspapers remain adamant that the reportage was accurate. These are serious and respected, not popular tabloid, newspapers. For a set-piece interview with the president of the Bundesbank they do not send a young scribbler still wet behind the ears. The Bundesbank had made some arrangement to see at least one of the interviews before publication – which may have left Dr Schlesinger more relaxed and less discreet than he would otherwise have been – and the reports originally came from a piece in *Handelsblatt* trailing the full interview to be published in a later edition.

Some UK Treasury officials later put about the notion that Schlesinger had deliberately subverted sterling out of revenge for the humiliation he had suffered from Norman Lamont at the earlier meeting in Bath. That would have been out of character. Dr Schlesinger did not become president of the Bundesbank by indulging personal animosities. Moreover, it ignores the climate of opinion in Germany at the time. The Bundesbank, famously independent of the politicians, was nevertheless being accused on having 'gone soft' on inflation and having yielded to demands for an interest rate cut unwarranted by Germany's own economic fundamentals. Moreover, the rules of the ERM frequently required the Bundesbank to intervene not only to succour the failing currencies but also to weaken its own. That intervention threatened to bring in its train an inflationary increase in Germany's money supply, which was persistently above its target range.

'Black Wednesday' saw the pound start the day at its lowest permitted value within the ERM – DM2.7780 – and, despite intervention by the Bank of England, the Bank of France and the Bundesbank, fall to close in London at DM2.7500. Overnight interest rates had been raised to 100 per cent a year, the Bank's minimum lending rate from 10 to 15 per cent and the Bank of England had used the equivalent of £7 billion from the reserves, depleting them by one third.

By 7.30 p.m., with no sign in New York's early afternoon trading that the selling pressure had abated, Norman Lamont capitulated and suspended sterling's membership of the ERM. Interest rates were immediately cut from 15 back to the 12 per cent level to which they had been raised at 11 o'clock that morning. In New York trading the pound fell to 9 pfennigs below its now abandoned ERM floor, closing there at 2.6875. Next morning, interest rates were again cut, back to the 10 per cent they had been two days earlier. The lira temporarily withdrew from the ERM and the Spanish peseta devalued 5 per cent.

One plan contemplated during the fracas had been for the

pound and lira both to quit the ERM until the next weekend, at which point their values against all other EMS currencies would be re-fixed. Downing Street, meanwhile, cited five instances where, it claimed, the Bundesbank had deliberately undermined the pound.

A quarter century earlier, when a Labour Government had been battling desperately and eventually unsuccessfully to avoid a sterling devaluation, the then Prime Minister Harold Wilson had coined the phrase 'Gnomes of Zurich' to encompass the sinister alien forces he was fighting. Satan's familiar had changed residence to Frankfurt.

'Having joined (the ERM) we were right to endeavour to stick with it; and, in the circumstances which evolved, we were also right to withdraw,' pronounced an inherently dis-passionate Robin Leigh-Pemberton, then Governor of the Bank of England.

For the markets the possibilities had been clear ahead of the French referendum: if the French endorsed Maastricht then major currencies within the ERM might well hold their parity against the Deutschmark. If the French referendum rejected the treaty – and opinion polls showed that was a better than long-odds possibility – several currencies would devalue, with the pound and lira the likeliest candidates. In neither set of circumstances would other currencies appreciate against the Deutschmark. It was a one-way bet. Thus for the Bank of England, on the other side of that bet, the odds were over-whelming.

This is not to say that the bank dealing rooms made money out of events that day. Peter Maltz, head of spot foreign exchange dealing at Barclays Bank, comments: 'We have to service our client base. On Black Wednesday we didn't make money, we were too busy doing customer business.

'It happened so unexpectedly I don't think that people gen-erally speaking ever believed that sterling would be out of the ERM so fast. And they didn't see the value of being short of the pound anyway because it was right on its floor

'Don't forget that a lot of the corporate business the banks were doing: their customers – after the general election there was this big euphoria with the Conservatives returned to power – a lot of people bought sterling. And a lot of the fund managers were worried about their exposure in sterling and a lot of people were just saying "Let's stay square" and not necessarily going short of sterling. A lot of them were caught wrong, they were just squaring up.'

Squaring-up was enough to sink the pound. Because they had earlier bought it speculatively, those investors were holding disproportionate amounts of sterling. Now they were selling merely to get back into balance, not necessarily selling aggressively short.

In May 1993, two reports – by EC central bank governors and by central bank and finance ministry officials – blamed Germany, UK and Italy for what had gone wrong. They also argued for closer monitoring of economies and exchange rates so that when the two diverged there would be early warning signals and countries could realign more readily. Those reports were first presented to, studied and welcomed by EC finance ministers. Perhaps appropriately this meeting, like that which had prescribed in 1987, was in Denmark, this time at Kolding.

The attack on the French franc had already begun. It started immediately after the pound and lira had fallen. Three days after the French referendum had endorsed Maastricht the Bank of France raised its benchmark short-term interest rate from 10.5 to 13 per cent. The franc remained at its ERM floor. As with the UK earlier, the markets could see that there was a conflict between the low interest rates France needed to counter recession and the interest rate needed to keep the French franc at its ERM exchange rate against the Deutschmark.

The stresses took until the following July – almost a year – to become overpowering because the French economy was transparently in better condition than the German. Inflation in France was only 1.9 per cent, less than half that in Germany, where it threatened to persist as growth of the money supply was still above target. The French budget deficit was smaller as a proportion of the whole economy than that of Germany and its current account on international payments in balance.

A franc devaluation against the Deutschmark seemed irrational. The divergence of policy needs in terms of interest rates took time to resolve.

Incidentally, there was a bizarre parallel with the UK. French finance minister Edmond Alphandéry bragged in June 1993 that with its superior underlying statistics the franc should and might replace the Deutschmark. John Major's similar claim for sterling had been in early August 1992, a month before it left the ERM. M. Alphandéry also called for coordinated interest rate cuts in Germany and France. The implication was that as the franc was strong the French could talk to the Germans as equals. German finance minister Theo Waigel promptly cancelled a Franco-German economic meeting.

'Alphandéry made this speech – doing the same as Major had done about the pound the previous year, it was so funny' recalls Dr Jim O'Neill, chief currency economist at Swiss Bank Corporation. 'It was on a day when the franc was at its midpoint in the EMS and strengthening and French interest rates were right at the same level as German rates.

'I'd been a big fan of the franc and was talking to our equity analyst, who was getting increasingly bearish on French corporates. And I thought, "This is a mistake." It was one of the better calls I made that year.

'And in the next two days he made speeches calling for US-style interest rates in France. Putting bits and pieces together, it was quite clear to us that the French corporates were leaning on the government saying "We need to get our interest rates down desperately."'

The Bank of France had cut nine times between April and July 1993 the interest rate at which it intervened on the money markets. The investor could borrow French francs and sell them for Deutschmarks which she could then invest to earn enough to cover her interest charges on borrowing in France. If the franc devalued against the Deutschmark she would then be able to sell her Deutschmarks for more francs and so be left with a profit on repaying the loan. If Germany cut interest rates then the investment she held in Deutschmarks would show a capital gain instead. With unemployment in France by now reaching 12 per cent, a rise in French interest rates was inconceivable.

It was a case of heads you win and tails you don't lose. The franc could devalue but not appreciate against the Deutschmark in such circumstances. But the franc just did not devalue. There was a real tussle in the market, with some pointing to the policy conflict over interest rate needs and others to the French economy's robust characteristics. The Bank of France and sometimes the Bundesbank intervened and held the franc *fort*.

'The reason why the French franc was finally forced out of its narrow band in the ERM was probably because, until about a week before, nobody thought it was going to happen,' suggests Jim O'Neill. 'Everybody had given up on the idea and the final event was actually started off by French corporations taking protective decisions to hedge their exposures because suddenly they realized that perhaps there was a slight danger and they hadn't thought about it before.'

Anthony Stern, treasurer of the brewery and hotels group Bass, recounts how on 14 July he attended a French bank's Bastille Day luncheon party for clients. 'They had a lot of French treasurers there at the time,' he recalls, 'and as I talked to people around that room it became increasingly clear to me. The subject of the conversation was the ERM and the strains which were then appearing. The French treasurers were all saying "It's going to go. There's no question about it, we can tell it. And we've all put positions on to protect ourselves in case it does."

'My view before going there had been that the ERM would probably hold together and that the French and Germans would somehow find a way of seeing the thing through. After I'd been to that lunch – where I'd talked to people who were not speculating, it was simply a market view and they were all placing their money – I came back and said to our team that it did sound to me, if what these people were saying was true, that there is going to be a movement in the franc against the Deutschmark and we'd better take some protection to ensure it didn't hit us.

'As soon as that happens it just bursts out into action. Once people get the idea that there's only one way the market can move, they don't deliberately do things to make the market move, they merely protect themselves against its moving and the sheer number of people doing that make it inevitable.'

The *denouement* came swiftly. With pressure against the franc mounting once more, the Bundesbank council met on Thursday 29 July. It would have needed a major and dramatic move in Deutschmark interest rates – discordant with Germany's domestic economic needs – to have reversed the market trend. Instead they made only minor technical adjustments to interest rates. This provoked what may well prove to have been the final crisis of the ERM. At the crucial meeting in Brussels over the following weekend, the Germans suggested widening ERM bands to 6 per cent but France said that would leave speculators with a still-tempting target.

The French counter-proposal was that the ERM should drop its anchor currency by letting the Deutschmark float on its own. This found no more favour. The Netherlands and Belgium insisted they would peg their currencies to the Deutschmark rather than to an ERM with no anchor. Spain's proposal to scrap the ERM altogether came close to acceptance.

The negotiations were protracted and fraught, largely because of a desperate anxiety to avoid a franc devaluation. Only minutes before markets reopened in the Far East on Monday morning – late on Sunday in Brussels – the French won agreement that currencies would trade within bands 15 per cent above or below central rates. They argued this was likely to confuse speculators and leave room for a 2 per cent cut in French interest rates.

The inevitable *communiqué* on the outcome of the meeting declared: 'This measure of limited duration is in response to speculative movements which are exceptional in amount as well as in nature . . . the ministers and governors therefore reaffirm support for the current parities and are confident that the market rates will soon approach those parities again.' It later came to light that the finance ministers and bank governors agreed during the weekend that until ERM narrow bands were reinstated – which they expected to be by January 1994 – central banks should strike informal currency pacts with each other.

There were widespread predictions at the time that France would cut its interest rates from 6.75 to 4 per cent so as to re-stimulate its economy. Under the Maastricht rules, however, currencies must remain within 2.25 per cent of their central ERM rate for two years before joining in full monetary union. To keep the European Monetary Union timetable that would mean the EMU founder currencies returning to the narrow bands by January 1994.

Within little more than six months the franc had returned close to its original ERM parity against the Deutschmark. The original French argument that there was no fundamental need for devaluation thus becomes more convincing and the evidence refuting any need to cut interest rates – which ostensibly was why the speculators sold the franc down – appears conclusive.

Comments Chris Dillow, economist at the Nomura Research Institute's European headquarters in London: 'One thing that surprised many people including me was the policy response of governments. Many thought the French would do the same as the UK: see this as an opportunity to cut rates. But that doesn't appear to have happened.

'Is this because the governments are trying to play under the old rules, pretending that the events of July 1993 didn't happen? Or did they have a deeper logic? It may be that they have a deeper logic which is that the events of July 1993 happened so late in the economic cycle that they don't need lower interest rates.'

This whole episode leaves us with a question the answer to which may apply far beyond Europe and the particular instance: with the need for lower French interest rates disproved and with the franc proving to be worth its original exchange rate, why then did the ERM fail?

The markets had become convinced that France needed to cut interest rates and therefore the franc would devalue. Events have proved the markets wrong on interest rates and only briefly right on exchange rates. Is it true that even when they are driven by fallacy – even when they're wrong – markets prevail?

The markets had first believed that the ERM would work and currencies converge into eventually a single currency. Investors felt safe. Normally, high interest rates reflect a high inflation rate and therefore the risk of devaluation. What you gain from earning higher interest on your money you lose on the devaluation. But with the ERM they were persuaded there would not be a devaluation so it was safe to borrow in low inflation and low interest rate currencies, sell them for high inflation currencies where you could invest to earn a high interest rate.

Jim O'Neill of Swiss Bank Corporation notes, 'A lot of pension funds and economists – I'd blame myself a bit here – got sucked into this idea, because it was becoming quite easy, that the European Monetary Union theme was a nice one to participate in. And a lot of people kidded themselves that foreign exchange risks were becoming less among European currencies.

'Many of these fund managers in the States would consistently buy assets in high-yielding European currencies and fund them in the low-yielding ones. We saw it particularly: they would use the Swiss franc, because of its low rates, to finance all these other high-yielding assets like Italy.

'And because for four years there was no realignment – it wasn't until the Danish referendum shook people up – nobody thought there was any chance of anything happening and so four years' accumulation of unhedged investments was suddenly all trying to get out the same exit.'

Howard Flight, joint managing director of fund management group Guinness Flight, avers, 'It was a French idea that pegging and fixing the ERM as really a fixed system with very narrow bands would be successful in causing inflation convergence and therefore a path to a common currency. While that appeared to be working and economically satisfactory, then quite naturally markets went along with it.

'Six months at least before September 1992 it was very clear that that was no longer the case and various economies were going through tremendous real and unacceptable distortions.'

Once the markets became convinced they had been wrong, then to have realigned currencies would merely have confirmed their fears. Regardless of whether economically justified, only interest rate changes would meet the situation.

'The perception quite naturally became that either Germany had to change its policies to accommodate a wider European context or the thing had to blow apart,' concludes Howard Flight.

From that viewpoint, the ERM blew apart because Germany could not, at the critical point, meet the demands of the Deutschmark's role as the anchor to the European Monetary System any more than, two decades earlier, America had been able to support the dollar's pivotal role in the Bretton Woods system.

At Swiss Bank Corporation Dr Jim O'Neill, a currency economist seasoned by seeing his theories tested daily on the forex dealing desks, remains suspicious about the 'accident' which befell the ERM.

'The central banks were at fault to some extent because they didn't see it coming,' he told me. 'And they tried to kid themselves that they could resist it until the very last minute.

'That either means that they don't understand the markets any more or that, despite what they said, quite a lot of the central banks were quite happy for it to have happened.

'I'd buy some support for the idea they were quite happy for some of the moves to happen. Otherwise they would have been more sophisticated.'

Certainly, the finance ministers failed abysmally to live up to the foresight they showed at Nyborg, Denmark, in 1987 that the ERM needs the full support of member countries' fiscal policy – where was that in German reunification? – and to spot the need for any realignment early so that they could act before the markets saw the possibility.

Are attempts to lock currencies into fixed relationships doomed? It is too early to judge for the European Monetary System. Even if it were to progress eventually to European

Monetary Union, that would need time to be tested. Evidence from currency blocs elsewhere around the world is scant. The number of currencies pegged to the dollar, the Deutschmark and the yen is, in each case, small. We have seen the emergence, however, of looser relationships – currency zones – not usually created by deliberate policies but emerging from trade flows. Thus Hong Kong, South Korea and Taiwan, for instance, peg their currencies loosely to the American dollar even though all three are geographically closer to Japan.

'There's a natural tendency for these to emerge,' suggests Chris Dillow, 'because despite the greater liquidity and ease of trading today there's still a lot of hassle in changing currency. So it's natural for people to focus on one currency and say "Let's pay each other in that and avoid the hassle." And it's natural for that currency to be that of the biggest trading country in the area.'

There have been other consequences for the foreign exchange markets and for the world in general of this tendency for currency zones to develop. International trade has grown but trade within a bloc such as the European Community or NAFTA tends to become more important to the individual member countries than their trade outside the bloc. As a result, movements of exchange rates between the major currencies has less economic impact. The $:yen rate might become less important to the US economy as the North American Free Trade Agreement – NAFTA – develops. Mexico is almost unaffected by what happens between the Deutschmark and the dollar. The £:$ rate is less important to Britain today than before we joined what was then the European Common Market.

These major currency zones have developed since the breakdown of the Bretton Woods exchange rate regime. When currencies were directly, or through the dollar, convertible into gold it did not much matter which reserve currency a central bank held. Now, given that reserves may sometimes be needed to provide financing of imports – especially for less developed countries – and because, when intervening in the foreign exchange markets, it is the value of the currency against that of the major trading partners which matters, most central banks prefer to hold these currencies. But they can no longer trust any major currency to keep its value free of political waywardness by its host country. As a result, central banks may move their currency portfolios – that is, the choice of currencies they hold in their official reserves – to reflect changing expectations, just like another investor restructures her portfolio of shares.

'While a reserve system based on a number of reserve currencies can enable countries to reduce their exposure to exchange risk, it can also lead to instability through the switching of reserve currencies in response to changing, and perhaps ephemeral, expectations . . .' says an IMF report. '. . . the combined pattern of interest rates and expected exchange rate changes is in principle an important determinant of countries' reserve policies.

'As a result, official trading in the currency markets does not necessarily and in all circumstances exercise a stabilizing influence'*

In other words, central banks themselves are among the speculators on the foreign exchange markets. What they need – what may persuade them to renounce currency speculation – is to find a reserve currency which eliminated all such risks. It would be:

- free of political interference
- independent of the performance of any single economy or even group of economies
- accepted without question as a means of payment
- the amount available must grow in line with the expansion of world trade

It was partly because gold fell down on that last proviso that the Bretton Woods gave a role as substitute for gold to the dollar, which eventually failed the other conditions.

---

* 'The Role of the SDR in the International Monetary System', Studies by the Research and Treasurer's Department of the IMF, March 1987.

Here's an analogy. A person with funds to look after might choose to put them into a single investment or pick a handful of investments which look safe. The problem is that today's safe bet can too readily become tomorrow's loser. Fixed interest investments may see their real value eroded by inflation. Shares? General Motors and IBM, once corporate paragons have since been what Americans (showing no canine political correctness) call 'dogs'.

The person trying to preserve a small capital sum can invest it in a unit trust or mutual fund. They will then get a spread of investments across more companies than is practical for any individual. The portfolio may even be designed and invested in such proportions that it replicates the market overall, that is be indexed. Likewise, in international currencies, a central bank might find it attractive to hold its reserves in a unit of money which replicated the world's various currencies, which had the positive characteristics of gold but the supply of which increases to keep world trade lubricated. (In fact this would be even better than my analogy. The investor in securities markets might find that worldwide they have all fallen. But you cannot have such a universal decline in currencies. If the dollar falls then the other currency against which it has fallen must obviously have risen.)

The nearest we have to this ideal is SDR – Special Drawing Rights – which is often referred to as 'paper gold'. The need for something of the sort became obvious a few years before the collapse of the Bretton Woods system. The world's central banks were not holding a large enough 'float' of reserves to cover the needs of growing international trade. As reserves existed so that a country could keep importing without suddenly having to bring down the shutters because of a hiccup in exports, then the way to judge the adequacy of reserves was what proportion of imports they would cover.

The world's central banks held enough official reserves to cover almost six months' imports in 1959 but only three months and four days' imports by 1969. About half of those official reserves in 1969 were directly in gold, the output of which, however, was growing more slowly than world trade and the dollar was proving an increasingly unsatisfactory substitute. The need was therefore for a universally accepted reserve currency.

Special Drawing Rights (SDRs) are a form of currency issued by the IMF. The IMF simply credits a participating country with holding so many of these units. That country holds them – and is required to keep a certain minimum – in its reserves and can use SDRs to settle its dealings with other central banks and the IMF. If all agree more international liquidity is needed the IMF just creates more SDRs and credits them to the member countries' accounts.

Some poorer countries have had the problem that to pay interest on the money they have borrowed overseas and to build a good cushion of official reserves they have needed to keep up large trade surpluses. That's meant holding down consumption by their (already poor) people so as to curb demand for imports and release goods for export. An allocation of SDRs enables them to have official reserves without having to generate a balance of payments surplus.

Creditworthy countries no longer need SDRs. The international capital markets have grown to such an extent that a creditworthy country can borrow by issuing international bonds denominated in reserve currencies. Portugal, for instance, embarked in 1993 on a big international programme: borrowing Y75 billion in January, DM1.5 billion in June and $1 billion in September. If a creditworthy country like Portugal borrows like this it can boost its foreign exchange reserves without affecting its international credit standing. On one side of the national balance sheet are those debts and on the other side the funds lenders have advanced. The cost of so augmenting the official reserves – useful in case of a rainy day for exports – may be very small: it will be the interest Portugal has to pay on the bonds, minus the interest earned from investing the funds. Portugal borrowed that money by investment banks selling the bonds to investors around the world, just as if the government were a private corporation issuing a debenture. In other words, this activity has been privatized.

But that's of no help to the poor soul shuffling around

Europe getting ripped off by the banks and bureaux de change every time he crosses a border. It is a severe encumbrance to the development of Europe's single market that a company buying supplies from elsewhere in the region, unlike its American counterpart which buys and sells across fifty-two states with a single currency, must juggle with so many variations of money.

What chance for the ecu?

It was being used by Italian businessmen when the lira was inflating so fast that they weren't even able to give the normal thirty days' or sixty days' credit. The ecu was an accepted store of value. Agree with your customer how much they would owe you in ecu and you knew what it would be worth when eventually they paid.

The prospects for the ecu developing as the single currency for the whole European Union appear to have been affected very little by the widening of the ERM bands which was otherwise such a setback to monetary union. Germany's constitutional court approved the Maastricht treaty in October 1993 and so removed the last uncertainty. The ecu was free to become the common European currency by the end of the century. The day after that court ruling the EC (now EU) itself endorsed the point by raising a seven-year loan of 1 billion ecu.

The turnover in ecu-denominated international bonds grew tenfold between 1989 and 1992. According to the Bank for International Settlements, the ecu outstripped all other currencies except the dollar and Deutschmark. Then first the Danish vote and later sterling and the lira's departure from the ERM awoke investors to the risks.

Until this time, they had held the view that the interest rate on ecu bonds should be in line with the weighted average of interest rates on component currencies. Ecu bonds might even be attractive at a lower rate than that because they represented a diversified currency risk. But the widening of ERM bands widened the currency risk and the danger that ecu bonds might be worth less than bonds denominated in Europe's strongest currency, the Deutschmark. For the time being they may prefer to have an investment denominated in Deutschmarks because the Bundesbank has an enviable track record in defending the value of that currency. The ecu is a currency which will be controlled by the new central bank for the whole of Europe but it has no track record. The Maastricht treaty makes no provision for the new European Monetary Institute to evolve. Overnight it will become the EU's central bank. Likewise the ecu, which has been a basket of currencies issued by their various central banks, suddenly becomes a single currency in its own right, issued by the new and unproven central bank for Europe.

At least to start with, investors will view the ecu as riskier than the Deutschmark and therefore needing to offer a higher interest rate. Until the new central bank has established its anti-inflation, sound money, credentials it will err on the side of caution. Combine these two facts and you have a bias towards deflation.

This threatens to create conflict. The French and the British, the Spanish and the Italians, say, may lean towards a more accommodating central bank which allows a little more inflation and lower interest rates to alleviate unemployment. Germany and the countries which through all recent travails have stuck with the Deutschmark may not be willing to relax stern Bundesbank disciplines. The Bund freier Bürger (BFB) or Free Citizens' Alliance, was a party formed to campaign in the June 1994 European and October 1994 Bundestag elections for preservation of the Deutschmark. Polls showed 75 per cent of Germany's electorate anxious that the Deutschmark should not be subsumed into the ecu.

Sir Michael Butler, who was Britain's permanent representative at the EC headquarters from 1979–85, argues, 'The Germans' position – as indeed all the actions of the Bundesbank, if not its words – has always been consistent with their hoping that the impetus towards EMU will die away again as it did in the 1970s.

'The only kind of monetary union attractive to them is one in which a Deutschmark zone, managed by them, is gradually extended to the Benelux countries, Austria and perhaps France. But there's the rub.

'The attraction of EMU to France is to have an equal say with the Germans in managing European monetary policy, instead of having slavishly to follow them, as at present.'

Bundesbank president Hans Tietmeyer told the annual meeting of the World Economic Forum in Davos early in 1994 that the Bundesbank would not pass any of its reserves to the European Monetary Institute (notwithstanding the Germans' success in winning its locus in Frankfurt). Maastricht permitted central banks to do this but, said Mr Tietmeyer, 'The Bundesbank will not do this. We feel we are equipped to manage our reserves in the appropriate way. Of course this will change when we move into a situation of a European central bank.'

4

THE DOLLAR

Buddy, Can You Spare a Yen?

'The almighty dollar is the only object of worship'
Philadelphia Public Ledger, 2 December 1836

Not any more it isn't. Since it came off the gold standard just over twenty years ago the dollar has declined:

- in importance as a reserve currency, as it may be a smaller proportion than gold in the reserves of developed countries
- and in its value against other currencies

Moreover, though the statistics are too sparse to show any meaningful trend, the dollar's still-dominant share of world currency trading has eased slightly. It figured in 83 per cent of foreign exchange trading in April 1992, compared with 90 per cent three years earlier.

When Nixon suspended the dollar's free convertibility into gold at $35 an ounce the greenback was valued at DM3.660 and Y360. In 1992 it touched DM1.3862, in mid-August 1993 Y100.8, and in November 1994 Y96.05. This has been the undeniable trend, but the dollar has experienced both extremes of fortune on the way. It doubled against the Deutschmark, for instance, between 1980 and 1985 and its value against the average of all the world's currencies rose by one third in that period.

Washington's reaction to its fluctuations has remained consistent. Each time the exchange rate has been seen as a problem – too high or too low, no matter which – there have been calls for protectionist trade measures and for other governments to do unto their own economies what the solons of Capitol Hill thought would be good for them. Nixon threatened an import surcharge in 1971. Reagan's administration made protectionist noises to extract from trading partners help with dollar difficulties in 1985. US Trade Representative Micky Kantor threatened a breakdown of the GATT Uruguay Round in 1993 as the dollar came under increasing pressure. In early 1994, Clinton tried to extract from Japan a guaranteed level of imports from the USA by threatening to drive up the yen's value against the dollar.

As befits its status as still the world's major currency, the dollar has been the focus of heavier coordinated intervention, involving more central banks, than that mustered for any other currency. Some of those episodes have passed into the annals of financial history.

The bid to curb the dollar's seemingly inexorable five-year rise culminated in the Plaza Accord of September 1985. It came only six months after a former luminary of the President's Council of Economic Advisers, Dr Alan Greenspan, had told a House of Representatives sub-committee, 'As for central bank intervention in the foreign exchange market, it too appears to have little sustained effect when there is strong movement towards a currency.

'Such intervention may temporarily disconcert speculators and discourage speculation in the currency for a while. Resources available to central banks are limited and repeated massive intervention simply is not feasible.' Dr Greenspan was chairman of the Federal Reserve Board when, on four days in 1992, it used the equivalent of more than $1.25 billion as the US contribution to a larger coordinated intervention supporting the dollar, and when in November 1994 it used a reputed $1–1.5 billion in one day.

Concerted intervention – in the vernacular, central banks ganging up to rig the currency markets – was first mooted during the Group of Seven summit at Versailles in 1982. That was early in the dollar's rise and only a year after Beryl Sprinkel, Treasury under-secretary for monetary affairs, had announced on 4 May 1981 that the USA would henceforth practise 'clean floating'. This meant that markets alone would determine exchange rates and central banks would not interfere. However, Dr Sprinkel – realism honed by his earlier experience as chief economist at one of America's leading banks – admitted to me wryly at the time that he could speak only for the USA, 'not what other central banks might do to the dollar in manipulating their own currencies'. The next G7 decision on the subject was only a year further on, at Williamsburg in May 1983, when they agreed to undertake coordinated intervention whenever necessary.

'In some ways the persistent strength of the dollar has seemed to defy economic explanation,' commented a paper presented to a Congressional meeting.* Most popular explanation, described by the paper as supported by 'mainstream economic thought', attributed the dollar's sharp rise to the US government plunging into the red. Under President Ronald Reagan the US government spent considerably more than its tax revenues and needed to borrow. As the budget deficit grew faster than private savings – which were sluggish – the rest of the funding came from overseas and it was this inflow of foreign money which was driving up the dollar. US Treasury Secretary Donald Regan denied this was cause and effect, calling it instead a vote of confidence in the US economy also reflecting the appeal of America's political stability compared with uncertainties in most other parts of the world. But that paper to Congress argued, 'There is limited merit to the argument that the dollar has appreciated as the result of funds coming to the United States in search of a 'safe haven' from political disruption abroad. For this to be more than a short episode there has to be a sustained increase in the degree of instability abroad.'

Whatever its cause, the high value of the dollar was simply pricing American exporters out of foreign markets and often meant that imports undercut the prices US manufacturers tried to charge in their domestic market.

* Overview by Alfred Reifman, Congressional Research Service, presented to conference 'The Strong Dollar: Causes, Consequences & Policy Implications' co-sponsored by the Joint Economic Committee of Congress and the Congressional Research Service 29.11.85.

Kodak sent a letter to its stockholders, for the first time in its 105-year history in the spring of 1984. It said that the dollar's rise over the last four years had cost Kodak $1 billion in profits. Eastman Kodak president and chief executive officer Colby Chandler told New York Senator (David) Patrick Moynihan that there was no question of unfair trade practices by Japan, where Kodak had a 15 per cent market share and competed fairly with Fuji, but in West Germany, Kodak film cost 60 per cent more than Fuji film.

'It is simply a function of the arithmetic of the exchange rate and we can't compete.

'You will always be able to buy Kodak products in the United States. Our plans are not in any sense to leave this market. But if this keeps up just a little bit longer our products won't be made in the United States. We will become a marketing company.

'We won't necessarily build our plants in Japan. We could build them across the lake in Ontario.'

The USA's merchandise trade deficit had swelled from $36 billion in 1982 to an expected $100 billion in 1984. Excluding oil – sharps swings in crude prices at the time distorted economic statistics – the trade balance had deteriorated by $90 billion between 1981 and 1984. The US Treasury estimated $20 billion of this was cyclical – economic recovery and a pick-up in demand earlier in the USA than elsewhere in the world – and $25 billion was due to the LDC (Less Developed Countries) debt crisis which had been sparked by Mexico's near-default on its international loans. The other $45 billion the Treasury attributed to the dollar's rise.

Notwithstanding that, there were movements afoot in Congress towards imposing a new discriminatory tariff against countries thought to be unfair in their trade practices. Dr Martin Feldstein, then chairman of the President's Council of Economic Advisers, appeared before a Senate sub-committee on international trade in March 1984 and argued against such measures. Counterbalancing the trade deficit, he pointed out, would be 'a capital inflow that adds to the pool of investible funds in the United States. This year we expect an inflow of about $80 billion, enough to finance about half of all net fixed investment in the United States. . . .'

'A larger inflow is particularly helpful now, this year and in the next couple of years, because of the very large budget deficits, which are currently absorbing more than half of all net domestic savings. That is why I hesitate to use words like 'overvalued' in describing the dollar today. It is clearly above the value that is sustainable, it is clearly above the value that balances trade; but if we didn't have the dollar at its current levels, we would have very different problems. Our exporters and importers would be better off but the interest-sensitive domestic industries – the investment goods industries, the construction industry – would be much worse off.' Were it not for the supply of investment funds from abroad, interest rates would be higher.

It was a point Alan Greenspan endorsed a year later when he appeared before a House sub-committee on domestic monetary policy. 'The level of interest rates and the level of inflation that we currently experience would be higher with a dollar which had not been rising at the pace of recent years,' he said.

'As a consequence of that, I think capital investment has been higher. So while we are clearly very aware of the job losses that are occurring as a consequence of the strength of the dollar and as a result of imports displacing some competing goods in the United States, it is by no means clear to what extent, if any, the strength of the dollar has, in fact, created a net job loss as such.

'There is no doubt that the extraordinarily large flow of funds either by foreigners or by Americans invested in the United States has been a significant factor in creating a much more tranquil environment in the capital and financial markets than would have existed without it. So while we may, in fact, be looking at the strong dollar as something which is creating problems, I suspect that if the dollar were to turn around and go down, the problems that would occur as a consequence would make the problems of the strong dollar insignificant in comparison.'

That was not an argument persuasive to Senator Moynihan who related Kodak's experience in arguing his case for the USA to develop a Strategic Foreign Currency Reserve which would 'correct market imperfections' by buying foreign currencies with dollars to 'reduce the extent and slow the pace of exchange rate movements, resist further increases in the dollar's price and assist its gradual decline'. It would be able to moderate any sudden drop in the dollar by reversing the transactions, using the stock of foreign currencies to buy dollars.

In fact, the Federal Reserve already held significantly more than $1.1 billion worth of foreign currencies and the Treasury Exchange Stabilization Fund a further $1.7 billion. Using some of those reserves to try and halt the dollar had not proved efficacious. Despite some Federal efforts earlier in the month to boost the Deutschmark at the dollar's expense, on 21 September 1984 the dollar hit an eleven-and-a-half-year high of DM3.1765, provoking the Bundesbank to intervene as aggressively and as visibly as it could. The Fed returned to the attack during the next week, selling $135 million for Deutschmarks in three days.

By mid-October the dollar had bounced back to its earlier levels. It quickly resumed its rise so that by January 1985 the Fed was ruefully noting that the dollar had risen by an average of 8 per cent against all other currencies in the last six months alone.

The bewilderment this movement engendered showed in a report the Federal Reserve Bank of New York – the reserve bank through which the Fed in Washington conducts all its market operations – sent to the Federal Reserve Board in May 1985. 'Interest differentials *vis-à-vis* the German mark, for example, though still favourable to the dollar, had been just about cut in half,' it said. 'Under these circumstances, expectations developed that the dollar would weaken during the latter part of 1984, but these expectations failed to materialize. Each time the dollar started to move lower, it quickly recovered.'

The What Goes Up Must Come Down school of economic

thought was already in evidence. As early as August 1984 the Congressional Budget Office updated its report on the outlook for budget and economy with a brief note entitled 'The Effects of a Sharp Dollar Depreciation'. Ascribing the currency rise to inflow of capital from abroad, it cautioned, 'Should these capital inflows cease, the dollar could drop dramatically on the international exchange market. Domestic inflation and interest rates could rise and growth in real output could slow temporarily.'

The worry was growing that quite apart from whatever economic damage an overvalued dollar might be doing, the further the pendulum swung the more sharply and farther would it be likely to swing in the opposite direction, with equally irresistible force and devastating consequences.

These fears were piqued when an Ohio savings and loan institution – akin to a building society in the UK – failed in March 1985. Fears that other 'thrifts' would follow triggered a panic. The dollar fell 2.4 per cent in twenty-four hours.

A fortnight before, Dr Greenspan had warned about both the consequences of a sharp fall and the difficulties of managing a moderated decline in the dollar. He opined on how the Fed should respond if long-term interest rates were to rise steeply but he said that 'a more likely scenario is an eventual weakening of the dollar, which could develop into a speculative downturn in the exchange rate. This would, in turn, put short-term interest rates higher and stifle further economic growth.' With the dollar already 30 per cent overvalued, demand for it was unlikely to be sustained indefinitely.

'History suggests that there is little the Federal Reserve can do to nudge the foreign exchange value of the dollar lower in an orderly fashion,' he warned. 'The attraction of the dollar as a safe haven vehicle appears to outweigh the effects of relative interest rates.

'As was evident late last year [when the dollar had bounced despite the Fed's and the Bundesbank's efforts and in defiance of interest rate disincentives] lowering interest rates on dollar-denominated assets, relative to those denominated in other currencies, does not necessarily cause the dollar to fall.

Moreover, should the Fed try to push US interest rates down significantly to weaken the dollar, the monetary expansion which would be required to achieve this under present economic conditions could intensify inflation pressures and inflation expectations.'

Senator Pat Moynihan advocated his Strategic Foreign Currency Reserve to produce quick results. For the longer term, his solutions included, '. . . the governments of all industrialized nations representing the major trading currencies must coordinate their macro-economic policies.' And, he demanded: 'The governments of foreign countries with underpriced currencies must stimulate economic growth.' Setting aside other objections about economic strains in those countries, this begs the question of who shall decide – and how – that a currency is underpriced and to what extent. Even for the dollar this was a problem.

One of the proposals examined by a Congressional conference* was to adopt a target zone for the dollar which would produce a long-term, sustainable balance on international trade in goods and services in the presence of full employment and reasonable price stability. If the dollar moved out of the zone, the Fed would have to change its monetary policy to move it back in.

'Setting a target zone presents almost as difficult a set of problems as keeping the dollar in the zone once it has been established,' the paper noted. 'The calculation of the zone depends on what is considered full employment and reasonable price stability abroad as well as at home. And the question arises as to whether a 'sustainable equilibrium' in the balance of payments calls for balance, capital exports (a trade surplus) or capital imports (a trade deficit).'

Greenspan's verdict was that, 'It is easier to point to techniques which will not be too effective, such as excessive monetary ease or sporadic intervention, than cite the things which the Federal Reserve might do to effectively bring down the value of the dollar.

* Alfred Reifman (see page 87).

'It would appear that the best thing that the Fed could do is to be patient, awaiting the emergence of market forces away from the dollar. That is likely to occur sometime this year, although it is very difficult to pinpoint the actual timeframe.'

But as the Federal Reserve itself reported, the markets themselves were beginning to take note of how the high dollar was affecting America's trade balance. The patience of politicians who are so oft-inclined to berate the short-termism of financial markets was wearing thin.

In early September 1985 President Ronald Reagan – that disciple of Adam Smith and advocate of free trade – echoed the Nixon of fourteen years before. He would launch investigations into alleged 'unfair trading practices' by Japan, the EEC, Brazil and South Korea. This was widely seen as an effort to head off protectionist pressures in Congress which the Republican majority leader of the Senate, Robert Dole, referred to in a speech the next day. He had, he said, 'never known such Congressional pressure for restrictive trade legislation'.

Just as Nixon had threatened a 10 per cent import surcharge and eventually got results, a fortnight later James Baker, who had taken over from Donald Regan as US Treasury Secretary, met with his counterparts from Japan, Germany, France and the UK for the weekend at the Plaza Hotel in New York. This meeting of the Group of Five (G5) finance ministers agreed to step up concerted intervention. There was little effort to veil the threat under which they had acquiesced. The post-meeting statement referred explicitly to the need for the dollar to depreciate so as to help reduce the US trade deficit.

'Some further orderly appreciation of the main non-dollar currencies against the dollar is desirable,' they said. All G5 'stand ready to cooperate more closely' to bring this about, probably by direct intervention in the foreign exchange markets. Added Federal Reserve Board chairman Paul Volcker: 'I do think exchange rates are important and must reflect economic fundamentals. Intervention must be useful at certain times.'

During the previous week, the UK had strengthened its

reserves by raising $2.5 billion with a floating rate issue in the Euromarkets and this was now seen as ammunition.

That Monday morning the dollar fell more than 3.5 per cent in a few hours to its lowest level since June 1984. It was one of the steepest falls on record. The only intervention was a token sale of $8 million by the Bundesbank. The dollar had fallen from Friday night's DM2.8430 to DM2.6885 by the close of trading on Monday evening in New York.

Why did it work with so little intervention? Partly because the markets could see the major central banks all lined up and determined to make it happen. Partly because the dollar had been so over-valued there was little attraction in buying it and it was probably ready to fall with little encouragement. It was close to a foregone conclusion. Most important, however, was that the central banks were only adding to a trend which had already begun. Note that phrase in the G5 statement 'some *further* orderly appreciation of the main non-dollar currencies against the dollar'. The dollar had peaked already and any intervention would only add to its downward momentum.

This quickly went too far for the participants' comfort. The dollar was down to DM1.83 and Y153.65 by the time the G5 finance ministers plus their Canadian counterpart reached the Louvre Accord over the weekend of 21–2 February 1987. This was in fact a G7 meeting: the G5 together with Canada and Italy. However the Italians – who by now were arguing that as their economy had overtaken in size that of the UK they should therefore replace it in the G5 – refused to cooperate. They took umbrage at what they saw as the slight to them and Canada that, they alleged, the G5 ministers stitched up an agreement with which the enlarged group would be presented as *fait accompli*.

The Louvre Accord was to intervene to prevent any further slide in the dollar and to stabilize all major currencies at near to present levels, keeping them in future within – unpublished – target zones. (Hadn't anyone read that earlier Congressional paper?)

This attempt to scare the markets into submission was based

on intervention and the effect of threatening it. Underlying policies remained unchanged. It was all mouth and no treasuries.

Five years later, with the dollar at new record lows against both Deutschmark and yen, the Fed was to call in aid concerted intervention just to persuade the markets that the dollar's weakness was not part of the USA's underlying policies.

The greenback now was getting what Americans are wont to call a 'double whammy'. There were the inevitable uncertainties of a presidential election but the dollar was also an exogenous casualty of Europe's currency turmoil in the summer of 1992. The year's early promise of a vigorous US economic recovery faded and with it the dollar began to wilt. Its initial spurt from DM1.50 to DM1.68 and Y122 to Y135 by April turned into a sharp decline. Between May and July it was more than 10 per cent off against the Deutschmark and down nearly 5 per cent in yen terms.

As the Federal Reserve Bank of New York later commented, 'With the dollar rapidly approaching historical lows, a July summit meeting of the leaders of the Group of Seven nations heightened the market's focus on official policies toward exchange rates. The absence of any reference to exchange rates in the summit's concluding communiqué, coupled with what appeared to be ambiguous official statements during and following the meetings, led some market participants to conclude that the G7 was unconcerned about the dollar.'

After all, Japanese authorities had been explicit in favouring a strong yen and the last meeting of the G7 – in April – had been equally explicit that 'the decline of the yen . . . was not contributing to the adjustment process.'

Now the ERM storm clouds were beginning to gather. First with the Bundesbank raising its discount rate and so widening the interest rate differentials which were already so unfavourable to the dollar. 'In this environment, market participants began to adopt large short-dollar positions on the premise that the dollar faced little risk of an appreciation but good prospects of a further decline,' the New York Fed narrated. 'This perception of the dollar as a one-way bet, coupled with the absence of any source of strong support for the dollar in the marketplace, caused the currency's decline to accelerate.'

It was getting out of hand. The central banks banded together and intervened, the US contribution alone being to buy $170 million, selling Deutschmarks, on Monday 20 July. The dollar bounced that week from DM1.4470 to DM1.50 by Friday but a week later was back to DM1.4745, having thus lost half its expensively bought advance.

Within weeks, the Fed was intervening heavily, buying $1.1 billion against the Deutschmark in just four days of August, again buttressed by further buying support from other central banks. 'Selling pressures were somewhat blunted by the interventions,' said Fed vice-president William McDonough, who was managing the System Open Market Account through which the transactions were made, 'but the operations did not interrupt the tendency of the dollar to decline . . . when these operations did not appear to discourage the bidding for Deutschmarks, the US authorities refrained from further intervention.' The dollar hit a new record low of DM1.3862 on 2 September. Its fall against the yen was just starting.

Japanese banks hold huge blocks of shares in their customer companies and have done for years. When they come to calculate whether they have adequate share capital for the amount of business they are doing – their capital ratios – those banks are allowed to include 40 per cent of the profits showing on those shareholdings, even though they haven't sold and realized the gains and if they were to do so would immediately depress the share price.

At this time, the bureaucrats running Japan were concerned that the low level of share prices might drive banks' capital ratios too low. Together with suspicions that the banks were concealing the true extent of the bad debts on their books, this might perhaps trigger a banking crisis, adding to the woes of an already troubled economy. The bureaucrats engineered support for the stock market, driving Tokyo's Nikkei index higher. Foreign investors took note and began moving their money into yen assets. In addition, Japanese companies were repatriating capital to make their accounts look good at the fiscal half-year point which came at the end of that month. The result of all this demand for the yen was that on the last day of September the dollar saw an historical low of Y118.6.

No sooner had Japanese corporates completed their book-cooking and turned off their heat against the dollar than it got roasted in the latest wave of European speculative grilling. 'Transactions related to the financing of official European intervention were perceived as affecting the dollar,' notes Bill McDonough. 'Throughout the period [from November through January] market participants reported that both in the course of rebuilding official reserves and in transactions related to financing official borrowings, a number of European central banks were heavy sellers of dollars and that, at times, this selling pressure restrained the dollar's upward trend against the Deutschmark.'

Every cloud has its silver lining, however. The Fed and the Treasury admitted that in that three months to the end of January 1993 they realized profits of $135 million from foreign exchange activities and their unrealized gains were well over $3.5 billion.

More to the point, foreign central bank activities were no more than moderating the dollar's recovery against the Deutschmark. As July turned to August 1993 and the ERM was being emasculated, the dollar climbed back to DM1.73. Its downward trend against the yen had persisted, however. On the 27 April the fall to a new record low of Y109.15 – despite the Bank of Japan having that month bought $6 billion in exchange for yen – provoked another dosage of the Louvre Accord: this time with a spot of paradox stirred into the formula. The official statement from the US Treasury was: 'The Administration believes that exchange rates should reflect fundamentals and attempts to artificially influence or manipulate exchange rates are inappropriate.' That might be read as abrogating intervention. However, the statement continued:

'Moreover, excessive volatility is counterproductive for growth. Therefore we are monitoring developments closely and stand ready to co-operate in exchange markets with our G7 partners as conditions may warrant.'

In case, perhaps, their statement had caused confusion or the markets did not run scared at such Draconian threats, that same day the G7 bought the dollar aggressively: the US to the tune of $200 million. The market reaction was extraordinary, if not quite what had been intended. The dollar bounced almost 2 yen to Y111.05 before plunging at the rate of a yen a week – despite further intervention to the tune of more than $1 billion by the USA – to hit its record low of Y104.8 in mid-June. By mid-August it was down to Y100.8. It was saved further immediate depreciation only by the fall of the Miyaza government presaging the end of thirty-eight years of Liberal Democratic Party rule and political consistency in Japan. Slowly, hesitatingly and how enduringly only time will show, the dollar crawled back against the world's two other major currencies.

At some point during all this – probably more as a dawning realization than a flash of insight detonated by a specific event – the US authorities came to understand that intervention was not working. No longer was it of itself expected to achieve any desired end, rather it was an instrument of reassuring the markets about US policy. Thus the New York Fed rationalized the latest official forays. 'The US authorities intervened on three occasions during the period, purchasing a total of $1,067.5 million against the yen to show that they were willing to co-operate with other monetary authorities as appropriate and were not favoring a weak dollar as a matter of policy.' Not even the dollar, the world's most widely held and most heavily traded currency, backed by the resources of the US Treasury and the Federal Reserve Board and, in turn, supported by central banks of the world's seven most advanced economies, could defy the markets.

This verdict still holds good. In late April and early May 1994 the dollar was under pressure again. This time, with the rate down to DM1.6570 and Y101.2 even after intervention by the Fed and the Bank of Japan, a fresh effort involved concerted intervention by no fewer than seventeen central banks. Expectations arose that after this episode the G7 summit in Naples held early in July would agree a plan for concerted interest rate moves and coordinated intervention to support the dollar. When this failed to materialize the markets became convinced that Clinton's policy towards the dollar was benign (questionably) neglect. In mid-July the greenback touched Y96.80 and DM1.5235.

As I write, the dollar remains vulnerable to speculative attack at any time. Successive US governments have given the impression that they are willing to use the currency as a trade weapon, would consent to its decline to stimulate economic activity at home (especially ahead of a presidential election) and lack the political desire or power to force through austerity measures if such were needed to support the exchange rate from collapse.

The dollar, in other words, has a credibility problem which is growing. When he failed to negotiate promises from Japan that US exporters would be guaranteed numerically specific shares of Japan's markets, President Clinton – like Nixon and Reagan before him – tied currency values to foreign trade. He threatened that unless Japan conceded to his demands the USA would drive the yen higher.

One senior US Treasury official explained the latest inter-vention as April turned to May in 1994 as being 'to counteract a negative psychology that had developed on the basis of false perceptions that the US was trying to drive the dollar down . . . or was somehow indifferent to where market forces took its currency.'

The market misperception might just conceivably have arisen from that earlier threat to drive the yen higher and a failure to appreciate that, whereas the yen was to rise against the dollar, the dollar was not to fall against the yen. Notwith-standing his President's earlier imprecations, US Treasury Secretary Lloyd Bentsen said the dollar's decline had 'gone beyond what is justified by economic fundamentals . . . This administration sees no advantage in an undervalued currency.' As, by that time in the life of the Clinton administration, the dollar had fallen 18–20 per cent against the yen, misunder-standing about this point is hardly surprising.

5

THEORIES ABOUT EXCHANGE RATES:

What Makes Money Move?

'Any Economic Theory or Principle of Accounting
which cannot be explained in plain English as
Applied Commonsense, is bunk.'

Roberts: Second Law of Money

How do we make sense of the way exchange rates pop up
and down like the proverbial undergarments? As Roger Bootle,
chief economist at Midland Bank, more befittingly expresses
it: 'The extremes to which both the pound and the dollar got
in the mid-1980s as a product of the action of the exchange
markets were clearly daft.

'It can't make sense for the pound to be DM5 in 1981 and
as low as DM2.33 in 1982, and with the pound to dollar rate
the range was $2.50 in 1980 to $1.05 in the mid-1980s, with
very little justification from the economic fundamentals.'

Sterling may be an anomaly — Britain's economic decline,
loss of Empire and all that — but how can you justify the
transmutation of the dollar:yen rate from $1:Y360 to
$1:Y100 in little more than twenty years? The Japanese eco-
nomy has outperformed that of the US in the period, granted,
but by three and a half times? And what of the dollar to
Deutschmark rate, the most liquid on the foreign exchange
markets? It doubled in the five years to 1985, then halved
again in the next seven. Markets may be forever maverick. Is
there some commonsense basis on which to value one currency against another?

Next to the main elevator shaft of the Rockefeller Center in New York is a vending machine from which you can buy, among other things, Coca-Cola. A standard twelve-ounce can of ordinary no-holds-barred Coke will cost you a dollar. An exactly similar can (the same size, but here it's called 330ml) from a vending machine at Frankfurt railway station sells for DM1.75. On that basis $1 = DM1.75. That is Purchasing Power Parity, the exchange rate at which the price of a basket of goods in one country equals the price of the same basket of goods in another. It depends on no fancy economic hypothesis and relates to our real lives.

I chose Coca Cola to illustrate the point because it is the biggest of all global brands, sold freely in many parts of the world and so is a liquid (sorry) market. The *Economist* newspaper has been using the Big Mac hamburger as a currency index since 1986, comparing the price in local currency with the dollar price in the USA to give an implied PPP of the dollar in each currency and comparing that with the market exchange rate to indicate whether the currency might be under- or overvalued. In April 1993, this index suggested that the Russian rouble was 50 per cent undervalued at 686 to the $1. As a year later it took more than 2000 roubles to buy one dollar perhaps it is as well that the *Economist* has always characterized the exercise as light-hearted.

More august support for the use of PPP comes from the International Monetary Fund. It previously compared the total economic output, the Gross Domestic Product (GDP) of countries by taking their value in local currency and converting those into a common currency – the dollar – at market exchange rates. This approach was responsible for the nonsense which the Canadian economist Dan Usher had remarked on more than twenty years earlier: people in many less developed countries had annual incomes which in those dollar terms would not be enough to keep an American alive for a week; yet they lived tolerably, if very simply.

IMF figures calculated on market exchange rates suggested Asia's share of world output fell between 1985 and 1990 whereas this had been the fastest-growing region by far. The solecism resulted from some Asian currencies having declined against the dollar. So the IMF recalculated its sums using PPP. This showed, for instance, that China's previously estimated 2 per cent of world output was really 6 per cent or more and that developing countries as a whole produce more than one third of the world's GDP rather than the 18 per cent previously credited to them.

Why the difference? People in less developed countries rely much more on locally produced goods and services, much less on those which are internationally traded. When it comes to goods and services which can't be moved across borders – restaurant meals, taxi services – even bigger divergences are possible. In poorer currencies non-tradable products tend to sell at very low prices compared with tradable goods.

This disparity does not only apply to poorer countries. Securities house Jardine Fleming's analysts in Tokyo calculated in mid-1993 that the yen's PPP was Y170–90 to the dollar for the consumer goods industry, which is relatively sheltered, but Y100–115 in exporting industries such as motor cars.

Theoretically, if the price of that can of Coke in one country produces a PPP exchange rate far enough out of line with the market exchange rate then a trader would buy in one country and sell in the other, profiting from the arbitrage until the flow of Coke drove prices and exchange rates into line. That's scarcely a practical proposition even with an international product like Coca-Cola. Moreover, the can of Coke sold from a New York vending machine for $1 sells from an exactly similar machine in Atlanta for 60 cents. What's the PPP for the Deutschmark now?

Purchasing power parity is based on the idea that if prices are far out of line then arbitrage will align them. Someone will buy where prices are cheap and sell where they are dear until their buying demand raises the low prices and the extra supply where prices have been high drives them down. If the prices are in two different currencies the arbitrage trader will sell the currency he receives on selling the goods and buy the currency needed to pay for them.

So, when the exchange rate is $1:DM1.60, you start out

with DM1.60 and convert it into $1. You buy a can of Coke for $1 in New York and sell it for DM1.75 in Frankfurt – and you end up with DM0.15 more than you started off with. You can do that on a much larger scale until your constant selling of Deutschmarks and buying of dollars will move the exchange rate to $1:DM1.75.

That's the theory. It makes sense. It doesn't work.

There's the cost of moving the goods from New York to Frankfurt, the price – exchange rate – disparity may be quite wide before it would be worthwhile for a trader to transport the goods. In many cases, too, manufacturers restrict the franchise to sell their products, and governments impose regulations on imports.

An increasingly important factor today is that services rather than goods account for a growing proportion of the more developed economies. Once we have enough to eat and wear, find we can drive only one car at a time and have no need of more than one dishwasher in the household, we tend to spend our money on paying others to take the drudgery out of life, on travel and on other services which do not increase our consumption of material goods. As currency economist Dr Brendan Brown, head of research at Mitsubishi Finance, puts it: 'Purchasing power parity is low down the list of most people's perceptions when they're appraising currencies. It exists but it's a fairly distant anchor, setting a limit of plus or minus 25 per cent for an exchange rate.'

There can sometimes be another complicating factor which Dr Alan Greenspan – now, as chairman of the Federal Reserve Board, the USA's central bank governor – pointed out during his evidence to a Congressional hearing. 'The US dollar in foreign exchange markets is approximately 30 per cent above its so-called purchasing power parity.'

'The problem with the calculation is that it is very rough and that it presupposes that the US dollar is not the reserve currency for which there is constant accumulation. So the exchange rate will always, under such circumstances, be above so-called purchasing power parity.'

*   *   *

Time was when you could always bank on the trade figures. As Harold Wilson's Labour Government struggled desperately to resist devaluation of sterling in the mid-1960s (and lost in 1967) their first line of defence was the trade figures. One of the new government's first measures was a controversial requirement – contrary to international law – for an advance deposit against the cost of imports. They launched the Queen's Award scheme to encourage exporting and started throwing knighthoods at individual exporters.

Every month I could bank on Trade Figures Day. As a young City editor of provincial dailies I knew that my editors would give me extra space and want something for their front pages – often as the lead story. Rarely would the *Financial Times* fail next morning to give this news pride of place. Those learned scribes, and even we humble hacks, knew that a key point, usually *the* key point, would be the reaction of the foreign exchange markets. The markets never failed to react.

Today, a month's trade figures may pass almost unremarked, often causing little more than an hour's flurry in the markets and attracting little, even broadsheet, reportage. Trade figures don't move currencies. The dollar soared in the first half of the 1980s almost in parallel with the US trade deficit. The French franc came under pressure in late 1992 to July 1993 notwithstanding a trade balance arguably more robust than that underlying the Deutschmark and certainly improving, whereas Germany's appeared to be deteriorating.

The relationship might be in the reverse direction only: that currencies drive trade balances. It is this thinking which has made the US and Japanese governments nurture the yen's strengthening against the dollar in the belief that they will thereby reduce Japan's hefty trade surplus – a record $135 billion in 1993 – especially with America. The US concern is not only to reduce its trade gap with Japan but also to keep the yen so high that Japanese exporters will be at a disadvantage against American rivals elsewhere in the world.

Even this relationship – a high exchange rate pricing you out of export markets and imports into your market – is being called into question. The short-term effect of currency appreciation is well known. At first a more expensive yen causes Japan's trade surplus to widen as it boosts the dollar value of Japanese exports and lowers the value of imports. If politicians lack patience or simply panic, they may try to 'remedy' the short-run effect by pushing the yen even higher, giving a further twist to the spiral.

William Cline at the Washington-based Institute for International Economics says* that a rise in the yen's real exchange rate leads to a fall in the trade surplus two years later. (The real exchange rate is akin to the real interest rate: it is the nominal or apparent rate, adjusted for inflation. Thus where interest rate is 8 per cent and inflation 6 per cent, real interest rate is 2 per cent. Likewise the real exchange rate reflects the reality that if prices rise faster in America than in Japan, the USA's competitiveness deteriorates unless the exchange rate changes to compensate.)

Cline argues that when the yen rises that cut in the trade surplus reduces economic activity – exporters find they are not selling so much abroad and in the domestic market manufacturers are having a tough time competing with imports – and as economic activity declines so do savings relative to investment. The extra finance for the investment is an increased capital inflow or decreased capital outflow to match the shrinking trade surplus so that payments overall balance.

But Ronald McKinnon of Stanford University points out that Japan's trade surplus has been rising steadily over the years while the yen has appreciated†. The overvalued yen has been keeping the economy relatively deflated and so curbed demand for imports (as well as forcing manufacturers into export markets more than if home demand were buoyant). By this argument, the Bank of Japan should ease monetary policy – cut interest rates – so as to boost the economy and thereby demand for exports.

---

* 'Japan: Trade Adjustment in the Pipeline' by William Cline, Institute for International Economics.
† 'Dollar & Yen: The Problem of Financial Adjustment between the United States and Japan' Ronald McKinnon, Stanford University, USA.

Which argument is right? Each is logical, based on equally reliable evidence and requires no obvious assumptions or presuppositions which might be invalid. Each on its own seems cogent and, frankly, I find it impossible to choose between them. Fortunately, as this debate is about the influence of currency rates on trade surpluses and our concern at this juncture is whether trade today drives exchange rates, we can leave the academics to this possibly inconclusive argument.

With the BIS survey of foreign exchange dealing showing it to be more than twenty times the level of world trade, perhaps it is not surprising that trade surpluses and deficits have so little influence on currency rates.

'A fundamental change has gone on in our understanding of the markets,' comments Roger Bootle. 'Years ago people thought of forex markets as the markets for currency which became available as a result of international trade. Parasitic financial activities had grown on that but the main driving force was international trade and therefore the exchange rate was an equilibrating mechanism between the supply and demand for currency arising from that real economic activity.

'Owing to the growth in internationally mobile funds it is now appropriate to regard the exchange rate as a price which instead equilibrates the international demand for different countries' stocks of assets. What that means is that in the old days the focus of attention was the trade figures and the focus of capital flows was the trade figures. That has gone. It is now the market's valuation of the fundamental attractiveness of assets denominated in these different currencies which drives exchange rates.

'But there is a still a residual influence from trade flows. They set bands of plausible levels for the exchange rate but I think they're very wide. You couldn't get the pound above DM3 or below DM2 because the market perception would be that those prices were out of line with real trading relationships, so there would be massive stabilizing speculation the other way. But that's an enormously wide range.'

Britain lifted – actually, suspended – exchange controls in

1979. Since then UK pension funds, insurance companies and individual savers (usually through the medium of unit trusts) have been free to invest heavily overseas – and they have done so. US pension funds have dramatically increased their overseas investment in recent years and around the world countries have relaxed capital controls, both by welcoming foreign investment which was previously excluded and by allowing their own investors to venture their funds abroad.

When trade drove exchange rates the importer and exporter had very little decision to make about a currency. They based their buying decision on quality and what the cost would come to in their own currency; they decided their selling price overseas on the basis of what the market would bear and how much that would convert to in their own currency. The only currency decision to make was whether to secure the foreign currency: as soon as they ordered the goods; when they actually arrived; or when payment was due, perhaps some months later; whether to exchange expected foreign currency receipts 'forward' – in anticipation of payment – as soon as the export order came in or, at the other extreme, when the foreign currency was eventually payable. These so-called 'leads and lags' apart, trade realities determined exchange rates.

Today, with investment a more important factor than trade in affecting exchange rates, the investor looking overseas has several variables to consider. An order of priorities arises from research which appears conclusive and, if it is not, has such widespread acceptance that it has become self-fulfilling. Least important in terms of investment performance will be the choice of individual security: which bond or the share of which company. More important will be to get right the directional trend of that particular market. Buy a duff share in a rising market and the overall rise will probably let you come out without loss. Even the best-performing share is unlikely to show you a profit if the whole market is falling. But most important for investment performance is the decision about the currency. Here it is worth recalling that observation by Guy Hurley, proprietary trader in Barclays' dealing room: 'You're having to express two opinions at once. It's not a simple liking or dislike, as with a share at a particular price. Here you have to say not only 'I like sterling' but also 'I hate the dollar'.'

Governments have made themselves increasingly vulnerable to the currency likes and dislikes of international investors. As, through the 1980s, the US budget deficit burgeoned and was financed by a swelling inflow of funds until the world's richest nation became also the world's biggest borrower, fears arose about when the music would stop. Before each auction of US Treasury bonds, rumours flew around Wall Street that this time, yes this time, the big Japanese securities houses — Nomura et al — which had been granted the status of prime dealers able to bid direct at the auction, would not be buying. Japanese investors were regularly buying a quarter and on the odd occasion a reputed 40 per cent of the bonds on offer.

More recently, it has been Europe's governments which have had to scour the world's markets for money. For all the pious pledges made at Maastricht limiting the size of budget deficit and overall indebtedness as a proportion of GDP, this has not precluded an increase in absolute terms. In many cases compliance with, or even convergence towards, Maastricht criteria has been nugatory.

In two years Germany's total public sector debt grew almost 30 per cent — from DM1,050 billion at the end of 1990 to DM1,350 billion at the end of 1992. The proportion held overseas rose from 21 to 26 per cent. Of France's public debt repayable in seven or more years, the foreign-held share rose from 17 to 27 per cent between January 1991 and April 1993, while for short-term debt the increase was even more dramatic, from 29 to 43 per cent.

With foreign holdings so high, the potential for action on a market-dislocating scale is clear. The risk is that when they are holding such a high proportion of the government's bonds, if foreign investors take fright about the currency, or even just fall in love with another currency, their selling would be on a larger scale than the market could absorb without prices collapsing. From that perspective, what might make the music stop for France and Germany?

Brendan Brown believes that a key influence in exchange rates today is relative real interest rates. How does the interest rate in the USA, after allowing for inflation, compare with the similarly inflation-adjusted interest rate in Germany? This approach helps to explain why some of the casualties in the ERM imbroglio fell despite offering higher interest rates than the Deutschmark. The problem it poses is that while the nominal interest rate at the time is clear, how much should you allow for inflation and how long a view does the market take of inflation rates?

When in June 1993, for instance, the French franc was suffering less inflation than the Deutschmark, and French finance minister Edmond Alphandéry was calling for it to take over the anchor role in the ERM, Bundesbank president Helmut Schlesinger pointed out that the Deutschmark's role as a reserve currency arose largely from its inflation record over the past twenty years, with which the franc could not compare.

So if the markets work on relative real interest rates they have to decide:

- over what time span to calculate the inflation rate
- what that is likely to be
- what is the appropriate relationship between the real interest rates on two different currencies

Chris Dillow, economist at the Nomura Research Institute's European headquarters in London, confesses, 'I don't know what the real interest rate is, to be honest. There are only two countries in the world with meaningful real interest rates and that's the UK and Australia. They are the only places that have index-linked bonds. Real interest rates elsewhere are a nonsense because we don't know what expected inflation is.'

Federal Reserve Board chairman, Alan Greenspan, has in the past warned – in evidence to a Congressional hearing concerned at the dollar's then unwonted strength – that real interest rates may be ineffective as a tool for shaping exchange rates. 'The attraction of the dollar as a safe haven vehicle appears to outweigh the effects of relative interest rates. As was evident late last year [when the dollar had bounced despite the Fed's and the Bundesbank's efforts and in defiance of interest rate disincentives] lowering interest rates on dollar-denominated assets, relative to those denominated in other currencies, does not necessarily cause the dollar to fall.'

Beyond the bounds of all economic statistics is a factor which may sometimes be decisive and is always an influence on the foreign exchange value of a currency: fear. This propensity to funk off into 'safe' currencies has sometimes reached such extremes that, for instance, Switzerland in the 1960s imposed negative interest rates: you paid Swiss banks interest to keep your money in Swiss francs (and in those days of exchange controls it took exceptionally fiendish ingenuity to hold any meaningful quantity of Swiss francs other than in a Swiss bank).

Currencies which have the somewhat ambiguous benefit of safe-haven status will be subject to extreme movements during international crises. Such unpredictable extraneous factors add complications to the lives of the host countries' international traders and central bankers.

Other currencies are subject to what you might think of as less positive speculation. 'What makes currencies most vulnerable to speculation,' says Chris Dillow, 'is uncertainty about economic policy. For many European countries there is often thought to be the risk at any time that the government will use the currency as a means of stimulating the economy. Speculative attacks against the Spanish peseta, or sterling, or the Swedish krona are more likely because these are large open economies where the governments have a benefit from letting the currency go. That's in contrast to the USA, where you don't get speculative attacks on the dollar because nobody perceives that a weaker dollar is extremely bullish for the economy in the way that a weak peseta is helpful for the Spanish economy.

'Another factor is the liquidity of the currency. The legacy from having been a reserve currency – like sterling – is that the amount traded is far greater than the amount of the host country's real trade and that creates the potential for volatility. A further factor is the extent to which the real economy is volatile. For many small economies the growth rates, inflation rates and suchlike have swung about to an enormous extent. That is magnified and reinforced for foreign exchange markets, because if economic growth could be between nothing and 3 per cent next year then expectations of economic growth are going to be even wider and, therefore, attitudes towards the currency are going to be even more dispersed. Thus there's an even greater chance of the currency moving in extreme directions.'

Brendan Brown points to the heavy dependence of some economies – and therefore their currency values – on a single commodity. Crop failure or the gyrations of copper, oil or other commodity prices may produce even more pronounced swings in the currencies of the producing countries. Both the Australian and Canadian dollars are heavily influenced by the fortunes, if not of single materials then of commodity demand overall.

'The Canadian dollar has been described as the casino currency of the US dollar – the casino neighbour – because you have a huge amount of money going into the Canadian dollar simply attracted by its being called a dollar. It is assumed to be close to US dollar and it offers a more attractive interest rate. That matters a lot when US rates are low. If US rates rise again then there is less interest in going into the Canadian as the high-interest neighbour. That variability in demand from such a huge neighbour gives the Canadian dollar natural volatility. It's a currency condemned to be more speculative.

'But equally important in making a currency vulnerable to speculative attack is a lack of political stability and the prime example of this must be Italy.'

Given the unpredictability of politicians and the impotence of even the US government to buck the markets, can we advance our mission of trying to comprehend what drives exchange rates by looking at some bigger picture of a country and its currency?

Some feel FEER is the key, or at least the nearest you'll find to one. It stands for Fundamental Equilibrium Exchange Rate. Chris Dillow explains: 'Markets do have some vague notion of fundamental equilibrium exchange rates in that people will say that in the long run the currency can't stay where it is because the economy is in recession or because the current account balance is massively positive or negative. They have that sort of vague notion.'

If the UK is running a trade surplus – exporting more than we import – and very low unemployment, most people would regard that as ideal. (We have only fleetingly enjoyed such a state.) If we have a trade surplus but high unemployment then it is arguable that there is not enough demand in the economy – the trade surplus arises because our demand for goods is less than our output – and the government should consider lowering interest rates to boost demand, part of which will create extra jobs and part be met from imports which will balance our trade.

If we have a trade deficit and full employment than it may be that the economy is overheating. The trade deficit shows demand exceeds our current earning capacity. A rise in interest rates would reduce demand for imports and will either make our manufacturers look overseas more for sales or perhaps trim their workforce. But if you have a trade deficit and high unemployment that shows the economy is in fundamental disequilibrium at that exchange rate. Raising interest rates to reduce the trade deficit would reduce demand and so aggravate the already high unemployment. Lowering interest rates would increase demand which the trade deficit shows is already greater than our ability to earn abroad at that exchange rate. Devaluation to restore the equilibrium is then all but inevitable. That was the case with the UK in the summer of 1992 and was why Chris Dillow and his peers were able to predict sterling's inability to keep within its ERM bands.

'What surprised me was the speed and timing of sterling's devaluation,' he recalls. 'In most of what I wrote before September I said that sterling was overvalued and there was a long-term risk of devaluation. What struck us all as so strange was the speed with which it happened.'

The problem with fundamental equilibrium exchange rate is that it requires assumptions about what is the natural rate of unemployment. Some unemployment is inevitable and deciding whether unemployment is unusually high or unusually low is a very subjective judgement. The nature of the labour force, the skills it has and the skills required are all constantly changing. It also begs the question of what the long run equilibrium is in the economy and what is the real exchange rate consistent with that. If the nominal exchange rate should be £:DM2.60 that is a long-run figure but it is not obvious that it ought to be DM2.60 when the economy is clearly not at equilibrium, such as when we are not at the natural rate of unemployment.

If FEER is based on the real exchange rate it does not tell you whether you should achieve it through changing the nominal exchange rate or by adjusting domestic prices. Thus when the US Congress was once considering ways to keep the dollar at the 'right' exchange rate – within 'target zones' – a Congressional research paper at the time warned: 'The calculation of the zone depends on what is considered full employment and reasonable price stability abroad as well as at home. And the question arises as to whether a 'sustainable equilibrium' in the balance of payments calls for balance, capital exports (a trade surplus) or capital imports (a trade deficit).'*

So if even FEER fails us, what can we rely on as a guide to exchange rates? Howard Flight, joint managing director of the Guinness Flight fund management group and no tiro on the subject of foreign exchange, believes the search is as misguided as that for the philosopher's stone.

'The bottom line is all about money flows around the world,' he asserts. 'Where you get the pressure of money flows one way or the other way – moving faster or even slower than the mechanisms to deal with them and the natural offsetting

* Overview by Alfred Reifman, Congressional Research Service, presented to conference "The Strong Dollar: Causes, Consequences & Policy Implications" co-sponsored by the Joint Economic Committee of Congress and the Congressional Research Service 29.11.85.

economic factors – then you get pressure one way or the other on exchange rates.

'The various factors which determine money flows and exchange rates keep changing in their relative importance the whole time. Whereas for a period interest rate differentials were the crucial thing, suddenly they're not and something else is. It's highly dangerous because suddenly the ball game changes. Even the way interest rate differentials are perceived suddenly turns on its head.

'If anyone tries to make a black box of it – create a formula and put in assumed standard weightings for any of these factors – they'll fail. Any neat attempt at a mathematical economic model or some form of technical-investment-decision-taking model can only hold good for a short period of time. It's got to be dynamic and allow for the impact of different factors to be greater or less at different times.'

Exchange rates are also signalling to us how our economy is holding up in the world. If factors deciding the exchange rate are forever changing, constantly shifting in relative importance, what of the feedback which the exchange rate is giving about the economy?

'The exchange rate as a single statistic may not be very meaningful on its own,' says Bank of England associate director, Ian Plenderleith. 'It is a summary reflection of a host of factors and underlying forces, some driven by fundamental economic developments, some responding to movements in relative interest rates and asset prices, some moved by technical or seasonal conditions, and some reflecting longer-term trends. Understanding these factors can give us useful information about how economic agents are responding to the monetary stance we are pursuing and hence how far we are succeeding in pursuit of our monetary objective of price stability. But the information is inevitably jumbled and laced with a great deal of extraneous 'noise'. It needs to be decoded.'

Alan Greenspan of the Federal Reserve Board might envy him. Shortly after the Fed had raised interest rates by a tiny 0.25 per cent – but upset the bond markets mightily by so doing – Mr Greenspan gave Congressional testimony.

American savers had seen interest rates on bank deposits fall so sharply that they had endeavoured to restore their incomes by switching to other investments which did not, however, figure in the US money supply. The message was so fogged by this that the Fed didn't know whether its monetary policy was tight or loose. Bereft of its usual Deutschmarks and guiding stars, monetary policy depended on 'ongoing assessments of the totality of incoming information'. The Fed was closely watching among other indicators 'the price of gold, which has been especially sensitive to inflation concerns, the exchange rate and the term structure of interest rates'.

The quest for an explanation of how the markets behave – and, more importantly, for a predictor of how they will behave – is as old as the markets themselves. Some of the theories have found favour in the foreign exchange markets and the size of their following makes them influential.

There are Fibonacci retracement numbers. Says Tom Elliot, head of foreign exchange trading at the bank in the Nomura securities leviathan, 'Fibonacci retracement numbers have become very popular since the early 1980s. They were initially used in the Chicago markets, on the floor of the IMM, and they've become a self-fulfilling argument.' The IMM – International Monetary Market – opened in 1982 and deals in monetary futures.

Mr Fibonacci was a Swiss–French mathematician who became very interested in all sorts of markets, no matter what security or commodity they traded so long as prices moved. He came up with a theory that of any move in one direction there would be minimum retracements. The minimum retracement levels are 31.8 per cent of the original move and more often than not a 66 per cent retracement of the entire move. The theory does not specify the time involved in these retracements, however.

Judging what is a move, when it began, how much of it is the original, whether it has actually ended or whether the latest price change is merely a pause within the context of the continuing big move may seem easy and mechanical until you actually draw up a chart – of gold prices, of the £:$ rate, of cocoa prices, of German interest rates or the Dow Jones index of share prices on Wall Street – and try to apply the theory in practice.

There's another problem. It's a variant of Goodhart's Law. This says that whichever monetary aggregate a government chooses as a target variable becomes distorted by the very act of targeting it. Some would extend this to say that if a government bases its economic decision-making on any particular statistic – the exchange rate, the money supply, inflation rate, the balance of payments or even something as remote as the number of housing starts – that statistic will ineluctably become distorted for as long as it is the focus of policymaking decision.

Likewise with Fibonacci, the canny Tom Elliot observes: 'As more and more people pay attention to the percentage retracement, the traders are waiting for them to happen and indeed provoking those type of recoveries. The traders will anticipate a retracement.'

Some proponents would argue that the retracement numbers concept belongs within an alternative approach to investment and markets: technical analysis, otherwise known as charting. This is the great divide, if not as great as that 'twixt communism and capitalism in the depths of the Cold War, certainly engendering animosities as great as those which led to the Battle of Blefuscu which, *Gulliver's Travels* recounts, arose from disagreement over which end to open a boiled egg.

The blunt enders are the fundamentalists, with whom we've been concerned to this point. They are looking at economies and the fundamental values which lie behind currencies and the demand therefore. When fundamentalists analyse shares they dissect individual companies' accounts, assessing the true worth of the share. In commodity markets, they study crop reports, mining returns and the changing pattern of demand in consumer countries. In all cases, there will, of course, be as many different schools of thought about the relative importance of various factors as Christianity has sects.

Fundamental analysis is concerned with value. Over time,

says the argument, relative value asserts itself: markets must come back to reality.

Technical analysis – popular at the sharp end of the foreign exchange markets, at the dealing desks – is concerned with price, regardless of value. The performance of a price, plotted on a chart, will give a picture of how people are behaving towards that currency, commodity, or share. This approach says that value is of no practical relevance: it may be that a currency is overvalued but, if people take it into their heads to keep buying it, then it will just become even more overvalued and if you are trading a currency what matters is the price you pay to buy and the price you get when you sell. A shopkeeper offers you a kilo bag of sugar and explains that it is worth £1.50 because of the wages which were paid to the workers who produced it, the calorific value it offers in your diet, its wide utility in cooking and the ease with which you may measure out precise amounts. So the value is really £1.50 but the price in the shop next door is 60p a bag . . .

There are numerous theories based on studying price movement regardless of value. Best known, perhaps, is the Elliott Wave.

Ralph Elliott was a retired Californian accountant in the 1930s who made an exhaustive study of stock markets' hourly, daily, weekly and monthly movements. (This for entertainment value must have ranked somewhat below watching the grass grow but above his previous occupation.) He decided that the market moves in waves. Each upward wave has three upward moves and two downward. Each down wave has two downswings and one up. Again, the problem is – when you study a chart – deciding which of the various squiggles is a major wave and which is a contrary move within a large trend in the opposite direction.

Several of these theories of technical analysis have one factor in common with the Kondratieff cycle. Nikolai Kondratieff was a Russian government official who, in 1922, promulgated a theory that no matter how mankind arranged its affairs, there was an immutable boom-bust cycle of between forty-five and sixty years which determined events. As we have not been collecting statistics long enough to analyse several cycles of such duration, Kondratieff's theory shares with those of Fibonacci and Elliott the characteristic of being neither provable nor disprovable. (Kondratieff, for his pains, was sent to Siberia.)

There is a more general psychological theory behind technical analysis. People behave irrationally. You can say that the difference between price and value is the irrationality of human behaviour. Alan Greenspan came to saying this when, years ago, he pointed out to a Congressional hearing that people were funking into the dollar as a currency hedge and in those circumstances a fundamental change such as an interest rate cut might have no effect.

The economist John Maynard Keynes – no slouch as an investor – said the movement of share prices was analogous to a newspaper competition in which you had to predict the rankings of a beauty contest. The art was less in judging the comparative beauty of the contestants than in guessing how they would rate in the eyes of the judges. Just as one minute skirts reach to the ankles and the next are a mere pelmet from the waist, men's ties kipper-shaped or bootlaces, so investors fall for the charms of particular market sectors, then out of love with them. Suddenly, everyone was buying Australian nickel mining shares, property developers, electronics and computer manufacturers. Biotechnology stocks had their turn, so did pharmaceuticals. Fickle as Don Juan, investors fall out of love with one sector and give their affections to another.

Charles Dow – immortalized in Wall Street's Dow Jones index – was an early exponent of charting and is credited with having observed that there is a certain rotation in which types of sector most find favour. Chartists say that a price chart reflects the net effect arising from the myriad attitudes, emotions and decisions of traders and investors about that currency, commodity or security. It will also show how attitudes and behaviour have been changing, and certain patterns emerge. Thus a currency may have a long and steady, perhaps steepening, rise until some holders worry about when the trend may reverse and decide to take their profits. The price makes a small peak as it falls back. The profit-taking exhausted

– perhaps some deciding they'll wait for the currency to get back where it was – buying drives it higher again. But when it matches the previous peak that is when those who deferred selling, now remembering how last time they missed the boat, get out fast. And potential buyers are deterred by the recollection that the currency previously failed to go higher. Thus a second peak forms to make what in chartist jargon is a 'double top': it is a signal that the long upward trend has been reversed and the currency is likely to fall, perhaps far. The literature of technical analysis is strewn with such patterns: head and shoulders, reverse head and shoulders, double bottom, flags and pennants, dead cross, diamond patterns.

Then there are those who study how the particular price is performing compared with others, its relative strength. And some will plot on the chart whether the trend seems to be gaining or losing momentum, often by comparing a moving average with the price movement. There are as many different theories and formulae in technical analysis as there are practitioners.

Guy Hurley, proprietary trader in Barclays Bank dealing room, graduated in Slavonic & East European History, then took a Master's degree in Finance & Decision Sciences from an American university. How does he apply such a wealth of learning to his job? He doesn't. He relies on charts. Why?

'I've no idea why. No idea at all.'

Except, of course, that for him they work. Presumably Barclays would not have recruited him from a rival and be hazarding a not inconsiderable sum of capital on his judgement if it were otherwise.

There are, he asserts, three kinds of traders:

'There are flows traders who look at the screens, hear what the salesmen are saying and deal off the back of that. If they see an order for £200 in dollars to Deutschmarks, they'll say, 'It isn't going to go up, is it? I'll sell some, too.' Some of those guys are really, really good and make a lot of money. Frankly, I've found that whenever I tried to do that, I always get buried.

'Second is the fundamental trader who'll say 'Look at the balance of payments, look at growth differentials, interest rate differentials and in view of the Russian situation this is what we should be doing.' Those guys they make money sometimes but for every one who's made money there've been nightmare examples of people being buried.

'At the time of the Russian coup, for instance, the dollar was clearly going down, for fundamental reasons, and there were fundamental players out there who had big shorts on.' [Not attire, they had sold the dollar 'short'.]

'They came in on Monday morning and they'd been wiped out, although technically it was clear they should have gone home long that weekend. I did but I didn't make very much out of it because I didn't have a very big position. But technically it was a screaming buy on the Friday afternoon. It had broken chart points and was going up. Now whether that was because the Russian was buying and forced it up or whatever I've no idea.

'The third type is the technical trader and he trades almost entirely off the charts. That's me.

'I think what it really comes down to is psychology. The markets are all about psychology. It's not about how intelligent you are. It's about how lucky you are and how well you can read what the next guy's trying to do. And charts are just a map of supply and demand and a map of where people are long and where people are short. It gives a discipline.

'You work very hard at your charts. You look at them twice a day on a consistent basis across a variety of currencies. And you try and work out what's going on.'

The Bank of England Quarterly Bulletin of November 1989 carried the fruits of research by Professor Mark Taylor and Mrs Helen Allen into how influential – and how successful – technical analysis is in the foreign exchange markets. They found that for forecasting over the shortest time horizons – from less than a day to at most a week – 90 per cent of dealing institutions used some charting. For two thirds of those institutions, charts were at least as important as fundamentals. When making judgements about longer-term movements – a year or more – 85 per cent said fundamentals mattered more than charts, with 30 per cent relying on fundamentals alone.

How useful had technical analysis proved to be? '. . . Some chartists' forecasts were remarkably good and could not be improved upon by a range of alternative forecasting procedures.'*

They also found that chartists' forecasts were so far apart that there was probably 'an insufficient consensus among chartists to influence the overall market strongly in any particular direction . . . chartism is unlikely to have a destabilizing effect on the market.'

Many chartists reckon that the balance of supply and demand will keep a currency rate between a lower – 'support' – level and an upper – 'resistance' level and that if the exchange rate breaks through one of these barriers it will continue for some time in the same direction. Riccardo Curcio and Charles Goodhart of the London School of Economics tested that against hourly data in the foreign exchange markets for twelve weeks and found it was true.†

Now and again you'll hear broadcast reports refer to the FTSE, or Dow Jones index or whatever, breaching a 'psychologically important' barrier which will always be a round number, usually of hundreds or thousands. It was part of the stock in trade which we used on BBC Radio years before, I must confess, there was any evidence to suggest that round numbers had any psychological significance.

However, Paul De Grauwe and Danny Decupre of the Catholic University of Leuven, Belgium, crunched foreign exchange data through a computer and found that traders tended to avoid exchange rates ending in round numbers. There is, of course, no economic – fundamental – justification for this. Once the rate broke through a barrier it accelerated away from it.‡

* 'Chart Analysis and the Foreign Exchange Market', Professor Mark Taylor and Helen Allen, Bank of England Quarterly Bulletin, November 1989.
† 'When Support/Resistance Levels Are Broken, Can Profits Be Made? Evidence from the Foreign Exchange Market' by Riccardo Curcio and Charles Goodhart, LSE Working Paper, 1992.
‡ "Psychological Barriers in the Foreign Exchange Market" by Paul De Grauwe and Danny Decupere, CEPR Working Paper, 1992.

Perhaps it is not so surprising. If you are leaving instructions with a dealer to act on your behalf are you not more likely to specify that they should buy or sell at, say, £:$1.50 rather than $1.4985 or $1.5015?

Finally, there is the efficient markets theory. This says that at all times markets reflect the aggregate knowledge and judgement of all market participants. Only unexpected events make any difference, therefore, so it is pointless trying to predict market movements. That's one for the academics, the rest of us ordinary folk know that nothing – least of all a market – is perfectly efficient and people don't always behave with perfect logic.

6

EUROCURRENCIES
Money in Exile

It is not trade which makes exchange rates change, it is capital. Some of that capital may be invested ultra-short-term or at extreme risk, in either case qualifying for the soubriquet 'speculation'. While capital is free to move around the world, politicians' efforts to regulate exchange rates are vitiated. Since the ERM was wracked by turmoil, European Commission president, Jacques Delors, and others have suggested reimposing capital controls, restricting everyone's freedom to move their capital – invest their savings – at will.

The Eurocurrency markets grew out of governments' efforts to control capital movements. Some argue that it was the growth of Eurocurrency markets which undermined exchange controls to the point where they had to be abandoned. Might they have the capacity to repeat that effect?

What is Eurocurrency? A dollar bill is a dollar in the USA; outside its country of issuance it is a Eurodollar bill (the term applies even outside Europe, for example, the Euro yen in Asia). You create Eurocurrency when you take sterling abroad and when you bring back home francs, pesetas, drachma etc. left over from your holiday or business trip. Today the Eurocurrency market is a $7,000,000,000,000 affair. It's more than left-over holiday money.

The Eurocurrency market has its sources some thirty years ago, out of the confluence of two forces. Firstly, the USA persistently spent in trade overseas and invested abroad more than it earned. That left surplus dollars sloshing around the rest of the world. In the simplest terms (caring not for economists' sensitivities on the finer points) the foreigners who held those dollars were not just going to keep them in a drawer or under the mattress. They lent the money so that it could earn interest. They may have deposited it in banks outside the USA, which then lent it around the world – Euroloans – or they may have bought IOU's – Eurobonds – issued by companies which wanted to borrow dollars.

Secondly, governments imposed regulations and controls on the movement of capital. In particular, the US government imposed an 'interest equalization tax' of 15 per cent on the interest foreigners were getting on the deposits they held within America. So investors, who still preferred to hold their funds in dollars, simply moved their money out. They withdrew the dollars, in effect, from America and lent them to foreign corporations and governments. These are offshore funds. They are not regulated. They are taxed lightly, if at all. If they are to be taxed, there are usually loopholes.

The saying in Euromarkets twenty years ago was that the typical buyer of a Eurobond was 'the Belgian dentist': a high-earning professional person, with some undeclared income or capital to invest beyond the view of nosey tax men. The attraction of Eurobonds to such a person is that they are 'bearer': there is no proof of ownership or title except physical possession of the document, no central register of bondholders through which ownership and, therefore, liability to tax can be traced. They are usually paid without deduction of tax. The mechanics are often that the owner takes her Eurobond, which is printed with coupons attached, to the paying bank, perhaps in Luxembourg or some similar fiscally permissive centre. The bank clips off the coupon now due for payment and hands over the cash.

Legend has it that on certain dates in the financial year the railways attach a few extra coaches to the trains between Luxembourg and several other European cities, so as to accommodate the numbers of discreetly prosperous individuals making the return journey on the same day with no more luggage than a leather portfolio. Certainly, the immediate environs of Luxembourg station, otherwise not particularly salubrious, are notable for the multitude of banks.

Because they would pay no tax, investors would accept a

lower interest rate on a Eurobond than on a domestically issued bond where interest was liable to tax. The lower interest rate payable made this an attractive form of financing for a company which wanted to borrow, particularly if it needed to raise funds for an investment overseas. If it borrowed in its own currency and invested in assets denominated in another currency, the company exposed its balance sheet to the risk of exchange rate movements lowering the value of its assets relative to its liability to repay the loan. It may sometimes be more convenient or more efficient to raise the money in the Euromarkets rather than directly in the country where the investment is to be made.

After the Third World debt crisis in 1982, many US commercial banks became reluctant to lend overseas, thereby encouraging companies to by-pass the banks and seek capital direct from investors. Some have suggested that today's Eurocurrency investors are far more sinister than the stereotypes implied by the 'Belgian dentist'. Wayne Marr, associate professor of finance at the Freeman School of Finance, Tulane University, and John Trimble, assistant professor of finance at the University of Tennessee in Knoxville compared Eurobond issues with those made in the US domestic bond markets.* They suggested that an important factor making it more than 1 per cent a year cheaper to borrow through Eurobonds rather than domestic bonds was because of the secrecy which drug traffickers, fraudsters, insider traders, tax evaders, arms salesmen and terrorist organizations value in bearer bonds.

'Half of the Euromarket's demand for bonds comes from institutional investors, many of which are likely to have legitimate preferences for anonymity,' they acknowledged. 'The other half is from retail investors, some of whom no doubt require anonymity for legitimate business and personal motives.

'Another part of the retail demand stems, however, from the desire to hide illicit activities. These investors include participants in international drug trafficking, fraud, insider

* Joint article, "Journal of Applied Corporate Finance," Continental Bank, September 1988.

trading, tax evasion, capital flight and covert government operations such as arms sales and state-sponsored terrorism.' Among the supporting evidence they cited was the experience in 1984 when the US Treasury tried to get the benefits of lower interest rates on the Euromarkets by offering an issue. At the behest of the Internal Revenue Service this issue broke the Euromarkets convention and instead of being bearer was in registered form so that the owners would be traceable. The bond issue did not sell until it was amended to partially-bearer form.

The two academics concluded that Eurocurrency activity would wane if governments cooperated against drug trafficking, tax evasion and international terrorism.

How did governments respond? They went in there and got some of that cheap borrowing for themselves. Public sector borrowing was less than 5 per cent of all international bond issues when that report was published in 1988 but more than 40 per cent by 1992, according to the Bank for International Settlements.

When the ERM upheavals left a number of European governments bereft of foreign currency reserves, several found that the cheapest and quickest source for a top-up was the Euromarket. The growing move among governments, moreover, is to turn a blind eye on tax. Increasingly, as they find they have to compete for the funds of investors who focus on nett returns, European governments are making their bond issues tax-free to everyone except their own residents. Governments have learnt that there's not much point in their doing otherwise. They have to compete in the international markets for the funds of savers who invest on the basis of the nett return after tax.

Let's suppose that the international market rate appropriate to that government's creditworthiness is 9 per cent. If the government is going to tax the interest by deducting it at the outset – what is known as witholding tax – at 10 per cent then it must pay 10 per cent gross which, after 10 per cent witholding, is 9 per cent nett.

But now look at matters from the viewpoint of that country's own savers who have been buying the government's bonds in the domestic market for a gross return of 9 per cent subject to income tax, let's assume, of 25 per cent. Thus they were getting 6.75 per cent nett. They would switch from domestic bonds to the Eurobond paying 10 per cent gross and as the 10 per cent witholding tax would be credited against their 25 per cent tax rate, would be left with 7.5 per cent nett. To compete, the domestic bonds must, therefore, now offer 10 per cent gross and the government will have raised the going rate of interest on all its borrowing. It will pay out more in extra interest than it collects in witholding tax, Moreover, all other borrowers in that country – companies issuing bonds for instance – will have to offer higher interest rates to compete, thus inhibiting investment by industry and depressing demand for labour.

One important effect of the Eurocurrency markets, according to an IMF report, is to have weakened the link between a reserve currency's status and the balance of payments of its country of issue.* 'For example, other central banks could increase their dollar reserves but instead of that being a direct claim on the USA it might be met in part by an increase in the dollar liabilities of non-US residents. Only the transfer between US residents and the foreign central bank would show in the US balance of payments.'

The existence of so much offshore money makes it very difficult to assess and understand what is happening to a country's money supply and, therefore, the threat of inflation, notes Dr Brendan Brown, head of research at Mitsubishi Finance.

'The activity offshore and demand for investments offshore has to be considered as part of the total picture if you want to understand what's going on behind the scenes,' he advises. 'To look day to day just at the US capital account data produced in the balance of payments in order to work out what's happening on fund movements into the USA is totally unsatisfactory because a lot of what shows up in the US balance of

* 'The Role of the SDR in the International Monetary System' Studies by the Research & Treasurer's Departments of the IMF, March 1987.

payments is a residual determined by the genuine demand for and supply of dollar assets outside the USA.

'For example, if you get a big increase in demand for dollar deposits in Europe – which allows banks in Europe to repay their dollar borrowing from banks in the USA – what you'll see in the US balance of payments is some reduction in inter-bank lending from the USA to the rest of the world. That's meaningless in telling you what's going on but if you could somehow get the total picture and see that there was a big increase in non-bank demand for dollar deposits in Europe that would give you more idea of what were the forces behind the dollar's strength or weakness.'

Some central banks seek to regulate or restrict the use of their currency as a Eurocurrency in the belief that it can produce distortions. Dr Jim O'Neill, chief currency economist at Swiss Bank Corporation, notes, 'The Bundesbank have never been entirely comfortable about the amount of what they regard as speculative money going in and out of Germany and how it impacts, not necessarily the Deutschmark but the German money supply. At the time of the first pressure on the French franc there was a big rumour going round – which had some substance to it – that the Bundesbank was considering reintroducing some controls so that they would reinvigorate the EuroDeutschmark market.

'This would, at the time, have allowed them to have forced EuroDeutschmark rates to collapse while at the same time keeping domestic rates high and so stop all this speculative money going into Germany.

'It's not a dead issue and, of course, when it comes to bond issuance governments are constantly concerned about the relative amount of Eurobond issuance compared to domestic. A lot of it is to do with pride and supporting domestic business as opposed to international business. And in some cases there is a genuine concern about what it might mean for liquidity creation and their control of the money supply.'

One effect of a Eurocurrency emerging may often be on a country's banking system, exposing it to competition and thereby making it more efficient, to the benefit of the currency as a whole. Brendan Brown reckons, 'The Japanese government doesn't have any particular feelings about the yen being a reserve currency but does about the dangers posed by internationalization of the yen markets to particular cartels inside the Japanese financial system. The more you internationalize, the less powerful do any domestic cartels become.'

The Euromarkets grew out of governments' imposition of regulations, and controls on capital grew because many market users – including governments themselves – sought to avoid the adverse effects of those controls. They were also fed by trade imbalances because it is impossible to distinguish between capital and a trade credit and to discriminate between those which occur offshore.

Says Howard Flight, joint managing director of fund management group Guinness Flight, 'It was the mechanism of inventing the Euromarkets, originally to get round the problems of exchange controls, which accommodated the return to free international capital markets. You've really moved on to where actually it's forced exchange controls to go because they were increasingly irrelevant anyway.

'Central banks which are trying to control issuance of Eurocurrencies are barking, basically. They're pissing into the wind.'

The lesson of the Eurocurrency markets is that if a government tries to reimpose capital controls – if, for instance, it follows Mr Delors in trying thereby to reduce currency speculation – it may prove self-defeating. Says Kim Schoenholtz, head of economic and market analysis at the investment bankers Salomon Brothers International: 'In the 1980s it was common to have a deviation between Eurofranc and domestic French franc interest rates and in periods like that the valuation of the franc might depend more on Euromarket than on the domestic market.

'But in the past decade Europe has moved to open and liberal capital markets – the degree of openness is probably greater today than at any time since before World War One. The result is that there is no special relationship that one would think of between Euro interest rates and the behaviour of

exchange markets that would be different from what one
would expect from the domestic interest rates and the foreign
exchange markets.'

7

INTERVENTION

When Governments Step In . . .

'Foreign exchange intervention works only if it is profitable and if it is profitable then it is unnecessary.'

Market adage

The Bank of France was throwing the equivalent of $100 million a minute into the market in its vain effort to keep the franc above its Deutschmark floor. This, on Friday, 30 July 1993, was the heaviest one-day haemorrhage of currency reserves in history. The Bundesbank's decision the previous day to make only a token change in interest rates was fracturing the ERM. At the weekend this fracture finally occurred; but not without a battle.

As, on Friday morning, German finance minister Theo Waigel and the top four executives at the Bundesbank met their counterparts in the French finance ministry headquarters at Bercy in eastern Paris, the markets were preempting the decisions they postponed. By lunchtime the Bank of France had exhausted its DM30 billion credit line with the Bundesbank but by then the franc had dropped to its intervention trigger point. Under ERM rules both central banks must intervene and the Bank of France could borrow automatically without limit from EMS central banks.

By the end of the day the Bank of France had used the equivalent of more than FF300 billion – FF5,263 for every man, woman and child in France* – had wiped out the

---

* Equivalent at the time to £588 (£:FF8.94) or $894 ($:FF5.89). Income/capital $18,100 = £10,300 in 1991

country's foreign currency reserves and incurred debts which left it with a net deficit of more than FF180 billion. All to no avail.

They had been warned. A month earlier, the Bank for International Settlements (BIS) had published its annual report covering the year during which sterling and the lira had retreated from the ERM. It remarked, 'The events of last year confirmed that any hope that official exchange rate commitments, when seriously tested, could be defended by intervention alone was unfounded.'

Why can intervention not be relied upon to straighten out the markets? We elected these politicians, why do they let the policies on which they were elected, be it Britain's membership of the ERM or France's *franc fort*, be blown adrift by unseen currency traders? The French economy was strong enough to justify the franc's value at its old ERM rates in 1993, as its later return to around those rates demonstrated. Yet even unprecedented commitment of foreign currency, supported by the Bundesbank, was overwhelmed.

Does intervention fail:

- because it is too small, in that central banks have built up reserves which are inadequate in the context of today's markets?
- because of how it is done?
- because there is something inherent in intervention, that it is bound to fail; that it is even counterproductive?

Through intervention a central bank tries to change the market price of its currency, perhaps without the government making other changes in the economy. Instead of moving interest rates, imposing regulations to restrict bank lending, or the government making any of a number of other changes to influence the whole economy as well as the exchange rate, the central bank goes into the market and buys or sells the currency. But by intervening in the market – buying or selling its own currency to sustain or depress the exchange rate – the central bank ineluctably affects the rest of the economy.

At the Bank of England the man responsible for any intervention is Terry Smeeton, chief manager of the foreign exchange division. It is a sensitive activity, based on using frequent day-to-day dealings for intelligence-gathering. 'Our operation is, compared with other central banks, a very active one,' he told me. 'We are in the market all the time, dealing with counterparties for customers we have.

'We put a very high price here on information. We want to know what is going on in the sterling market and so we do deal around a small base, with commercial banks overseas, in order to gauge the temperature of the market the whole time. And so we're active in the market on a day-to-day basis.

'From time to time those activities – if there is a sharp movement in sterling which we want to encourage or resist – those activities will be either curtailed or stepped up in order to achieve an intervention effect.'

Central bankers cannot know what forces they are up against or how those may be augmented by others who are waiting to join in once they think they can guess the outcome. There must always be the tantalizing doubt about whether just a little more, one last thrust, might not turn the tide.

In Frankfurt, Lisbon, Madrid, Milan and even (grudgingly) Paris, European central banks regard the Bank of England as an adroit operator in the markets. ('They've had a lot of defending to do,' jibes Dr Frigyes Hárshegyi, deputy president of the National Bank of Hungary). There's a balance to strike, a fine judgement to be made. Is this latest shift in the exchange rate just a blip which can be left to correct itself and where intervention might adversely affect market sentiment or, if it is left uncorrected and unchallenged, might it develop market momentum which would be much more expensive to counter? Is there a big order out there, a trade payment or large capital investment going through the market? Success on even a limited scale depends on keeping a close ear to the ground, detecting early a shift in the market's tectonic plates.

'That's where the information I was talking about comes in,' notes Terry Smeeton. 'It's clearly inadvisable to go into the market to try and defend a particular level if you gather that there's a huge amount of selling coming out of some particular bit of the world or a very large corporate commercial order likely to be transacted which will swamp whatever you may choose to do. So it's a question of judgement on the basis of information you've got.'

He had been in the heat of the battle to keep the pound in the ERM in September 1992. As with many battles, the outcome was not obvious from the outset. Smeeton and his team used their varied tactics, deploying all the skills they had developed in many a skirmish on the foreign exchange markets, believing they just had to hold the line until the equivalent of the cavalry arrived, in this case in the shape of the French electorate.

'The period in question was one which seemed to us to have a finite conclusion with the French referendum on 20 September,' he told me. 'Part of our general philosophy at the Bank is that we are happiest undertaking intervention when we can see where we're going to end – where we're bridging to, as we would put it – and have some take-out situation. And, as far as we were concerned at that time, 20 September clearly was going to be a major event which would lead to unknown changes, undoubtedly some changes. Our objective in a sense was to bridge from wherever we were to that point in time. We gave up before reaching that point because undoubtedly the forces did come to too much to resist.'

How could the forces become irresistible? If the Bank of England lacked the firepower and was overwhelmed in September 1992, what about the confrontation ten months later when the combined forces of the Bundesbank and the Bank of France – able to call in as aid the resources of all other ERM members – were defeated and the ERM itself torn asunder?

Hence the suspicion that interventions fail because they are half-hearted or that central banks lack the firepower to match the growth of international currency trading. This is a subject which has taxed the Solons of the BIS:

'As to intervention itself, the question necessarily arises as to whether it was, in some sense, insufficient. Or was it simply ineffective in the new globalized financial world? . . .

Technology, innovation, free capital mobility and investors' desire for international portfolio diversification have by now all combined to increase vastly the potential for shifting large amounts of capital around the world, and across currencies, at great speed. For, even leaving aside outright speculation and also the relatively new highly leveraged 'hedge funds', far more investors now have an interest in exchange rate developments than formerly.

In other words, even the managers of the traditionally conservative institutions such as pension and insurance funds, as well as retail investors, must now necessarily take account of perceived exchange rate prospects – and they doubtless do.'[*]

Direct investment flows into the twenty-four leading industrial countries, the members of the OECD, totalled $91 billion in 1991; investment flows from them during the same year amounted to $162 billion. Borrowing on international capital markets that year came to $525 billion. Are foreign exchange reserves adequate to reflect this? Have governments, which until 1989 borrowed less than five cents out of every dollar raised by international bond markets but, by 1992, were mopping up 40 per cent of international bond issues, armed the Terry Smeetons of this world with enough reserves to intervene effectively?

Stephen Bell, chief economist at Morgan Grenfell, notes that when all Europe's weak currencies were knocked out of the ERM, their reserves were exhausted. 'But however large their reserves had been,' he suggests, 'the market could have knocked them out.'

---

[*] Bank for International Settlements 63rd annual report to 31.3.93.

Official Reserves*
(All countries) (SDR bns[2])

	1986	1987	1988	1989	1990	1991	1992
Excluding gold	419.0	507.8	543.0	591.1	637.9	672.0	691.9
Gold[1]	304.6	323.3	289.0	287.7	254.6	232.3	234.5
	723.6	831.1	832.0	878.8	892.5	904.3	926.4†

[1] at London market price [2] SDR (Special Drawing Rights) = $1.37 (end 1992)

Banks in the UK dealing in foreign exchange agree with the Bank of England a ceiling to the amount they can have outstanding in the foreign exchange markets overnight: their exposure limits. On one critical day during the ERM turmoil, he recalls, two large orders from clients that evening took Morgan Grenfell to its exposure limit.

The BIS survey of foreign exchange markets shows, of course, that over the last six years international currency dealing has grown much faster than trade or investment. 'The firepower of the central banks – the amount of intervention which they can plausibly deploy – has grown much more slowly than the size of the markets in which they are intervening,' notes Roger Bootle, chief economist at Midland Bank. 'Therefore intervention seems to have become that much less powerful.

'It's important to stress that it's the relative size that's changed rather than anything particular about the act of intervention itself, which has really brought the diminution of power.'

Does this mean governments should build reserves to a level which would match the amount needed to resist all market forces?

'What are the reserves there for?' challenges currency economist Dr Brendan Brown of Mitsubishi Finance. 'There's a much better functioning international capital market than thirty years ago, so access to borrowed money is all the greater and the readiness of investors to lend money across borders is

---

* IMF Annual Report 1992

† Bank for International Settlements 63rd annual report to 31.3.93.

so much greater. Also, you are on a flexible exchange rate system so you should have less demand for reserves relative to economic size than was the case twenty years ago. For a country to invest its wealth purely in reserves is not the most productive form of investment.'

Terry Smeeton himself acknowledges that in managing Britain's reserves he is neither running a dealing room like that of a commercial bank nor pursuing maximum return. 'We're driven by different motives,' he told me.

'The commercial banks' dealing rooms are there to contribute profits. Our main responsibility on the foreign exchange side is stability of sterling. The principal objective is that it should remain relatively stable and certainly not move in such a way as to jeopardize the inflation target, which is the overall government objective.

'The reserve management function flows from that. We have a pile of assets − about $40 billion worth of currency, gold, SDR reserves − which we have available if necessary to support the pound if sterling comes under pressure. We had, of course, to draw on them heavily when we were in the ERM up to the period of our departure. Having taken some pressure at that time, they are rebuilt, so to speak.

'They are invested to ensure the best secure return we can gain, commensurate with a high degree of liquidity so that we can use them to intervene should we need to do so. Whilst we try not to incur a loss in any of our business, the profitability of what we undertake is not the prime objective.'

The ineffectiveness of intervention can seem puzzling from one perspective. Since the total amount of foreign exchange dealing is many times the level of world trade and cross-border investment, the great preponderance of currency dealing is between banks and (other) speculators. For them overall it must be a zero-sum game. One bank's gain on a rise in the Deutschmark against the dollar is matched by another speculator's loss on a fall in the dollar against the Deutschmark. The only factors which make the net sum above zero are whatever can be skimmed from traders in goods or investors of capital together with intervention by the central banks. If, aside from this, currency dealing balances out, why doesn't just a modest amount of intervention tip the scales and change the exchange rate? This seemingly persuasive idea overlooks the difference between goods prices and assets prices. Goods (and services) prices move because of relative supply and demand. The price of an asset doesn't.

The supply of an item is determined by completely different factors from the demand. Different people are supplying for different reasons from those for which you are buying; but for an asset it is all the same. The demanders for the asset are often the suppliers as well. They are all paying attention to the same factors. For example, when you go for a haircut you are looking at the length of your hair and the price the hairdresser charges. The hairdresser is looking at how many haircuts she can do in a day and how much profit she can get. But when you sell Deutschmarks you are paying attention to interest rates, inflation rates and the same factors as the person buying those Deutschmarks. For this reason foreign exchange markets can move dramatically without any great change in trading volumes because everybody comes to the same conclusion about the various influential factors at once. All are buyers of one currency and sellers of another. With no counterbalancing selling of the first and buying of the second: no deal. There is, therefore, no correlation between price changes and volumes.

Dr Jim O'Neill, chief currency economist at Swiss Bank Corporation, believes that in the ERM crisis Europe's central banks could have held exchange rates with intervention. It was not the resources – foreign exchange reserves – but the will to use them that was lacking. He argues that the speculators were not – and are not – in an impregnable position, for all their resources, because they rely so much on borrowing.

'If the central bank is smart it'll know these guys are leveraged and they can't keep their position for very long at all.' He says, 'And if floating is absolutely clean – so that central banks don't stand in there and satisfy some of the pressure – the market will move against these operators and when they want to buy their position back they will have it move against them again.

'I would argue that even with fixed exchange rates, if these governments really, really believed in the levels that much, then because these hedge funds are on leverage the central banks should be smart enough to realize that these guys can't continually run open leveraged positions and have to take it back in two or three weeks.

'I do think that given leveraged money some of these funds push to the extreme on some smaller currencies.'

Brendan Brown agrees: 'I don't think the adequacy of the reserves was an issue. France with an AAA credit rating could have borrowed another $50 billion or whatever without much problem. Agreed it wouldn't be good to put all that number of bonds into the capital market in one go but borrowing wasn't the issue.

'More of an issue was that politicians may get somewhat anxious about going out and doing anything on that scale when they've already been criticized for having lost $4 billion in a day or whatever. They're risk-averse, like most people. It's more the growing fear of ultimate huge loss, rather than inability to fund the whole operation.'

Countries' currency reserves today are gross rather than net. A government borrows foreign currencies and these are an asset on one side of the balance sheet. On the other side is the liability to repay the loan. The funds are available for intervention but, if so used, must eventually be replaced.

A central bank can build gross foreign reserves to an extent limited only by its capacity to borrow in international markets. It may even, given the credit rating which the UK − but not, for instance, Italy − enjoys, borrow more cheaply than the rate earned on the foreign government bonds in which it invests the funds and so run a profit. The Bank of England could borrow heavily in ecu, for instance − issue ecu long-term debt − and if it simply reinvested that short-term in exactly the ecu's constituent currencies the net reserves would be unchanged, but it would have gained liquidity.

The loss incurred when intervention fails is much misunderstood. The Bank of England may have used $30 billion intervening on 16 September 1992 and the Bank of France

FF300 billion on 30 July 1993 but each was exchanging for its own currency, pounds and francs. The loss will arise only when it comes to rebuild its reserves, buying foreign currency again in exchange for its own now devalued currency, and when it comes to repay foreign currency loans.

Suppose the Bank of England is trying to keep sterling at its old ERM floor of DM2.7780. It could take from its reserves, or borrow from the Bundesbank DM2.7780 and use it to buy £1. Sterling then devalues and when the Bank wants DM2.7780 to repay the Bundesbank loan or replenish its reserves then, if the new rate is DM2.50, the £1 it holds will buy only that quantity of Deutschmarks. For DM2.7780 it must now pay, at the new exchange rate, £1.1112. The loss is thus 11.12 per cent. Another way to express it is that the Bank sold DM2.7780 for a £1 which then bought only DM2.50 so the loss is DM0.2780 on every DM2.7780, which is 10 per cent.

The risk of loss if intervention fails limits how much a country may be willing to borrow in the defence of its currency. There's also a limit – in addition to credit risk – to the amount of its own currency the Bundesbank (or other central bank) will want to create for these operations. In simple terms, it is creating Deutschmarks and lending them to the Bank of France, which then sells them to the holders of francs who now hold and can spend in Germany the extra Deutschmarks which the Bundesbank created. That is inflationary, not popular with the Bundesbank or any other central bank.

If it is not a question of central banks lacking the firepower to be the arbiters of exchange rates, might the way they use their power be critical to its effectiveness?

When a central bank decides to intervene in the markets it can do so surreptitiously, deceiving dealers into thinking there is more bona fide demand for the currency. The alternative of letting the intervention be known, or even publicly announcing it, relies on the effect such information will have on sentiment, perhaps even scaring the markets.

The response to this approach, however, is unpredictable and it can even backfire, according to Chris Dillow, economist at Nomura Research Institute's European headquarters in

London. 'Some will say that it's just a smoothing operation and it will have no great impact; others see it as a signal that the government wants the currency higher and it can go higher, but others will say that the government are pissing in the wind – failing to face up to the economic facts of life – which means either that they should let the exchange rate depreciate or should be making fundamental adjustments.'

The man with the awesome responsibility of deciding – of guessing which way the market will react – is Terry Smeeton. 'It depends on the circumstances very much,' he told me. 'Overt intervention is successful at times and we used every tactic we had in late 1992 (and obviously failed in our objective). Overt was used very little in that period because the more you use it, the less effective it becomes. Diminishing returns set in very rapidly and we used it sparingly so that we would always benefit from the announcement effect.

'And we used it in conjunction with other central banks from time to time. Having the Bundesbank or Bank of France in support of you at the same time can be effective in adding to the appearance of the operation.'

The unpredictability of the market response to intervention, the change in attitude towards it to the point where markets will sometimes defy the central banks and dealers even talk of 'taking them on' is, in the view of Midland Bank's Roger Bootle, part of an intellectual revolution.

'That intellectual revolution hasn't only affected people in the markets, it's also affected people in the central banks,' he observes. 'If you have a situation in which most people in the academic community, in the markets, in the banks, in the central governments, the treasuries and the media believe (in Mrs Thatcher's words) You can't buck the market – and by and large that has been the character of these constituencies over the last fifteen to twenty years – then the effectiveness of a given amount of intervention is correspondingly reduced.

'In the old days it used to be suggested that if the markets knew the central bank was intervening their response was likely to be stronger. They were likely to go along with what the central bank was trying to do. Now the opposite is suggested. If the central bank is in then they automatically go in the other direction because they sense the action is unsustainable and they think that there's a chance for a profit because here's someone in the market not on profit-related criteria but for other reasons.

'In this climate the central banks must feel the same thing because they can't have any conviction, either, that they can stand out against the markets. And that imbues their own actions with a terrific sense of hesitancy and that's well understood in the markets. So when the central bank intervenes it's like dropping a piece of raw meat into a shark-infested pool.'

Is intervention doomed to fail? Does it contain within itself contradictions which will vitiate its effects? Might it even be counterproductive?

Remember that buying the currency in the foreign exchange markets is only one possible way to defend the exchange rate. Often it seems politically and economically less painful than the other methods, the most obvious of which is to raise interest rates. But, as the BIS pointed out*, holding down interest rates while intervening to support a weak currency just helps the speculators on the other side. Reflecting on the storms which tossed sterling and the lira out of the ERM, the BIS suggests that some of the defenders were handing ammunition to their enemies.

'In intervening on a large scale to defend currencies while attempting to limit interest rate adjustments, central banks indirectly accommodated the efforts of market participants to hedge exposures in weak currencies and to take open positions against those currencies.'†

The low interest rate made it cheaper for the speculator to borrow the currency she was then selling on the foreign exchange market.

'This is not to dispute the effectiveness of intervention as such,' suggests the BIS. 'Rather, it should caution against large-scale intervention with limited interest rate adjustments. Only

* Bank for International Settlements 63rd annual report to 31.3.93.
† ibid.

by vigorously adjusting interest rates can central banks create a disincentive to private sector operations with potentially easy profits.'

Whereas it often substitutes for economic measures which would have adverse effects, intervention is not a cost-free alternative. The problem lies with the central bank either needing some of its own currency for sale on the forex markets to drive down the exchange rate or with what it does with any of its own currency bought in supporting the exchange rate. This provokes the debate about 'sterilization'. Sterilized intervention aims to achieve the effects of intervention without affecting the money supply. But there is a strong body of opinion among economists that the very act of sterilizing it makes intervention ineffective.

Here's how it works. When the Bank of England intervenes on the currency markets – let's say to support sterling – it is buying pounds and selling foreign currencies which it holds in its reserves. The sale of those pounds to the Bank of England reduces the domestic money supply. Someone is withdrawing money from a bank deposit in sterling and selling it on the market to the Bank, which is then absorbing those pounds and effectively cancelling them and giving the previous holder deposits in Deutschmarks, dollars or whatever. That is unsterilized intervention. It is tightening up the supply of money, putting upward pressure on interest rates just when forcing up the exchange rate is having the disinflationary effect of curbing demand from abroad.

By sterilizing, the Bank of England tries to offset that effect by taking equal and offsetting action in the domestic markets. If it has bought sterling on the exchanges and wants to insulate the domestic money supply from the effects, it can use those pounds to buy money-market instruments, such as Treasury bills, various forms of bank debts or government bonds. That money then gets injected back into the economy because it is now held by the people who sold the Bank those money-market instruments and now have instead money in the bank.

Whether sterilized intervention works – is effective in supporting sterling in this example – is a point of argument among economic theorists. Monetarists say that it is the money supply itself and the changes in money supply which govern a number of macroeconomic variables, including the exchange rate. So intervention which is not accompanied by a change in the money supply – intervention which is sterilized – has no effect whatsoever.

'The notion that effects on the exchange rate depend crucially on whether the domestic public hold Treasury bills or bank deposits I find perfectly bizarre,' declares Roger Bootle. 'My own suspicion, which is more than a suspicion, is that it doesn't matter whether intervention is sterilized or not. What really matters is whether the intervention itself is credible. That begs a series of other questions: how sustainable the intervention is, what size it can take place in, what exchange rate it takes place at.'

Brendan Brown counters: 'Sterilized intervention is ineffective in practical terms over any lengthy period unless monetary policy is working in the same direction.

'Suppose the dollar is weak because the perception is that the US Federal Reserve is pursuing an easy monetary policy and taking on a considerable inflation risk into the medium term. Then many investors are lightening up in dollars because they're concerned with it not being a safe store of value. In that situation, if the Fed or US Treasury comes in and buys up billions of dollars, that would just be a straw in the wind because investors are not going to say "We now believe the dollar is a good store of value because the US Treasury is coming in." In fact they would probably say the reverse: "Well, the Fed is really determined to pursue an easy money policy and take inflation risks. We'll take advantage and get out while the going is good." So that would be totally ineffective intervention.

'But if, at the same time as the Treasury intervening, the Fed raised interest rates then you could probably get a huge turnaround in the dollar and it would hold. You have to see whether intervention is on its own or in harmony with a shift in monetary policy. If alone, then there's not much chance that intervention would withstand a large change in market sentiment.'

Nomura's Chris Dillow professes never to have understood the argument that intervention is ineffective if it is sterilized. 'People's views on foreign exchange movements are not conditioned by movements in relative money supply,' he asserts. 'The speculators against the pound, the lira, the franc or any other currency do not run computer models comparing money supply growth in each country.

'Foreign exchange intervention that doesn't change the money supply can be effective to the extent that it signals that the government doesn't want the exchange rate to be at this level,' he asserts. 'That requires governments to have some sort of credibility, which means that foreign exchange intervention may be effective in one direction only.

'I'm absolutely sure that were the government to signal that they wanted sterling to be twenty pfennigs lower then the market would oblige. Were they to signal that they wanted sterling to be twenty pfennigs higher then they wouldn't. Whether the intervention one way or the other is sterilized is not the point.'

Spain found the peseta soaring when it first joined the ERM but when faith in that was shaken the peseta devalued three times within a year. The Bank of Spain had a crash course in intervention techniques and their effect on money supply. As the ERM crisis was coming to a head at the end of July 1993 I visited the bank's director general, Jose Luis Malo de Molina, in the Banco de España edifice overlooking the Plaza de la Cibeles.

'Intervention alone doesn't solve the problems of exchange rate instability,' he averred. 'If you intervene to defend the exchange rate but don't fully sterilize the effects on monetary aggregates, then in the end you keep the potential factors explaining the instability of the exchange rate.

'Our experience has been that it is almost impossible to sterilize fully the effect of intervention. That implies that in the end it is impossible to solve through intervention the problem you have with the exchange rate. Normally what is happening is that the budgetary policy is inadequate or wage restraint is inadequate. And that kind of situation affecting the exchange rate is provoking the contradiction between the exchange rate target and the monetary aggregates target.

'When the peseta was too strong and we needed to intervene to prevent further excessive appreciation we had a problem of sterilization. We needed to weaken the peseta but at the same time we needed to mop up liquidity to avoid the overshooting of monetary aggregates. It is clear that the process produced a lot of damage not only for the financial sector but also for the real economy.'

In other words, intervention cannot have sustained effect if the overall thrust of economic policy is in the opposite direction. You cannot square the circle by market operations.

At the Bank of England, the deputy head of the foreign exchange division, David Ingram, acknowledges, 'A lot of the exchange rate movements that we have seen have been the result of some misalignment which sophisticated investors are now looking at very closely. They are telling us about something: about policy and our exchange rates. It's a much greater discipline, I think, on policymakers. You can't just fix the exchange rate. You have to make sure it is fixed in line with the underlying economic fundamentals.'

The problem with the EMS currencies in the July 1993 ERM crisis was the conflict between the interest rates they needed at home – to counter recession – and those needed to keep their exchange rate pegged to the Deutschmark.

As the BIS concluded, '. . . it is very likely that, to be successful, even in the face of an attack on a currency whose fundamentals are sound, intervention now has to be greater than in the past – perhaps far greater. It may also be that, to be effective, more of it would have to be accompanied by larger and more persistent interest rate movements than has been the practice so far . . . that would mean inappropriate domestic monetary policies.' This was almost prescient, being published before the final assault on the French franc which defused the ERM.

As soon as the Bank for International Settlements had published that report, French finance minister Edmond Alphandéry – finding neither intervention nor high interest rates alleviated the mounting pressure against the franc – contemplated an unorthodox move some advisers were urging on him. Instead of raising interest rates – which, as the BIS said, lacked credibility – he should cut them. He decided against it largely because the Bundesbank indicated that such an unconventional, even contradictory, move would forfeit its support for the franc, which had already become considerable.

Might it have worked? Chris Dillow thinks not: 'The people who said that high interest rates in France were causing the franc to fall were making a contentious statement. Their argument was that if the French were to cut interest rates sharply then the economy would recover and people's attitudes would be that they would buy the currency because they believed the next movement of interest rates and the currency was upwards. But it's by no means certain that if the French had cut rates to 3 or 4 per cent that the franc would have risen. There is every possibility that it would have fallen.'

Jose Braz, Secretary of State at the Portuguese Treasury, speaks quietly and fluently in English as we sit in his salon overlooking the Tagus estuary a year after sterling and the lira have been ejected from the ERM. Dark hair rising straight above a broad, sloping forehead, heavy glasses and moustache give him the appearance of an academic, almost the archetypal absentminded professor. The appearance is deceptive. 'I think that the attacks in the last couple of years have been well founded. If I had money to speculate I probably would have joined in speculating against currencies which were in a position of evident disequilibrium. Markets saw interest rates unsustainably high and politically impossible to keep there because of the rising unemployment.'

The BIS agrees:

'Market participants are well aware of the potential output costs of increasing interest rates enough to discourage the taking of positions against the domestic currency, and that monetary authorities may lack the scope for raising interest rates sufficiently.

Even if the monetary authorities increase their interest rates sharply to demonstrate their determination to defend an exchange rate commitment, their action may be ineffective if their ability to keep rates high is not perceived as credible. Such credibility will obviously depend on the strength of the domestic economy and on the ability to achieve consensus on appropriate budgetary policies.

Furthermore, if interest rates are raised only after extensive exchange market intervention, the move may even be interpreted as a signal that the resolve of the authorities to defend the currency has reached its limits. In these circumstances, the increase in interest rates may trigger further outflows and, paradoxically, itself make the exchange rate commitment untenable.'

As the franc succumbed to market pressure in mid-1993 Frenchman Jacques Delors, president of the European Commission, began to talk darkly about a conspiracy. 'The president of the European Commission has said it's the Anglo-Saxon speculators,' noted Jose Braz. 'I don't believe that.'

Chris Dillow contends, 'You can dismiss the conspiracy theory of the markets. We couldn't agree how many beans make five.

'We are not irresponsible. We don't set out to undermine government policy. The conflicts we have seen in recent years between government economic policies and movements in the foreign exchange markets have arisen because governments have tried, in a high-handed fashion, to ignore the underlying realities of economic conditions — but foreign exchange markets do pay attention to underlying economic conditions.'

Research conducted by the Bank of Italy on data it extracted from sixteen central banks suggests that intervention can be effective. This could be seen as somewhat like a doctor taking confidential patient records from a number of practices and pronouncing on the value of the medical profession. However, recent independent academic research suggests that intervention can work in the right circumstances.*

* 'Does Foreign Exchange Intervention Work?' by Kathryn Dominguez and Jeffrey Frankel, Institute for International Economics, Washington.

Kathryn Dominguez and Jeffrey Frankel had the full run of confidential data on intervention from both the Federal Reserve and the Bundesbank and ran it through a computer, comparing exchange rate movements before and after intervention. They concluded that intervention is most effective when two or more central banks act together and publicize the fact. The same amount of intervention was more effective if split between two central banks than when used by only one. The average amount the Fed and Bundesbank deployed in each foray was surprisingly small – $100 million to $200 million – but could move the exchange rate 1 or even 2 per cent. It is more effective when the market has been gyrating without a consistent trend.

They examined in detail eleven particular episodes between 1985 and 1991 and found that in ten the central banks moved the exchange rate in the direction they wanted and in six of those cases they even reversed the previous month's trend.

Dominguez and Frankel warn, however, that intervention:

- must be used sparingly, as a law of diminishing returns quickly sets in
- is less effective if it lacks a strong element of surprise
- will not work at all if the economic fundamentals point in the opposite direction

Thus all the intervention to hold the EMS Humpty Dumpty together failed on two counts. It inevitably lacked surprise. The very rules of the ERM said that intervention was obligatory when a currency pushed against its upper or lower bands. And it flew in the face of economic reality. As the BIS subsequently commented, '. . . several countries' real exchange rates had become misaligned and at a time when European economies were displaying signs of more or less severe weakness and/or financial fragility.'

Tom Elliot, head of foreign exchange business at Nomura Bank International, watched reserves blown away by the market as European central banks strove to batten their monetary system together with intervention. 'The economic pains were accentuated by the reluctance of politicians to cut interest rates and promote growth in case that was going to increase pressure on their currencies,' he recalls. 'Each and every currency had that problem.

'Invariably we had a period before each devaluation when there were penal interest rate structures to deter speculation. Inevitably that fails. Intervention failed, too. We ended up with the devaluation and then the interest rate structures which they needed – but had been resisting – to get economies moving again.'

The problem lies with the politicians' attitude towards exchange rates. That is something with which bankers world-wide, particularly those directly engaged in currency markets, are wearily familiar. 'It's still extraordinary how much govern-ments do see currencies as matters of national prestige,' Brendan Brown complains. 'Look at the way the UK and French governments were willing to wage what, except in real human terms of lives and injuries, were wars, and which financially cost their economies as much as small wars. For what? Just for the prestige of displacing the Deutschmark as the anchor in the ERM.'

Chris Dillow agrees. 'Chancellors of the Exchequer have always got this notion that a currency is a symbol of your economic manhood. You know: The pound was strong today.

'Therefore they like to have a stronger pound than is good for the state of the real economy. They like to pursue things like credibility and currency strength as an extension of their own virility.

'The real costs of the last devaluation were not the foreign exchange losses incurred on Black Wednesday but the fact that Black Wednesday did not occur three years earlier, because the output costs we had as a result of an overvalued exchange rate were absolutely enormous. And I'm not aware of any significant compensatory gains.'

Is it all pointless? Is nothing gained by the government trying to sustain – either by interest rates or by intervention – an exchange rate or should it just let the currency float, or sink freely?

Theoretically at least, the idea of intervention to prevent a currency sinking is that devaluation creates inflationary pressures. But the September 1992 devaluation of sterling did not lead to a fresh upsurge in inflation, although the markets expected it at the time. The bond markets, for instance, fell – inflation erodes the value of fixed income stocks – and that reaction lasted for almost four months. Then the markets realized that things were different this time and the cost of living was not soaring, or even rising particularly. Why was this? How did we escape the adverse effects of devaluation raising the costs of imports and spurring inflation and yet get the benefits of an economic upturn?

First follow the mechanics of how devaluation worked through the economy in the past. An exporter to Germany who needed to charge £1 had previously priced his goods at DM2.80. Now with the exchange rate lowered he needed only DM2.50 to get his £1. He could lower his prices. In time that would increase demand for his goods and he would be able to expand output.

A German company needing to charge DM2.80 would price its goods in Britain at £1. Now that £1 would give the German manufacturer only DM2.50 so it would have to raise its prices in Britain, reducing its competitiveness against British manufacturers.

The first effect, incidentally, is that the goods sold to Germany now earn only DM2.50 and the goods imported from Germany have risen in price, so the trade deficit with Germany grows initially – the 'J' effect – until the price changes work through and extra demand for exports to Germany together with reduced demand for imports from Germany works through. That can take time, often a year or more.

Moreover, the British exporter now finds he can raise his prices in sterling and still be charging less in Deutschmarks. This tempts him to make UK prices equally profitable by raising prices here, too. There is also the lasting effect that imports – some of which are essential and not price-sensitive – cost more, so boosting inflation. Working against this is the (sometimes vain) hope that with the extra overseas demand boosting output, costs per unit of production will be lower.

But now devaluation can change costs immediately, argues Chris Dillow, because multinational companies with spare capacity in every country can change production immediately. 'So the benefits of devaluation can occur within days, potentially, at the extreme. And because the benefits of devaluation come through much quicker, so unit labour costs improve and that offsets the inflationary impact of higher input prices.

'In consequence, when devaluations occur, profit margins increase because costs on balance are actually falling and because the effect of higher import prices is to squeeze marginal overseas producers out of the market.

'So it is possibly the case that a devaluation does have permanent effects in boosting economic output because it gives a pick-up in profits which can then be invested to produce a higher output in the future.'

The Bank of England has argued against this, claiming that any attempt to change the real exchange rate (the exchange rate adjusted for inflation differences between the two currencies concerned) simply by changing the nominal exchange rate doesn't work. The only way to change real competitiveness is by not allowing the total money supply to increase, or the exchange rate to fall to adjust for inflation. Then inflation is squeezed out of the economy.

To the argument that the 1992 devaluation did not boost inflation the Bank of England counters that it may have done. Inflation, although low, may still have been higher subsequently than it would otherwise have been. Lending credibility to this: some months before the devaluation a number of independent forecasters were predicting zero inflation or even falling prices.

If central banks do not intervene – or if their intervention is now less effective than it used to be – does that adversely affect the economy in a less obvious way: adding to industry's uncertainties by making exchange rates more volatile?

Whereas all recognize that exchange rates fluctuate more

than they did under the Bretton Woods agreement, there is no strong consensus on whether markets have settled at a particular level of instability or have grown, and are still growing, increasingly volatile. Chris Dillow suspects that the crucial point in this respect came with the Plaza Accord in 1985, to cheapen the dollar, and the Louvre Accord two years later when governments undertook to stabilize the main currency blocs. 'Since 1987 the fluctuations between the three main currencies have been smaller than in the preceding ten years,' he says.

The two major exchange rates – DM:$ and Y:$ – seem to have prolonged periods of moving within a very narrow trading range and then suddenly burst into life with a sharp shift within six months, according to Brendan Brown. At the time of the Gulf War, he points out, the exchange rate changed 20 per cent in eight weeks.

'The surprise to many economists has been that although inflation has come down everywhere to low levels, exchange-rate volatility has not come down,' he comments. 'A BIS research study says you would have expected the decline in inflation and the inflation convergence at low levels to have meant less exchange-rate volatility. But it hasn't.'

The problem is one of measurement. Statistical studies of standard deviation over a year, a month, week or day give no simple and conclusive answer. 'I'm not sure how you would measure volatility overall and it would be a statistical nightmare,' comments Roger Bootle. 'It's not obvious to me that rates have become more volatile over the years.'

Views about this possible need for intervention as a steadying influence have changed. The Bretton Woods agreement stabilizing exchange rates was based partly on the belief that exchanges and markets were potentially unstable and were characterized by people with unstable expectations. If you left them to their own devices they could drive exchange rates to levels that were unjustified by the economic fundamentals. Experience since the breakdown of Bretton Woods has led many people to believe that the exchange markets are fairly stabilizing.

'There are some circumstances in which you can say that's true,' opines Roger Bootle, 'but it seems to me that the original worries about exchange markets were right. They can drive currencies to levels which bear very little relationship to the fundamentals and they do so for all sorts of peculiar, self-justifying reasons. One of the reasons why they're able to get away with it is that they believe in themselves and that the central banks believe in them.

'If, by contrast, the perception of what they were doing were different, the result might be different. If the markets believed that they had the power to drive currencies to ridiculous levels and, indeed, that they were doing it, and if the central banks believed that's what had happened and were determined to stop it and the markets believed that too, then the reaction to intervention might be different.'

That doesn't mean that the central banks or their political masters would get it right, however. Bootle admits, 'There are instances when central banks have been trying to defend ludicrous exchange rates or have been trying to avoid taking necessary action in economic policy and the markets have seen that and said, "Yah, boo sucks! We're not fooled by that" and they've sold the currency and, in a sense, the markets have been behaving in an appropriate and stabilizing way and have been forcing governments and central banks into taking necessary action.'

This factor leads Chris Dillow to conclude that intervention – and even the foreign currency reserves to finance it – is unnecessary. 'The idea that we need large bodies of foreign reserves rests on the notion that governments are capable of knowing what the best way of managing the exchange rate is. I would have thought that the history of UK membership of the ERM and of other countries' membership is that they don't.

'The British economy is far better trusted to the hands of foreign exchange dealers than to the hands of Chancellors of the Exchequer, quite frankly. So we don't really need foreign exchange reserves and certainly would be better off without intervention.'

Intervention works only when it is supported by other economic fundamentals. The loss of reserves may encourage governments to face up to that reality. As the BIS puts it: 'When reserve losses reach an unsustainable scale, countries face the choice of whether to raise interest rates significantly and for relatively prolonged periods or to change their exchange rate policies.'

Intervention can be profitable. That happens when the exchange rate is aberrant and reality will reassert itself. In which case, why not leave it to the market? In the old adage: 'Foreign exchange intervention works only if it is profitable and if it is profitable then it is unnecessary.'

8

BROKERS

The Go-betweens

Where is the foreign exchange market? London is by far the world's largest centre for currency dealing, so where in the City can you visit it?

There is no marketplace. Traders meet only socially, never to transact business, which is all done through banks of telephones or, increasingly, through computerized systems on the pervasive screens.

The nearest thing to a heart or nerve centre of this market lies in offices like the one I visit on the eastern edges of the City and in a score like it dotted around the square mile. Tucked away within a characterless glass-fronted office block is MW Marshall & Company. Founded in 1868 by Mathew Marshall (whose father had been chief cashier at the Bank of England) it remains one of the most distinguished names in the City but is known to few beyond its specialist areas of the money markets. Currency market lore has it that one dealer on the $:DM desk at Marshall once did a turnover of $4 billion in a single day. Certainly, its business in this, the world's most heavily traded currency pairing, is such that Marshall has devoted to it two dealing desks, each in a separate office with subdued lighting, behind soundproof glass. The small room, in constant contact with 150 banks, handles deals no smaller than those in the larger room, with lines through to a further 240 customers and frequently contacting hundreds more. Presiding in the larger room, listening to the intercom which tells him what is happening next door, is Tony Martin, managing director of foreign exchange broking, thirty-three years old with thirteen years in the business, and a big man in every way.

Beside him is the more diminutive, bearded figure of Dave 'Alice' Cooper.

Dave bombs Dresden.

It's the Germans who ask for it mostly. So Dave gives it them. From Frankfurt, Dusseldorf, Hamburg or Bremen, in a quiet moment, they may come through direct to the desk: 'Alice.' (Dave's been stuck with that since the pop star came to fame.) 'We've got some visitors here. Bomb Dresden for me!'

If business is not too frantic, 'Alice' obliges. Down the line, unaided by props, he creates an impressive array of sound effects, heightened by a variety of equally convincing peripheral noises, which if it wouldn't stand as a solo turn on the television networks would certainly not disgrace a talent contest. The Germans – Austrians, too – love it.

Dave, forty and tireless – he's been in the market twenty years and those close to him reckon he's good for another twenty – is one of the market's characters. In foreign exchange broking that is not a human weakness. The human element is its strength.

Foreign exchange brokers buy and sell on behalf of the banks, never trading for themselves. A trader, such as Steve Harris in charge of the $:DM desk at Barclays, is free to deal direct with any or all the other banks in the market, may choose to trade through one of the electronic systems such as Reuters but can also use a broker such as Marshall.

'The big figure we're dealing is 1.74 and the 15–17 we're quoting is the points,' explains Tony Martin. 'If someone wants to buy dollars they'd have to pay DM1.7417 and if they wanted to sell dollars they'd get DM1.7415. Our banks give us orders, one bank tells us they pay 15, another banks says they sell at 17.

'That is our price and we show it to everybody around the world. We've got a network around the world and that price goes to everybody. Then if a particular bank wants to sell at 15 or buy at 17 they say to us, "We sell $10," and then we tell the bank that's bid us "You've got $10 million at 15 from X Bank," and that's basically what we do. We get our money from commission.'

But not without using a language of their own, stripped down to ruthless brevity. Thus you and I talking of a currency might mean the dollar or the pound, the Deutschmark or the yen. Here a currency means what is truly a currency pairing: the Deutschmark against the dollar or the dollar against the yen. Deutschmarks are 'marks' but the French franc is 'Paris' to keep to one word and still distinguish it from other nations' francs, such as the 'Swissie' (that last 'ie' being an indulgence when the pressure's not too intense).

Here, of course, there's no time for wordy explicitness such as, 'Buy dollars in exchange for pounds.' That's, 'Given cable.' The opposite is 'paid'. Nobody bothers to mention the word 'million' either, just 'ten pounds' or 'twenty dollars'.

The broking companies have had a key role in London's emergence as the world's major centre of currency trading. They were given this central role, initially, when foreign exchange dealing was to be revived after the Second World War. In return for undertaking to create a liquid market and quote several, then-minor currency pairings but promising not to deal direct with corporate customers, they gained the exclusive right to deal between banks. The scrapping of that cartel, freeing the banks to deal directly with each other, came expressly to ensure London remained competitive. As important, with sterling ceding its reserve currency role, the brokers led the move from quoting currencies mainly against sterling to dollar-based quotations. And they expanded abroad, wherever customers were to be found.

Marshall and its rivals are today global firms. Tullett & Tokyo has offices in Toronto and Brussels as well as across the USA, RP Martin is in Bahrain, Intercapital in Hong Kong, Babcock Fulton Prebon in Sydney and Marshall itself almost ubiquitous.

'The domination of foreign exchange markets on a global basis is by UK-based brokers,' claims Marshall's chairman, Michael Knowles. 'The reason for that is clearly because of the way London emerged in foreign exchange markets and the way UK broking operations expanded their presence on a global basis. We were invited by the Bahrain Monetary Authority to go into Bahrain; we were invited by the Monetary Authority of Singapore into Singapore to develop the markets with them, and in those early days we were the only broking firm with a licence there. We had an agreement with the Bank of America that we would commit ourselves to stay in Singapore for a minimum period irrespective of what happened to that market.'

That investment has paid off. Today the Bank for International Settlements rates Singapore fourth in the world – after London, New York and Tokyo – for volume of foreign exchange business.

But the BIS investigation of currency dealing showed that the brokers' share of total dealing had declined, particularly in the major centres to which business gravitates and where automated dealing systems are increasingly in evidence. Banks often find the fixed fees of the screen-dealing services produce lower transaction costs than the percentage commission they must pay a broker.

'They don't have to deal with the broker. Period,' says Michael Knowles. 'They haven't had to for the last fifteen or more years but they have chosen to and our business is expanding. The market has gained many new specialist players, with many different aspects and motives. In that wider expanding marketplace our market share has gone down but our business is growing every year.'

On the international currencies desk – dealing with a range of currency pairings – thirty-one-year-old Eugene 'Stan' Quinlan (the nickname from an alleged similarity of appearance to Stan Laurel of Laurel and Hardy) has begun trading the Greek drachma on Marshall's view that from previous obscurity it will blossom on to the international markets. Even as he explains to me his ambition to build this business so that Marshall becomes the first broker to call, a large American bank's London office calls to say it cannot take the credit risk of a small Athens bank which is on the other side of a deal. 'Stan' arranges a switch: putting a third bank, acceptable to both and accepting both, in the middle of the deal. When trading volume is heavy even the largest banks dealing in major currencies may reach the limit of credit risk – counterparty risk

– they will allow each other and a broker may find another bank to slot in between them. Russia's counter-revolution, for instance, begat a score of banks and a kaleidoscope of counter-party queries, provoking the international desk to keep a list.

'Stan' seems not much concerned by the threat of the screen systems taking his livelihood. 'I have very good customer relationships with people who will show me business that they wouldn't show a screen,' he tells me.

The dealer sees a screen and sees 31 bid for $:DM so he just puts it on the screen, whereas I go into the customer and say:

'Would you pay anything in $:DM? I've got a seller here.'

'I'll pay 30, I've already got it into the machine.'

'Would you pay 31 or 32?'

'Well, is he a good seller?' (Good meaning, in a worthwhile amount.)

'Yes, he could be.'

'All right, I'll pay 31 for them.'

'So I talk to the customer and get him to increase his bid side so that he gets them, whereas everyone relying only on the screen might never deal.'

Screens might be able to arrange switches where there are counterparty acceptance problems – where one side doesn't accept the other as creditworthy enough – but they can't feel out the inclinations of a dealer and his willingness to shift beyond the explicit figure on the screen for the sake of getting the business done before the market moves too far.

The screens and computer systems behind them have many advantages in eliminating tedious and inefficient paperwork, acknowledges Marshall managing director, Tony Porter. He says: 'There are screen systems which are very swift in acknowledgement and reporting of the trade. We have now a support system whereby, instead of brokers writing up tickets and support-area girls matching up the paperwork and putting it into the computer to confirm to the two parties an hour or two after, a screen system does it instantly but leaves the brok-ing to humans.'

Tom Elliot, head of foreign exchange dealing at Nomura Bank, finds brokers often unbeatable for unloading a large position. 'There may be one buyer in town – let's say Lloyds Bank – who wants to buy dollars at 25. [That is, are willing to pay DM 1.7425, only the last two digits needing to be mentioned, the 'figure' of DM1.74 being implied.] There are twelve brokers round the broking table, each in contact with sixteen banks; that's 192 altogether just at one broking firm.

'Everybody knows there's one buyer in town. But this way they don't know who it is. The broker's job then is to find for Lloyds a seller at a close price. The broker facility is always available but as principals we're not obliged to provide the broker with our running price.'

Thus Lloyds Bank in that example can use the brokers to pick up in small manageable amounts the dollars it wants whereas it might be unable to find a single seller of such a large quantity without having to pay dearly. In providing that service the brokers do not enjoy the privilege other market traders enjoy of being able to require a bank to deal at the prices it quotes.

Trevor Cass, who before he rose further in the Barclays hierarchy put in twenty-five years on foreign exchange, first as junior dealer and finally as the manager, says that only the brokers can get the business dispersed across the market fast enough when the heat is on. 'A dealer, when he decides to take major positions – in size – will very often get a group of his colleagues to call out to about seven banks.

'If you are on the receiving end of such a call, you may want to lay off the position but, knowing that the counterparty bank is probably already calling out to the market, will try to lay off through the brokers instead. If the market starts to move you've got to call the broker, you don't have time to call up another bank.

'The broker generally has a more immediate price, he's shouting prices all the time down the line, whereas when you call a bank it's going to take you five, ten or fifteen seconds to get one bank and do just one deal.

'You may deal on the electronic system as well, if there's a price there.'

But as I sat beside Barclays chief foreign exchange trader,

Andre Katz, dealing in £:$, I saw the difference between theory and individual practice. The array of equipment in front of him included a handful of small loudspeakers, each from a different broking firm and from each of which was coming a constant shout of prices. Experience has taught him how not only to hear what was being said, but to distinguish immediately between the different voices quoting prices.

A deal with one American bank had left him having sold dollars and holding £20 million which he certainly didn't want. He was convinced that in the quiet market conditions he could not sell that amount through the brokers without moving the price sharply against himself. 'As soon as you ask one broker he will shout out across his mike so everyone else hears what's going on.' That fact ruled out putting the whole £20 million into the hands of a single broker but allocating it in pieces across several brokers would have no better effect. 'The first broker would be shouting for a price in £6. Then to get the business done I'd be asking another broker to sell £6 and they'd be shouting and everyone hears the information.'

But in trading through a broker, a bank cloaks its identity until after the deal is done: nor need it disclose how much it wants to buy or sell.

As 'Stan' Quinlan explained, 'The bank comes on and says "What's $/Mark?". I say "12–15". [Meaning that you could sell dollars at DM1.7412 or buy at DM1.7415.] He might tell me, "I have an interest to pay 13 for $5 or $10" or just "I have an interest to pay." It doesn't have to be a specific amount.

'If he has an interest to pay he's buying dollars for Deutschmarks. If he has an interest to pay, he would just put the bid on. You would give him $10, it would be a minimum of $10 unless he specifies.

'But, first, I would put it into the market. Here on the desk and into my main $:DM desk. It would go in with an unspecified name that Marshall's pay 13. If I get given $5 I tell him and then he can drop his bid, or leave it there, or put it up. It's up to him. Quite often if you just give him $5 he'll probably say, "$5 and I'll pay 12 for $5 now." He might drop it.

'The market are looking for the keen price all the time – as we say, snipers.'

On Marshall's $:DM dealing desk shouting prices down a microphone is not enough. They also exchange between themselves hand signals, put up red and green lights and, when each deal is done, show plastic cards. Tony Martin explained it to me. 'If the bank calling us want to buy dollars we put the red light on to show we bid. To sell we put the green on.'

While we had been speaking the dollar had moved to 15–18: if you were selling dollars there was someone at that moment willing to pay DM1.7415 for them, and the red light at Mickey Roberts' place on the round table showed he had that bid. If you were buying dollars there was a seller around offering them at DM1.7418 and Dave Cooper's green light showed it.

The brokers at these desks were giving those prices – inviting people to do business at them – not only to all the London banks but also around the world.

'There's a lot of hand signals for buying and selling but I don't like that,' Tony Martin told me. 'I insist that we say words as well, because if there's a problem, everything's taped. If there's a problem you can't hear that [he moves his hand] on the tape. So I make sure that they say, ''Ten yours'' or ''Five mine'' and whatever is the name of the person they're dealing with. He might make a sign with his hand as well, that's just a natural instinct.

'This is all open line so everyone can hear everything that's said in the open market. But the banks don't want other banks to know what they're doing because it can affect the rate of the market. So if they deal I'll hold up the card with this bank's name on it and Mickey will hold his card up and all that our other customers will know is that it's been done at 18. They know that dollars have been bought but they don't know who's dealt. Afterwards, only the people who've dealt will know – we go through on the phone and tell them who they've dealt with – nobody else. It preserves the confidentiality of the market.'

Honest mistakes can happen and inevitably do. They may not even be misjudgements of the markets.

The worst mistake a broker can make, says 'Stan' Quinlan, is failing to listen. 'If someone says "Ten yours" and you get it as $20 or they say twenty and you get it as ten then you've got a problem. "$20? What are you talking about? I only gave you ten." Then the broker would have a position in $10 million. Then we'd have to unwind the position.'

When dealing is hectic some mishearings between broker and client or between two brokers in the same room are inevitable. There is a system for dealing with them, worthy of note because it illustrates the regulatory culture which the Bank of England has created in the City.

Tony Porter, managing director at Marshall, recalls, 'Before 1988 the way in which a lot of brokers, including ourselves, sought to remedy an error was to ask one of the banks involved, or even a third-party bank, to take care of the difference for us, within the banking system. Then when opportunities arose, on backwardation and so on, we would reflect the points back.' They would find a profit occurring by chance in the market and use that to repay the bank which had put right the mistake for them.

But after the Financial Services Act came into effect a solicitor advising the Bank of England came up with a snag arising from the law of agency, which has been on the statute book for more than a century. An agent – which in law includes a broker – may not take benefit from any situation other than fee. However, if the client knew in advance and indicated their acceptance that on the odd occasion an agent would take some form of benefit in kind where the opportunity arose, that would override the agency-law prohibition.

'So everybody had to be written to,' recounts Tony Porter. 'Our complete client list around the world got a letter from us, outlining the problem and suggesting that they write back and say they would be happy to be a participating bank. That still happens with any new customer.'

The cards which brokers show each other as they deal – used to identify the client without the rest of the market overhearing on the telephone – are coloured. A green card is for a bank which participates in the scheme, having written to waive the agency law prohibition. A bank with a red card has not.

'The alternative is a clear black and white approach which the Fed uses in the USA,' explains Tony Porter. 'There are no such things as points and if there's a problem you pay a cheque to cover the difference. If through an error you incur a profit then the bank pays you. Morally, that isn't quite as it should be. It creates temptation.' If you can pocket the profit of an error, how diligent does that make you?

Each desk must keep a ledger showing all such points transactions. The Bank of England makes spot checks. While it is mandatory for the brokers to operate such a system – because they are the agents barred from taking profits – for their customer banks, membership of the system is entirely voluntary. The Bank of England's Grey Book of regulations for this market says that if a bank is not participating then a broker cannot take benefit from them. That does not mean, however, that such a bank cannot profit from a broking error.

It struck me that a broker's skills in feeling out the market – having an instinct for which way banks were inclined rather than just the deals they were doing right now – could be used to his own account. He is trained to listen to perhaps a dozen people shouting at once, while at the same time listening to what is going on elsewhere and talking to the bank which is giving him an order. The skill of being able to pick up the best price for his client out of all those being shouted, and in closing the business before that price changes, could be turned to personal profit. In very hectic dealing with prices changing sharply it may very well happen that the normal relationship between prices would become inverted. Instead of getting only DM1.7415 for a dollar and having to pay DM1.7418 to buy dollars, an alert dealer might notice that somewhere in the room it was possible to sell dollars at 17 and buy at 16. This is what is known as a backwardation. Furthermore, if two brokers conspired together across the desk the opportunity for such instant risk-free profit would be enhanced. With prices moving so fast the risk of detection would be small.

Such inchoate suspicions were nurtured by whisperings

around the dealing rooms of some smaller fringe banks, themselves of dubious ethical standards, whose overriding emotions were jealousy and resentment that they could not get their snouts in the trough.

For a broker to take a profit out of the market by such a ploy is against the rules laid down by the Bank of England's grey book. This set of regulations also forbids brokers to take a position and trade as principal for their own account. They are confined to putting buyers and sellers together.

There's a practical problem confronting any intending transgressor in that he would need the cooperation of at least one of the banks involved in the transaction and, because the bank's dealer does not have authority to write cheques, the conspiracy would have to involve someone in the settlement system, too. As 'Stan' Quinlan pointed out to me, 'We certainly can't take money from the market because the two banks can't book it to an account. They can't book it to Eugene Quinlan account. Or even to Marshall.

'We can't say "You've dealt with Marshall." When we've done the deal we then have to tell each client who was on the other side.

'If you have a backwardation – someone willing to buy at 13 and someone else willing to sell at 12 – then generally you'd improve to the customer. You'd pick one of the customers and say, "You gave me the order I managed to sell 5 at 13 for you rather than at 12." Or you might say to the other that you managed to buy at 12 rather than 13.'

Such opportunities are welcome when they occur because for Tony Martin 'the real gut-wrencher' is exactly the opposite: 'When on a particular price we can't fulfil the orders, if we have to let people down.

'On this particular price, for instance – 17–18 – if four or five people tried to take us at 18 for lots of dollars – 100 million and you've only got 50 million – then you have to let some people down and we have to tell them, "You haven't dealt." That would be my decision to say around the desk here: "You've done this."; "You've done this."; "You've done this."; "You've done nothing."; "You've done nothing."

'How we try to do it then – of course, when it's hectic it's more difficult – is that the first one that deals gets it; the second one also does; the third gets some but the fourth and fifth, they've missed it.

'The orders that we get aren't there indefinitely. The banks change them, they pull the bids out and pull the offers out. So we have to report back to all the other banks and say "We're not there at that price any more, we're getting a new price." Then go back to them with a new price.'

A sudden hiatus like that prompts the broker to tell everyone with a shout of 'change'. It is not good news. Violent price movements are not good for the broker's business, according to Michael Knowles sitting away from the hubbub in the ordered calm of the chairman's office.

'The objective is to provide a very efficient way of doing business for the banks. In other words, to have a very liquid market so the bank can get in and out in the most efficient way possible, in the biggest amount possible, without disturbing the market because there's no mileage for us in the market being disturbed.

'We want a good liquid market. We don't necessarily benefit from these huge swings backwards and forwards. Nobody benefits.'

9

DEALERS

The Perpetual Poker Players

'Eighty-one to 88,' we can hear the brokers saying.

'83 to 88,' Andre says into the phone.

'83 to 88' is still the price from the row of small speakers on his desk.

'Morgan selling cable,' he calls into the room. Then to the intercom, opposite at eye level:

'Morgan New York give me cable at 83.'

But in the meantime the price is changing.

'83 to 85 in small.'

The brokers have only small bids and offers from client banks, probably less than $5 million or the equivalent.

'80 to 85,' Andre quotes to another direct line caller.

'Citi gives me,' he tells the room. Somehow he is listening at the same time to the market.

'Lower!' he calls out to tell colleagues the pound is falling sharply against the dollar.

'73 to 83,' from one broker's speaker.

'83 offered small.' Is that the same broker?

'80 to 85, small.'

That was how Andre Katz did the two deals I mentioned in chapter one and, as I explained, in forty seconds they gave him £10 million he had no wish to buy. He is 'long' of sterling, holding it having bought for dollars of which he is now 'short'. This is against his better judgement or intention expressed to me only a few minutes before. He had wanted – and still wanted – to be short of sterling and long of the dollar.

'Cable has moved ten points against me and that's $10,000,' he tells me now. 'And it's a quiet day. I don't want to lose my profit for a silly position really. You sometimes get £20 or £30 million positions but today's not the day really. Just try and nick a point here, nick a point there and keep the basic position.'

That, I had been seeing, was not always easy to do.

Andre Katz, thirty-one-year-old chief foreign exchange trader, is responsible for dealing in 'Cable' – £:$ – and £:DM at Barclays Bank. The dealing room (perhaps appropriately) is on the site of the old Royal Mint. A floor the size of a super-market encompasses also those who operate in the money markets buying and selling short-term loans, those who trade foreign exchange 'forward' for settlement at some agreed date in the future and those who trade in options, the right to buy or sell currencies.

In the spot market – foreign exchange deals where money passes from one bank account to another two days later – Andre and thirty-five other dealers answer to foreign exchange trading director Peter Maltz who, before reaching the age of forty is managing a turnover of $7–9 billion a day. That's equivalent to the turnover of the top thirty-eight companies in the 'Fortune 500' list combined. The world's largest company, General Motors, had sales of $132,775 million in 1992. Peter Maltz's team would match that in sixteen and a half working days.

Right now, that unwanted £10 million long position bothers Andre Katz. 'I can call other market participants and ask for their cable in five and see what they make me,' he tells me. By going on to other banks with whom Barclays has a direct-dealing relationship and asking their prices he might find a buyer offering a better price than in the market and would be able to shed some of the unwanted pounds without moving the market price against himself. He tries.

'He's just making me a market price really, not showing me a view,' he tells me after the first call. 'He's just making a price around the broker's price.

'If I hit him he'll just hit the brokers, probably. He is showing slightly because he's showing the bid where it is in the brokers but his offer's slightly higher. So he doesn't want to be paid.'

By sometimes very small disparities between another bank's quotation and those in the market, players like Andre Katz will judge which way rival dealers are moving and so hope to move ahead of them.

After a couple more calls he tells me, 'I'm a little bit more comfortable. I'm £5 million long and I'll hope to sell them out the figure 149.' That is, he will hope to sell the rest at $1.4900. According to the screen showing his current dealing position, that would leave him with a profit of £9000 for the day.

He had started that morning expecting the pound to fall against the dollar and had been right. During the day, according to reports in the next morning's newspapers, it had fallen from $1.4905 to $1.4885. But the fall had been broken with minor rallies, one of which had left the pound closing above its lowest levels of the day. Andre Katz had been trading on those minor flurries, always with an eye to the overall trend.

His ability to back his judgement is sometimes hampered – even thwarted – by the obligations which the Bank of England ordains he must discharge to other banks such as, for instance, the bank within the world's largest securities group, Nomura of Japan. There, Nomura Bank International foreign exchange dealing chief Tom Elliot explained: 'The Bank of England requirement is that if you want to appear as a trading bank in London you must make a minimum number of currency pairings as a market-maker. So between seven o'clock in the morning and four in the afternoon we are quite happy to be categorized as a market-maker in yen-related products.

'In return for that we require from Bank X that we can call them for sterling-related products or Bank Y for Deutschmark-related and people observe those requirements. There's no obligation to provide the broker with a price but there is an obligation to provide a price when someone calls you direct.'

So throughout his trading day Andre Katz must quote the prices at which he will buy or sell sterling for dollars. He quotes without knowing which way the caller is moving but is bound, for that moment, by his price. On hearing the prices the caller – another bank from anywhere in the world – is free to buy or sell and will then tell Andre which it is doing.

In return, those banks accept the obligation to reciprocate, so Andre can call them and deal at the prices they quote. How big each deal can be varies between currencies, with the obligation being smaller in the minor and thinly traded pairings. A rule of thumb is that the equivalent of $10 million applies for the general run of freely traded currencies.

'The market amount is not necessarily $10 million equivalent,' comments Peter Maltz. 'We have various relationships with different banks. We can rely on all these banks if we need to shift a big amount of, let's say, sterling. We can call twenty or thirty banks who'll make us a price in £5 or £10 and we can deal on that price. They have to make us a two-way price just as we have to make them one.'

The obligation extends to the spread between bid and offer prices, too. 'I usually quote a five-point spread,' Andre told me. 'I can go tighter but we don't go wider, really. If it's quiet we quote five points but even if it's busy and thirty or forty points wide in the market we still quote five points because we're consistent if nothing else.

'I'll quote a few people three points in £5 or even one point in £5. It's down to relationships.'

The result of all this is that, far from being people who can manipulate the markets, Andre Katz and his like are at the mercy of the market. He decides the dollar is going to fall so he wants to sell it and buy the pound. But a bank asks his price. He doesn't know whether it wants to sell or buy sterling. If he quotes a price just outside the market rate it may go in the opposite direction or turn him down and deal elsewhere. The caller has the choice whether to buy or sell at Andre Katz's prices and he must accept.

That can go on all day so that whereas he knew he should have been buying sterling and selling the dollar, he's chasing to try and get himself out of the opposite position having constantly had dollars dumped on him which he had then to off-load at falling prices.

Stephen Bell, chief economist at City merchant bank Morgan Grenfell, advises clients, the parent Deutsche Bank and his colleagues at the sharp end, dealing on the foreign exchange desks, on the outlook for the major economies and their currencies. He has a distinguished record in this respect but quoth he: 'It's a humbling experience for an economist to have to make a price on the desk alongside the traders.'

Andre Katz finds that this obligation always to make a market in his own currency can be so frustrating that, paradoxically, he may find it more profitable to speculate in those beyond his responsibility and in which he is presumably less expert. 'I'm quoting two-way prices to customers and banks alike that they can deal on. And sometimes it's not practical to take a position in the currency that you trade in yourself so you look around at other currencies where you can't get taken out of your position because you're not quoting two-way prices.

'You can take a position on your book and leave it there. You can say, "I think sterling's going to go down this morning" and I can take a £5 or £10 position and because I'm making a two-way price I may have one customer over there and I get sterling, make a bank and again get sterling and make someone else and get sterling again.

'I find I'm long and the rates will be lower and I can't find anywhere to sell my sterling. So sometimes in the actual currency you're trading it's not practical to take a position. It's difficult to maintain your position, especially at Barclays because we're high profile and quote a lot of market players and customers alike.'

Hence his use of the freedom to speculate on the bank's behalf in other currencies. 'I'll even take a Singapore dollar position if I think it's the right way to go,' he told me. For the past few days he had believed the Deutschmark to be high against the Italian lira and had run that position for a few days. Later he closed it out at a £15,000 profit.

But that does not mean the currency dealer can afford to be only reactive, just quoting prices apathetically and without some view of which way the currents are flowing. 'You need to come in with a view,' declared Andre.

'You can come in and see how things go but then you find with a market such as this one you'd be chasing yourself round and round, because if you don't have your own view the brokers can be quoting 40–45 and someone phones and you say they're 40–45. You get given 5 and you'll say 'I don't really want this 5 at 45 so I'll sell it the next bid.'

'So you're not going to get 40 bid, or if you do you're lucky. You'll be selling at 37, maybe 35 and losing money. If you keep doing that through the day you'll be losing money all day and end up down maybe 10 or 20 dollars.

'So if you come in without a view and the market's erratic you are almost certain to lose money.'

But how can he form a view first thing in the morning unless something relevant happened overnight?

'You can decide it's going to be in a range today and not decide on a definite trend. You can decide it's going to trade between 1.4830 and 1.4870. So you think, "If it gets anywhere near 30 I'll buy pound. If it gets anywhere near 70 I'll sell it," with a view to taking profits either side.

'Or you can think, "Cable's going to go up. Anyone who calls me I'm going to have to pitch it up slightly to them [quote a bid or offer price slightly above or below those heard in the market] and see what happens." And if people start passing [not dealing at the prices quoted] then they feel the same so you go and buy some and put it on the book so you're long ahead of the next move.'

I remarked on the absence of reading matter. Neither newspapers nor economic reports were very much in evidence.

'Sometimes you can read too much information,' he told me, 'and it clouds your judgement. It really does. I've had cases where you've sat down and you've read one thing; you read another thing; you read another thing, and you think "Well, what does that really mean? On one hand it means this and on another hand it means that." It's sometimes too much.

'Figures you can interpret one way or another. Inflation figures you can interpret to mean that interest rates are going to be put up, which would boost the currency, but then if inflation's high it's bad for the economy, so why should the currency go up? You get conflicting views.'

The brokers – many of whom will have left school at sixteen – may have as much influence on dealer opinion as magisterial pronouncements in the most respected journals. 'We all have feelings about what the market's going to do that day,' Eugene 'Stan' Quinlan told me at his desk in MW Marshall.

'We can see levels where there might be some support or we might see some selling interest or some buying interest. And we say to the banks, "I think the $:DM's been overbought today" and we give our opinion why we think the $:DM has been overbought or oversold.

'He may agree with us, he may not agree with us but at least he has an opinion and when you talk to your customer you get a feel for what they're doing. He might say it's a bit overbought and a lot of people think it's overbought and quite often the case is that it's going to go down that day because of the general opinion in the market.

'And he will be feeding that information to you. And from you.

'That's what they want, they want . . . you can't talk to a machine, you can't feel it out. That's why the banks have brokers: so that they can get a feel of the market.'

Across the desk from Andre Katz – with the banks of screens and equipment between them they can just see eye-to-eye without standing – Steve Harris heads trading in $:DM, the world's most liquid currency.

During the afternoon the latest retail sales figures for the USA emerged. 'They were really within most people's expectations,' he told me. 'So the market's more on people's positions and I think the market was a bit long of dollars going into the number – expecting a better one – and we thought the position was on the topside but the market was going down and finally the dollar's dribbled off.'

The backroom pundits – the economists you may see pronouncing sometimes on television news reports – may analyse and opine but when the figures actually appear there's no time here at the sharp end for considered analysis. All that matters is how they compare with the market position; is the market caught long or short of the currency?

'News is into the market – the information and the reaction to it – faster than any dealer could read more than fifty words of a report,' comments Andre. 'The other guy gets it ten seconds before you and makes money. From you. You lose it. So even in quiet times like this you pay attention to what's going on.'

Here it hardly matters how events should be interpreted. By the time that manifests itself a dealer could have suffered intolerable losses being 'right' but at the wrong time. What matters is how an event is moving the market, particularly what customers are doing. Customer business – from investors and traders in goods, rather than other banks speculating – presents both an opportunity and a risk. If they see a large order, dealers know to make sure Peter Maltz hears of it.

'We get to have to quote for some large business more or less on a daily basis,' he told me. 'I like to be around to watch so that we don't put the bank in a vulnerable position but quote the right sort of price for the right sort of amount in the right environment. If I hear of a big amount coming through the door I'll take an active interest in how we're going to quote it and how we'll get it out.'

Thus Andre Katz, fulfilling his obligation to make a market in cable, can suddenly be landed with a hazardous position. 'We may have to quote the price in £100 million,' he explains. 'The price will not be 09 to 14 for long. I wouldn't be able to clear £100 million through any one given broker, or even all the brokers at that price. The most that I could sell through the brokers in this market is probably £20 million so that leaves me holding £80 million I don't want. In that case I'd call other market players, either through Reuters or by direct lines in London where I can call up NatWest, Midland and others.'

But keeping an eye on such positions gives Peter Maltz valuable intelligence: 'I'm looking out for capital shifts, for what different types of customers are doing, what fund managers are doing, what investors are doing, to see if there's a particular trend forming so that we can take advantage of that trend as well.

'We encourage people to call us in big amounts because this

is a competitive market. We encourage them to bring us their business. You talk to people and you learn about their views, swap ideas before you do the business possibly.

'Obviously, our corporate desk are trying to encourage corporates to call us and it's really the mixture of all these calls and all these flows that you're seeing that creates an environment so that we can see whether the market's moving one way or the other. If you're seeing a lot of interest one way in a particular currency, that encourages you to take a position.'

'With the banks trading as principal I see an electrical analogy,' Trevor Cass told me on the basis of his twenty-five years' experience. 'The ebbs and flows of trade and investment related business I see as an electrical spike and the trading which the banks do on a day-trading basis as a condenser across those spikes; that's what it's designed to do.

'Obviously we make money out of it but it's designed to iron out these spikes, to make them manageable.'

I found Peter Maltz studying charts on his screens whenever he had no particular need to supervise one or other of the dealers closely. 'I look quite a lot at the charting,' he told me. 'We have numerous charting services.

'There are people who trade off fundamentals and others who trade off the feeling they have for the market and the flows. There's not one particular approach that a dealer should use. The dealers have access to all types of information which is necessary for them to trade. And they pick and choose what is important to them from the way they trade and their particular style of trading.

'I like to look at charts as a confirmation of something that I'm feeling anyway. If I feel strongly about something I look at the chart and say, "Is the chart agreeing with me, is it telling me that my timing's wrong or that I'm totally wrong?" So if I've got a strong view on something and am going to take a position I may look at the chart and say, "Yes, the chart's saying that's what I do as well." So it encourages me to take that position. I may look at the chart and say that the timing doesn't look too good.

'Another thing that I really find valuable is contacts in the market. I know a good few people in the market, talking to those people during the day. They'll say different things to us which will help you form a view.'

However formed, the view must be a detached one, free of sentiment or any concern about the effects of a particular currency movement. That, as Nomura's Tom Elliot puts it, is 'consistent with the way of life. You must be that sort of person and make your judgement on objective criteria.

'I had the business thrown in my face some years ago when I had a particularly successful day the day Ronald Reagan was shot. I happened to be long of sterling and short of the dollar prior to this occurring.

'Because nobody can predict anything of that nature, of course, I went home that evening and explained to my wife that life was rosy and I was really pleased with myself and so forth. And when she inquired why and I told her . . . she doesn't want to hear about my business any more. She thinks it's diabolical. From a humanitarian perspective she's absolutely right. It's a business though.'

Trevor Cass avers, 'You have to shed your beliefs. For example, over the last twenty-five years most people have made more money from selling sterling than buying it.

'If you're British you come out of the office and think "I don't like the fact that the currency is on the floor" but while you're in the building you've got to go where the market is going. And the market represents all traders in the world and national interests are outweighed in the aggregate.

'No country has more traders than the sum of the traders elsewhere. If there were as many traders in the USA as in the rest of the world then, given the way these guys are leveraged up, that might create a false market.'

Andre Katz's inclination was to believe that sterling was going down. 'There's a lot of talk of interest rate cuts again,' he told me, 'and a feeling that there could be a half-point cut within the next couple of weeks. Normally what happens is that people will start selling ahead of the fact and then when the fact materializes, then they want to take their profit and the rate goes the other way.

'That's what a lot of people don't realize about the foreign exchange market. A lot of the time it is like a bandwagon, you get a good idea and soon there are other people in the market who may be interested in the currency and so you get a snowball effect which moves the market.

'And the idea is you get in there, get on the bandwagon just before the others and take a profit before everyone else does. But the price moves too quickly sometimes.'

And all that assumes the ability to follow your judgement, which is something the dealer cannot be sure of. 'The most difficult thing is holding on to the position you want to have,' Steve Harris told me. 'You might want to be long of dollars so you've got $100 million in the bag. You bought your dollars.

'But you've got to make a market and if everyone keeps taking these dollars off you then trying to maintain your position at the level you want can be difficult to do. It's the skill, trying to keep your original position.'

Beside him, working in harness on the $:DM desk because the size of the market demands more than one dealer, sits Joe Green. 'You don't always have to deal well to make money,' he chips in.

'One of the most annoying things is that you can say to yourself: "This is what's going to happen to the Deutschmark. It's going to start off at $1.70. It's going to go up to 171. It's going to come back to 169.5." You can be perfectly right and still lose money because if you think you're right and you buy $20 million and then five people call you and they each buy $10 million. You're 70 short. To get them back you have to chase the price up there for them. All the time you're chasing the position.

'It can be the most frustrating thing because at the end of the day you can say, "I got this right all day, I knew this was going to happen and look at the P&L" and it's a loss showing.

'Conversely, you could be wrong and still make money on the day.' Andre Katz has been in the market for seven years and reckons that the worst aspect of the job is when you're losing money and then something causes a sudden break in prices, known as 'a gap' in dealer parlance. 'You've a wrong position and can't get out of it and everything that day seems to be going wrong. It can be horrendous.

'When you're making prices and you're making money and you're making the right prices, it's tremendous.'

This random element and unpredictability can be telling on the nerves when the level of trading is low and the dealer must just sit there not knowing what will happen next. Someone had discarded a roll of Sellotape among the few papers near Steve Harris's desk and from time to time he picked it up, broke off a strip and twisted it around his fingers.

'I believe it's my alternative to smoking,' he replied to my remarking upon it. 'I have this habit whenever anything's in front of me of just fiddling it about. There are people who are playing with pens, doodling. There's very few people who can sit there calm without letting it out.'

In all the bank dealing rooms I have come across around the City over the years, foreign exchange dealers have been at core calm and self-disciplined. That yob in rolled shirtsleeves you see screaming down two telephones at once whenever television news reports a sterling crisis is, for all the shouting and machismo gestures, surprisingly mature. They may not be particularly sophisticated (you will not find a Renaissance man among them) but they talk commonsense and their voracious environment tolerates few fanciful notions. 'The pressure on the individual has grown,' comments Steve Harris. 'It's very important – especially when you're working in a big team like we are here – that whatever you're feeling inside, it shouldn't always be shown. If you show that you're struggling to cope with the pressure three or four times a day you should be pulled to one side and taken off the position.'

There is also the simple reality that emotional displays give away information to the rival with whom you are dealing. 'It's all about how you display your image as well,' says Steve.

Unpredictability breeds superstition, too.

'We had one very good dealer and we had a building site just outside with a crane,' recalls Trevor Cass. 'And he'd say, "The crane's moving to the left, that's sterling going down, going to the right it's going up." People have their little ideas like that, as well.

'They're all a bit superstitious. When they've had a good day they think, what did they do? It's part of a pattern. They'll do that again and hope it brings another good day.'

But Peter Maltz disagrees. While remembering the dealer who followed the crane, he claims that today the market is 'such a monstrous animal, it's not like a game any more.

'If you were up against 50:50 chance on average, you would know you were a loser. Dealers here have 70:30 odds against them.'

Statistically, he's right but that doesn't preclude superstition – human nature hasn't changed. Early in the morning, as the dealers arrived at their desks, several of the tabloid papers they discarded were open at the astrology pages.

Moreover, while the banks' proprietary traders – with no duty to make a market – may speculate profitably on it, an event such as 'Black Wednesday' may bring no joy to the dealers on the desks. The banks may in aggregate have actually lost money, according to one bank's account. Certainly, several leading banks lost money on the day sterling was devalued . 'There was so much selling going on from corporates,' the London head of foreign exchange dealing at a leading Continental bank told me. 'We were trying to be short sterling but were getting clients selling as well. It was like a hot potato. And we didn't make money that day and I'd be surprised if any banks with good corporate business made a profit. They probably lost money on the proprietary trades that day. So many people were panicking to get out of the pound.'

A sudden flurry of activity as Andre spoke into his telephone, called across to his assistant dealing in £:DM and then to Joe Green on the $:DM. Afterwards, he told me what he'd done.

'I'm arbitraging. I'm given £20 in dollars.' (Bought £20 million in exchange for dollars.)

'I've managed to arbitrage some of that position at higher than where I've bought them because I've sold £:DM.' (Sold sterling and bought Deutschmarks.)

'Then I bought dollars and sold Deutschmarks.

'So I'm all square and made £1500. If I could do that ten times a day I'd be very rich but it doesn't all work out like that.'

We went through the figures. He bought sterling at $1.49 then sold that sterling at DM at 2.5452. He bought dollars at DM 1.7080. So the £:DM rate divided by $:DM rate produces a rate of £:$1.49016, compared with the $1.4900 rate at which he started. The whole process had taken less that twenty-five seconds and came because he had his wits about him and saw an opportunity.

Andre attempted my further education:

'The guy who's given me £20 at 1.49 knows something I don't. So by making that rate and seeing it I can get out quickly and make a quick turn of only 1.6 of a pip but across £20 million, which is a large amount, that's $3200. So that's £2000.' (Actually, it was more but I noticed that whenever we discussed any of his operations Andre tended to underestimate the likely profit.)

Arbitraging is the way a dealer will sometimes disperse across the market, without upsetting the rates, an otherwise unmanageably large transaction. It is particularly useful where the currency pairing is a small and relatively illiquid one. No need for arbitraging of the $:DM, as Joe Green told me. But on the $:Swissie, dealer Mark Hearne told me, 'The Swiss market sometimes gaps and the only way you can really cover yourself is through the $:DM and DM:Swiss and arbitrage to give yourself the $:Swiss. Yesterday there was a big order going through and we couldn't get the DM:Swiss either, so basically we got stuffed.' He laughed ruefully.

'You get some calculated moves in this sometimes which might then lead the $:DM, so basically you can give the Deutschmark trader some idea what's likely to happen in the next two seconds with him.'

One deal in one currency broken down to make deals in several others may raise the total level of activity in the room, acknowledges Peter Maltz.

'Once it becomes busy in one currency that feeds on to other currencies. If people are buying dollars against Swissie that can feed across to Deutschmark activity and dollar activity elsewhere,' he told me. 'There are so many facets to the market. People think it's a very simple process of buying one currency and selling it out again. We've got so many different aspects.

'What's become very active in the last few years and expanded is cross-currency trading, not just the basic cross currencies against EMS but more exotic-type crosses like Swiss against the yen or lira against the Danish krona and people are far more interested in these today.'

A quick-witted dealer might spot that trading in the $:DM and DM:Swiss will affect the $:Swiss but at the same time yen:DM and yen:$ are moving. Is that compatible with the yen:Swiss rates he sees?

Arbitrage activity, then, may have widespread if small effects on rates all around the market, as Peter Maltz endeavoured to explain to me. 'Somebody might be buying dollars in Swiss and selling them against the lira. There's no market in Swiss:lira really so they have to do it through arbitrage.

'Somebody may have a large order in DM:Swiss for instance, so they do something in $:Swiss and the opposite in $:DM, which is very confusing to people. So people see the dollar moving up against the Swiss, they'll be marking the dollar up against the other currencies.

'So somebody then comes along and sells a huge amount of dollars in the other currency. The dollar then goes down and that currency goes up and it gets quite complicated at times.' (I thought that was taking understatement a bit far.) 'It's a question of knowing your market and having contacts in the market so you know pretty much – well, you try and know as much as possible – what's going on.'

This frenetic activity can also contribute to another dealing room phenomenon which I call howl-round. That is a broadcaster's term for when the microphone is held too close to the loudspeaker. Instantly, the slightest sound the mike picks up it broadcasts out through the speaker, whence it feeds back into the microphone, augmenting the original, and this circular process goes on until it saturates the loudspeaker capacity. Likewise in a dealing room, arbitraging one deal will make several dealers active and raise the tempo of the room. Says Trevor Cass: 'The sheer level of activity may create more physical activity and noise, all of which have a physiological or psychological effect of making others more active. It's hard to sit there doing little if the tempo all around you has increased.'

At Nomura Bank, Tom Elliot explicitly recognizes the danger and seeks to avert it. 'That's my job. Because I'm not involved in the day-to-day market-making any longer, I try and act as the braking mechanism.

'If I think that the activity level has got to a pitch where we're in danger of losing control of our objectivity then I just pour cold water on things for a bit. I see that as one of my primary functions.' But the obligation to make a market – to quote buying and selling prices and honour them without knowing beforehand whether the caller is a buyer or seller – means that if trading rooms elsewhere are in a dealing frenzy and lack the mature steadying hand of their own Tom Elliots, the fever may prove contagious.

'One lapse of concentration and I've lost £10,000,' Andre told me suddenly. 'Nothing was going on until I was asked a price. I quoted 71–76 and I got given at 76. The next price should have given me a clue . . .' But instead of studying the market movement closely he'd been seeking information on the phone, and talking to Peter Maltz about some other business. The price had moved away from him. Announcement of an economic statistic was due shortly from the USA. 'I hope it's a bad figure for the dollar. Now I'd be paying away 30 pips and there's no point in paying away 30 pips now. I'd rather take another 20 points loss if it's a good figure rather than sell it here and see it go 30 points higher.'

The figures emerge at 1.30 p.m. London time, bang in line with expectations. Reluctance to deal just ahead of them gives way quickly to the briefest nervous pause before the level of activity swells. Everyone is dealing and the hubbub of voices now has grown continuous. But because there is no unexpected – sharp – price movement there's no shouting or excitement. They're all just doing business, or trying to find business.

During the afternoon the Bundesbank says that its press conference later in the week will be to announce next year's money-supply targets (some had earlier considered the possibility of an interest rate announcement) and the effect of that on the $:DM rate spills over into £:$, reducing Andre's loss from that slip to £3000. It seemed good to me until I realized that he could just as easily have had his loss increased by such extraneous developments.

More important over the day, however, is that the market has gone overall in the direction he expected and he was able to hold – more or less – the position he judged appropriate. He made money.

'The most frustrating is when there is actually nothing going on in the market whatsoever. The market is dead, you know, sitting there without a position for . . .' – this is Steve Harris talking – '. . . I mean you're in the office, for say, ten hours a day.

'If there's only one move that day in your currency, it might not occur until three o'clock in the afternoon and you might be sitting there without a position until three o'clock because you haven't got a strong view. And if you're not on that move at three o'clock – if you're not on that bandwagon – then you'll probably be caught. You're going to probably lose some money and it's going to be a very frustrating day and you'll go home that way.

'Other times your currency can be very, very busy from first thing in the morning. You can be busy quoting all day long. That's what's so good about it. No two days are the same.'

Steve, whose wife was expecting their first child in a few weeks (it was to be a girl, Emily) gets up at 6 o'clock and gets home to Shenfield in Essex at around 7 p.m. He will be at his desk by no later than 7.15 a.m. and quote to the market until 4 o'clock, before handing over to New York; but must still quote customers until 5.30 p.m.

Late in a frustratingly quiet afternoon he told me, 'I can be sitting here – I'm very relaxed at the moment – and suddenly a customer says to me "I need the $:DM in quarter of a billion dollars". It's very late in the afternoon, the market's becoming very thin and I've got to think. I've got to make this guy an offer. I'm either a buyer or seller.

'What's my easiest way of getting rid of this or don't I want to? If I think the guy's a buyer I'm going to go with him; I'm going to buy more; I'm going to buy half a billion dollars. Or, you know, if he gives me that's the side that's not too vulnerable. I can offer out these dollars.

'You're thinking like that and the guy wants a price while I'm thinking this to myself.

'I tend to sit here and think: What would happen now if they came in for a large amount? How would I pitch it? Do I want to receive dollars or do I want to lose dollars?

'At the moment, as nothing's happened for the last two hours, I would say I don't really give a toss whether he pays me or gives me. At the moment, there's probably enough liquidity to get out either side. But those are the decisions you have to make.

'I think the most important is that you're here ten hours a day and just keeping that concentration. Your currency can be doing nothing and suddenly there'll be one movement. If you're not aware of what's going on, it's going to be costly.'

Many people elsewhere work as long hours, many may even work longer. We pace ourselves, easing off when we can and summoning our concentration and energies when the situation demands. Our metabolism changes. A foreign exchange dealer has no control over, no ability to predict, when the next demand for ruthless fast decision-taking will hit him. The constant risk is of being caught off-guard. He can look for no mercy from rival dealers. That, day after day, is wearying.

Warns Peter Maltz, 'You have to be so flexible. It's all very well saying, "I think the dollar's going to do this or going to do that." You might be totally justified in taking that particular position.

'Something can come out at any moment to totally change that view. You have to be alert to anything like that.'

He works an eleven or twelve hour day at his desk, seeing little of his three children – from a newborn to a five-year-old – except at weekends. The foreign exchange markets around the world are shut only from nine o'clock Friday evening (New York closing) until seven o'clock Sunday evening (morning in the Asia Pacific region).

'You don't stop worrying about it during the weekend because something can happen and you can't respond quickly enough,' says Peter. 'That's worse actually. There's nothing you can do about it.'

Steve Harris acknowledges the need to have an idea what's gone on over the weekend and certainly what's in the weekend press but not to watch every news bulletin. 'The main thing is that if you've been working hard five days the two days you have off you must relax. Whether it means you play golf or spend five hours in the snooker hall or getting completely drunk – I don't know, whatever suits your fancy – you've got to get out of the market. We're encouraged here also to take holidays. There's some people work through seven or eight months without managing a day off work which is, I think, wrong. You need to wind down, basically.'

How the day ebbs and flows will depend in only small measure on the currency you trade. On the $:DM Joe Green starts between 6.30 a.m. and 7 a.m. as the Far East is approaching the end of its day. London provides just a limited service for the Far East as the business is mainly through Barclays in Tokyo (in which Steve Harris had a spell). Far Eastern interest in the $:DM is in any case small because it impacts little on the region's trade flows.

But pressure from that quarter adds to the early demand from mainland Europe as Steve and Joe begin full service quoting at 8 a.m. London time. That first hour is often hectic and the pace slackens only a little with the dwindling of Asian interest, with no real let-up until about 11 o'clock London time (noon on the Continent) when German and French dealers go to lunch. Then the Americans begin to make their presence felt and the day's busiest period usually runs from one o'clock until the mainland Europeans wind down at 4 pm. 'Between four and five is when you can get some very fierce moves,' says Joe. 'Europe's gone so there's just us and the States in it and it's a market all to itself after four o'clock our time because it just gaps – lifts up and down.

'We stop quoting other banks at four o'clock our time because it can get quite dangerous.' (The obligation under Bank of England rules ends then). 'The big American banks see a lot of flows and can just power the market one way or the other 50 or 60 points. In fact we've seen it move a lot more than that, especially on a Friday afternoon.'

Andre Katz heads back to Walton on Thames at about six o'clock. 'I pass my open positions to New York and ask them to take profit and stop-loss orders. If there's a problem they'll call us in the night.

'Some days if at ten o'clock in the morning it's quite quiet I book out for a game of squash in the gym. We have a gym here. We can be quite flexible. When it's busy you're at your desk and if you're busy for two months then you don't leave the desk at all, not for lunch or anything.'

Whereas some ascribe particular characteristics to different currencies, Nomura's Tom Elliot believes that is an illusion created by the time zones and characteristics of the dealers each brings into the market.

'It's not the currencies, it's the people and liquidity involved which create idiosyncrasies,' he avows. 'In Japan, for instance, the yen tends to be much more stable as a rule of thumb because of the commercial flows in Japan. Normally speaking the buyers and sellers, the import and export community, counterbalance each other unless there's a once-for-all shift. So the Japanese time zone tends to be quite stable.

'I would use a terminology regarding staff in European treasury operations as dealers. They're very analytical, they're into fundamental analysis and they recognise the strengths and weaknesses of the various economies and they'll trade on that basis.

'Go to New York and the people in the New York trading rooms are traders. They're punchy, geared to price volatility irrespective of the fundamental analysis. So we can have strong fundamental economic statistics coming out for the USA and if the dollar looks weak because Europe have all been buyers – and are looking partially to liquidate their position holdings to go home of an evening – and if the New Yorkers think they can drive the price down to force liquidation from the European side, they'll do that. They're much more driven by the price volatility than by the fundamental analysis.

'So there's a very different approach to the trading perspective from the European morning until about 2.30, then post 2.30 into the North American afternoon. Of course, post 5 o'clock London time the liquidity strains of the North American market are already very pronounced.

'Many of the banks refuse to quote after midday in New York because of the volatility. The price structure tends to become extreme after midday New York time, that's 5 p.m. London time. The number of market participants dramatically reduces as the Europeans close their book and go home.

'You can count those on the fingers of your two hands; the major market makers in New York and the rest of the market don't want to know. The rest of the market participants don't have a qualitative client base to depend upon for order flow because the qualitative clients tend to go to the ten or so major US banks or foreign banks in New York. So the price volatility in the New York afternoon can become significantly more pronounced as people get themselves set up for the return of the Tokyo market towards 5 o'clock New York time.'

Trevor Cass believes that the attribution of peculiar characteristics to different currencies tends to be self-fulfilling. 'If people say sterling always seems to come off the bottom at the end of the day, then it will, because they'll all be trading that way. There are traits in currencies. There are feelings such as that the yen always tends to be weak at the beginning of the week and strong towards the end.'

Peter Maltz agrees, 'The foreign exchange market loves its parallels. You know: you buy the dollar on any unrest in the world. I'm not quite sure the logic is quite there most of the time, but the market decides to do something which it traditionally always does. Any problems in Russia and you traditionally sell Deutschmarks because the Germans have made large loans and are in close proximity.'

But that scepticism about individual currency characteristics doesn't extend as far as a willingness to move dealers freely around the desks. 'People specialize in their particular currency so that they know the ups and downs and know their market inside out,' Andre Katz told me. 'We wouldn't swap over and I go and do the $:DM for a year and Steve come here and do cable. We don't do that sort of thing.

'There may be a need – it does happen occasionally – where a dealer is having a particularly rough time and needs a break from his currency.'

And they have their *esprit de corps*. Steve and Joe both told me proudly that $:DM is the biggest and most liquid of all the currency markets. And Andre reckoned, 'Cable is the number one currency for Barclays. There are bigger markets; but for prestige actually in the London market, to trade sterling for Barclays is still the main ambition. If anyone's got an ambition it's to trade sterling for Barclays. If anyone was approached and asked, "How would you like to come and trade cable at Barclays?" two or three years ago, they'd go, "Wow, I've reached it!".' They can become more possessive than a mongrel bitch with her pups.

Each dealer has limits within which he enjoys discretion to deal outside his own hours. An extraordinary number, free to leave with their counterpart's instructions to take profits or cut losses in the currency if it reaches a particular rate, will insist instead on being called, perhaps in the small hours of the morning – encroaching on their precious few hours' sleep, disturbing wife and offspring – notwithstanding that this means perhaps vital seconds or even minutes are lost.

'It's a twenty-four-hour market but there's still a twilight zone and the market is very thin at those times,' rationalizes Steve Harris in self-justification. 'You tend to find when you leave overnight orders that if everyone seems to be positioned the same way a lot of stop-losses tend to be triggered, unfortunately, during that time. That's the risk you take. That's why a lot of people tend to leave call levels rather than specific stop-loss levels.

'A lot of people hate to be cut out anywhere in that twilight zone because you get a lot of false moves there; because the market's extremely thin.'

Trevor Cass believes that often the dealer feels a need to be closely involved in realizing profit or loss on his own previous decisions. 'A stop-loss or take profit order effectively closes you out. In a sense it's slightly remote in that you're not actually taking a loss yourself but you're mandating somebody else to take it for you. Although that should be one and the same, it's not one and the same, actually.

'The real problem with cutting losses is not the small loss because we can all cut that. It's when the loss is enormous. Then the pressure is not to cut it.'

Peter Maltz calls all his dealers together for an early morning meeting each day just before they are obliged to start market-making. It usually takes no more than seven or eight minutes, sometimes as little as three. They exchange ideas and views about which way each currency is likely to go. It acts as a sounding board so that each dealer hears the views of his colleagues but is in no way bound by any policy line or consensus.

No sooner has Peter returned to his desk than in comes a call. 'We've just been asked for cable in 20 which is a bit of an awkward time because the London market doesn't open quite yet,' he told me. 'It's a bit of an awkward hour just before the London market opens so we're kind of stuck because we can't really get it out. We can normally call the Far East but most of the banks there are finished. So we're waiting until 8 o'clock. If the customer is buying a lot elsewhere with other banks it puts us in a very dangerous position.'

Might it be done deliberately, to take advantage of the market hiatus?

'There are unscrupulous people around, yes. Except it's not unscrupulous or even unfair really. It's part of the market. It's up to us whether we want to quote before we're obliged to at eight.

'There are people who take advantage of weak moments in the market.'

Later in the day, with a good flow of business coming through the room and the dealers, if not trading hectically, at least occupied, Andre Katz calls across to Steve Harris, 'He's a spoof to pay!'

This is a spoof as he later explained it to me:

'The market in the brokers is 95 bidder – 1.4895–1.4900.' (Thus he could sell sterling at $1.4895 – '95' or buy it at the 'figure', so called because it is $1.49 exactly.) 'The bank concerned is looking to sell. He wants to try and sell better than 95, so to create a false market he buys sterling through the brokers and pays the figure [$1.4900] for sterling so the brokers quote it higher.

'He gets calls out to the market participants – phoning other banks direct, that is – and hopes that they make him either figure to 05 or even 01–6. They're 99–04 and in this case he sells to everybody and he's improved his selling rate by as much as 5 points on that. He's selling them £30 or £40 and gets quite a reasonable result.

'It does work sometimes. It works more often than not, probably nine out of ten times. The thing to do is get the market to believe that's where the price is and then they will make you that rate and you sell to people and they realize that they've been conned, basically.

'I quoted him 97–02 – a lower rate than he was looking for, I think.' Within seconds, the rate was being quoted lower, 93–98.

What it comes down to is placing a number of very small orders with the brokers so that the market is misled into quoting a higher price, enabling the deceiver to sell at a higher price than would otherwise have pertained.

On the London stock exchange such a ploy would probably be illegal (though there has not been a successful prosecution this century for the common law offence of rigging the market). Here it is not even considered reprehensible or particularly sharp. In the securities markets it would probably also be impossible because each share deal is reported and seen.

The transparency of the market safeguards other dealers and investors alike against such a subterfuge.

Here in the foreign exchange markets a dealer knows only the prices others are making, not the size of the deals going through the market. He must feel in the dark for what is going on, helped perhaps by the broker. There are thus small differences of emphasis in the personal qualities required for the two roles.

MW Marshall managing director, Tony Porter, expressed the consensus view of what brokers look for in their peers: 'There's any number of personalities on the other side and any number of personalities have to be on this side to blend, win the trust of the principal traders. We work from university students down to guys who formerly worked in betting shops, because of their numeracy.'

To 'Stan' Quinlan, broking a number of currencies at Marshall's, it comes down to 'level awareness'. This for him meant keeping an ear to the rates being quoted in several currencies at once. 'It's knowing what's going on around you. We sit here ten hours. You have to concentrate for ten hours a day. We're aware where the business is coming from and going to and what's moving and what makes things move.

'A lot of people deal with other people because they're characters. They like to deal with them, they feel comfortable dealing with them. They trust them.

'It doesn't mean that broker is the best broker in the world but he is a good broker because he's got the trust of the customer and the customer feels happy. He might not be the sharpest broker in the world but because the customer trades with him, because he's comfortable with him, he's a good broker.'

But when Tom Elliot at Nomura Bank is recruiting spot foreign exchange dealers, he draws on seventeen years' experience of the markets and looks for someone who is self-motivated, self-disciplined and has a degree of leadership quality. 'So someone who has perhaps been captain of a football or cricket team, respected by their peer group, active in a social environment, maybe in a debating society or something of that order.'

But is the ability to trade foreign exchange something which can be taught or is it truly inherent? Are foreign exchange dealers born or made? I asked Trevor Cass.

'They're made but you have to start with the right ingredients which may not be in everybody born,' he replied. 'If you find people with those ingredients then you can make them.

'The ingredients are a sense of self-belief. You've got to have confidence in your own thought processes and an ability to come to decisions which you believe are right. That may not be an ingredient that you're born with, it may be conditioned by your success in early years. I'm a great believer that people who have success in their early years build on a very sure foundation and create more successes. So you've got to have this foundation of confidence and belief in self, which will be a combination of your upbringing, what you were innately given when the cards were dealt and what you make of it in the future.

'That is the core behind it. The attributes logically flow, which are: ability to take risk and to assess risk; an ability to decide when it's time to cut your losses; and an ability to decide when to take your profits.

'Again, as you build a foundation of success and you get these things right you get an incremental effect and it's a geometrically incremental effect: for every right decision you make you probably feel twice as right because of it, and so on and so on, until you come to, say, twenty-two, twenty-three or twenty-four when you've got a really very confident person.

'Now you can argue that that's quite dangerous. But I would say that in a well-controlled dealing operation where experienced people are running the overall risk profile, then as long as that is in place and functioning effectively then to get these young bucks in who feel confident, that's really what you're looking for.'

It is a predominantly male atmosphere to a quite extraordinary degree. The dealers themselves accept this without any liking for it. 'In the States and on the Continent there's a higher percentage of women dealers,' recounts Andre Katz reproachfully. 'Here we have one in thirty-five traders.'

The banks themselves have sought to redress the balance and the accepted wisdom of the markets is that they have practised positive discrimination. Without success.

'We tried to recruit females to leaven up the awful male atmosphere but they don't seem to have done well. I don't know why,' admits Trevor Cass. 'There are a number and there are some very good ones but pound for pound they have to be more aggressive than men and more unpleasant because they need a step change in their attitude and philosophy and perspective of life.'

Educational qualifications do not rank highly in the order of anyone's priorities in the spot foreign exchange market. They are much more at home talking of Spurs and Chelsea than Schubert or Chopin, the MCC than Iris Murdoch, golf than Goya.

'We've gone through a situation currently whereby there's been a bias towards university graduates,' notes Tom Elliot. 'I personally have mixed feelings on that. My feeling is that a university graduate has a very broad horizon in terms of their career expectation and need not necessarily commit them-selves wholly to spot foreign exchange. So I err on the side of looking at graduates as your career treasury banker: someone who will develop expertise in a broad consensus of trading tools within the treasury environment.

'Spot forex is much more focused and finite and I don't think that should preclude people who are school-leavers with A levels. A broad education is, of course, a prerequisite but I would never preclude people who have not gone to university. You need someone who has a sharp mind, is pushy and opinionated.'

Even within the august portals of the Bank of England, wherein are to be found many of the City of London's intellec-tual elite, such a view holds sway. 'Foreign exchange dealers are identified usually at a relatively early age – maybe in their late teens or early twenties – as having possibly the character-istics of a good dealer,' Terry Smeeton, head of the Bank's foreign exchange division, told me in his office beside the dealing room. 'And after a degree of training and testing they join the foreign exchange desk. Then they tend to remain there for some time, often for many years. Quite a few leave us to go into the commercial world in their late twenties or early thirties.

'It has been our experience that a bright school-leaver does make a good foreign exchange dealer. One needs to be careful about saying that too firmly. It is partly a function of the fact that we are dealing in a relatively limited range of what is now the foreign exchange market. The sort of business we do for the government and for central bank customers does not lead us into the more esoteric markets.

'Because we are not into the more recherché regions, we've found in foreign exchange the bright school-leaver type to be a very satisfactory person because he integrates very well with his counterparts in the market.

'It's very different in the reserve management functions which we run, where we have a team in a market which is more sophisticated. The dealing is less immediate, with less time pressure attached to it. It's better researched. It requires much more mathematics to decide whether a trade is suitable.

'And there we have found people with at least one degree, usually an Economics degree, maybe a Maths degree, to be the better sort of person for that type of job.'

Peter Maltz who – like several of his colleagues – joined Barclays from school, vouchsafes: 'On balance we find that people who've worked in the bank and worked in back office tend overall to be more successful. What we find with graduates is that a guy who's come through the bank, he's desperate to work here and he's seen this as the pinnacle of what he wants to do. He's not open, like a graduate is, to all choices in a working environment. And when a guy gets here he's so enthusiastic, so happy that he's finally made it.'

Recalls Trevor Cass, 'One of the things we used to look for was the grammar school educated person because they didn't have the level of innate security that meant: they weren't willing to take a risk; that they didn't understand that they had to work hard, and that they didn't feel that they needed to do things. But they were intellectually able to do it and therefore able to push themselves up and do really well.

'When you get to the guys who've been, one could say, born with a silver spoon in their mouth – to some extent public school people, people who've had a very sure foundation – that in a sense is a paradox and it doesn't always work in their favour because they don't feel sufficiently that they need to do it. They don't need to do it as hard as the grammar school guy.

'When you look at the London market, a lot of people say 'Barrow boys versus Harrow boys' in foreign exchange trading. There's no doubt that some of the barrow boys – some of the boys who came from the East End – made very, very effective traders; because they had come up in a hard school.

'They're the guys who'd taken chances – used their brains quite clearly, and a lot of them are very intelligent in fact – and made something of it.

'No need to be graduates, certainly not in forex spot trading.

'If you're looking at the more esoteric end of the market where you're considering things like derivatives – such as options, such as swaps – then you need quite clearly well developed mathematical skills to run the business.'

An options trader, for instance, has to consider simultaneously several variables, each of which will vitally affect the value of the option: how volatile is the currency to which the option relates, how does the price at which the option can be exercised compare with the current price, for how long does the option remain valid before it expires. This leads to the development of complex mathematical models. It can be an area for theorists, people who can contemplate the philosophy of risk in a structured and logical way. Sometimes they can be too theoretical for the market, however.

Tom Elliot muses, 'Some of the guys I've worked with over the years can think through a process very thoroughly, can come to a conclusion which defies criticism but when it comes to it . . . they can pull the gun out the holster, point it in the right direction but they can't pull the trigger. They don't like the responsibility of running that risk.

'And the guys on the trading desk are effectively self-employed. They are given limits within which to manage themselves. That's why I emphasize self-discipline, because it's not impossible but I think unnecessary to monitor the activities of every trader every minute of the day. So you have to have confidence in the people you are working with.

'But the reverse side of that coin is that you can't keep pushing people into assuming risk. If their analysis is thorough and defies argument then they should have the confidence in their own ability to manage risk on that basis. And many of the intellectual types are good at the analysis but when it comes down to the doing part they lack what it takes to go forward and assume the position they've thoroughly thought out.'

Each foreign exchange trader is treated as running his own business. The size of the open position – short or long of a currency – a bank may run is limited under Bank of England rules by the bank's capital. It then allocates so much capital capacity to each dealer and tells him to get on and use it as he judges best. 'That's the way we try and manage people,' explains Peter Maltz. 'We say, "You are running your own business with information and account flows. You've got costs – we make people aware of what the costs are – everyone is privy to the same information and it's a question of how you use it." You build up contacts in the market and encourage other banks to call you with the sort of business, the sort of calls, you want to see coming in.'

Paradoxically, while each is a business unto himself, there's an almost palpable team spirit in most bank dealing rooms. There has to be. Each dealer needs a close, almost instinctive, understanding of his peers. When an arbitrage opportunity lasts for only a matter of seconds, for instance, there is no time for discussing strategy, only for reflexes conditioned by knowing what a colleague – on whom you may in turn depend a few minutes later – is trying to achieve.

At the end of much confused shouting Andre explained to

me: 'I fancied sterling being a base at 80 and I made Bankers Trust London – which is a very big player in the market, like ourselves – 82–87 and taken. So I didn't want to be short.

'In other words, he bought sterling from me at 87, which was slightly above what the market rate was in the brokers. But I can't go in and buy sterling through the brokers because he's doing the same thing. There's no point. So what I did was again I used the arbitrage. I bought £:DM and sold $:DM to arbitrage and got my cable back at par really. And then the next price in sterling is 90–95 so it was lucky I managed to get out without a loss.'

He had escaped loss partly through luck with the market but largely because the two other dealers through whom he had arbitraged had reacted so instantly. Covering the cramped desk surface immediately in front of him a sheet of clear plastic is divided into squares in each of which is the name of a broker or bank. He enters each transaction on to his video screen by pressing the appropriate boxes with the point of a pen-like probe wired from its other end to the terminal.

On this screen one line shows the £:$ profit for the day so far, and another line all the other positions in other currencies, together with profit or loss.

He's now short sterling at this moment to the equivalent of £3,370,000; long equivalent $5,024,000.

On the $:DM desk they are $4 million short right now. The $:yen is $7 long. So everyone's got their own view.

Peter Maltz sees no need for the dealers all to be taking a consistent view and does not even try to prevent contradictions arising within the room where one dealer's position implies the dollar is overvalued against the Deutschmark, another's the opposite. 'Everyone is running their own business in their own currency,' he explains. 'Within the limits defined, they can run that pretty much how they want.

'If they think it goes down and I think it goes up I certainly won't say anything. So long as they've got pretty good reasons for what they think, then you give people the freedom to trade in the way they want.

'There's nothing worse, really, than stipulating to people

what your thoughts are and then doing something which they're not comfortable with. We normally find though that we're pretty much one way a lot of the time. People here will have the same opinion as other people and tend to be positioned that way.

'But quite often we have varying positions and we don't discourage that.

'All the dealers we trust enough to work within their limits and they're pretty much free to work within those limits themselves, without too much interference.'

But Lloyds Bank lost more than £40 million when two of its currency dealers based in Lugano, Switzerland, gambled and lost on the foreign exchange markets in the mid-1970s. About ten years later Midland Bank dropped the odd £100 million or so when one of its top executives guessed wrong about interest rates and exchange rates.

In the wake of their foreign exchange dealing in 1990–91 two ex-governors of Mongolia's central bank and three other bankers were eventually arrested and charged with dereliction of duty and abuse of position. They had virtually wiped out the country's entire foreign exchange reserves, losing $82m in ill-advised deals.

In the UK the Securities & Futures Authority banned indefinitely from the business an arbitrage dealer who incurred heavy personal losses at a financial bookmaker and then lost £1.7 million of his firm's money. Kevin Reed Morgan had repeatedly taken on far more risk than he was allowed when employed by two separate investment banks between July '91 and March '93.

After incurring heavy personal losses with the financial bookmaker in 1990, in July 1991 he moved to a new firm. In the ten days he was employed there he heavily exceeded his position limits, three times causing small losses to the bank. The last time was after he had already received a written warning. Mr Reed Morgan was made bankrupt in April 1993, two months after joining another City firm which had been advised of his earlier dismissal.

In March 1993, in a three-hour period in one evening alone,

he exposed his new employer to $400 million of risk in US government bond interest rate futures although he had agreed he would have no more than $5 million of risk at any one time. He got the direction of US interest rates wrong and cost his employer £1.7 million.

Those are only the more egregious incidents. From time to time banks around the world announce they have suffered losses from unauthorized dealing in foreign exchange or related markets.

As the inimitable Christopher Fildes once characteristically observed: it's funny how banks only ever seem to incur losses, never profits, from unauthorized dealing.

'Within the business itself the pariah is the guy who can't cut his losses,' declares Trevor Cass. 'He won't last long, either, because if he doesn't cut his losses he'll pull everybody else down as well. That really is very important, you've got to learn to cut your losses.

'In terms of is he a good judge of the movement of the market or not, then of course that's important but people will forgive you making mistakes in the market. But if you make mistakes which affect his bonus as well as your own then that's going to cause problems.'

Agrees Tom Elliot, 'The novice is the guy who makes a mistake and pretends it never happened. He's frightened to tell you because he knows he's made a mistake, he knows it's costing money. It's always going to become obvious during the course of the business day but he's hoping upon hope that by the time I or my opposite number elsewhere finds out about it the exchange rates will have moved sufficiently in the other direction so that the mistake is not a costly error but a profitable one.

'If that happens once, the chap is chastised for being a clown and not bringing it to anyone's attention; but if it happens again then they're out, because that's cheating on your employer. We all make mistakes, we're human beings and there is some latitude for human error; but if people lie to you or keep things from you there's no opportunity to manage the risk that we as an organization have incurred.'

Because of the limits within which they trade dealers are unable, in theory at least, to build up positions out of which their managers cannot trade without insufferable loss. Unless, that is, the dealer hides the transactions.

The computerized deal-entry system Andre Katz uses is popular in most active bank dealing rooms. Because the dealer enters each transaction live, the head of the dealing room can see every risk that his team has ongoing all the time. That is, unless the dealer does not enter the trade on the computer.

'So it comes down to trusting in reliable staff working with you,' concludes Tom Elliot. 'If somebody wants to be dishonest there's always the opportunity for them to be so.

'If it's in the system I can see it and raise a discussion about it. He's probably already taken remedial action and cut that position out at a small loss.

'The real howlers are the guys who are deceptive. That's a managerial nightmare.'

Technology has changed the way dealers learn the job and threatens to affect the calibre of tomorrow's traders. 'It's changed a lot over the years, with the growth of the electronic dealing systems,' comments Peter Maltz. 'We used to start people in the telex room for six months or a year – a lot of dealing was done over the telex in those days – but since we've had the electronic dealing systems there's no real need for the telex.

'Now we try to recognize a good potential dealer. He or she may come from anywhere; could be a graduate or could be someone from the branches.' Not only Peter Maltz himself but almost every dealer I met, not only at Barclays but in several other banks also, had started out as what the general public would call a bank clerk. By coincidence, Joe Green had worked in the same retail branch where his senior on the $:DM desk, Steve, had started his career.

'There's a few of us here who think it gives you a better understanding of the market generally if you know about basic accounting principles and the equity market and transfers and credits,' confided Joe.

Once Peter Maltz thinks a new recruit has the potential he

sits them on a currency with two other traders: 'Get the calls for them, check the confirmations, really do more menial type work; all the while analysing what these guys are doing. Once we feel that they have more than potential we send them on a one-month residential training course. They will continue to sit with the traders and make currency or on one of the smaller currencies.

'It's a fairly long process, I should say, before you're trading a major currency : a good three to five years usually before we let you loose.'

Tom Elliot mourns The Good Old Days when youngsters were properly taught the job. 'In the long and distant past when I was invited to come to London and join a treasury environment as a trainee' he recounts, as if it were fifty-seven rather than seventeen years ago, 'I was given a very thorough grounding before I was allowed to pick up a telephone.

'It's embarrassing to say that while there still is a demand for graduates and school-leavers to be involved in that in the very early stages of our business, the banks in general – because of the short-term revenue pressures that they're now under – the majority of banks now don't commit enough time, energy and resources towards training their people properly.

'Whereas when I joined seventeen years ago you could have as many months as you liked just observing – sitting with people, observing the techniques of trading and the fundamentals which impacted on price volatility – nowadays we're all governed by headcount. Headcount means cost. 'Is that efficient cost? What are we getting out of that person who is occupying that chair?' We're much more about the revenue side of the equation than about the educational side of the equation.

'So I'm embarrassed to say that organizations such as ourselves – we spend a great deal of money and effort educating Japanese trainees, who are given international exposure by the organization to come to Europe, New York – but in terms of local staff we don't. We would far rather go out and hire people who someone else has done the donkey work with, done the basic training with.

'Now if they show some aptitude for the business then I don't mind taking them on to my team; fine-tuning things and honing down the rough edges because I've got a raw article there which has been educated to a degree by someone else. So I'll go out and try and hire someone on that basis, who's done the very hard work. And there aren't too many of these banks around these days.'

Why? Why do they do it? What attracts people to the gruelling hours of often remorseless, unrelenting toil, the nerve-wearing unpredictability?

The money. Most mention that first and frankly. Given their backgrounds and conventional occupational attributes they enjoy higher remuneration, which is interpreted as a better lifestyle, than they could expect elsewhere.

There are other factors. And the appeal of these reflects their personalities, their competitiveness and controlled aggressiveness.

Steve Harris acknowledged that 'beating the competition' gives his job its main non-pecuniary attraction. 'I'd say that's probably more than anything else.'

How in such a market can he possibly know whether he has beaten the competition?

'You know. You know at the end of the day whether you've traded well. It's like a soccer player. You might play in the team that only wins one-nil. You know your part in that, you've played a tremendous part during the game and you know at the end of the day when you go home and reflect on the day whether you've traded well or not. I know at the end of every day whether I've traded well.

'And what everyone likes about the job is you can come in at the start of the day and you never know what's going to happen. You can never anticipate. No two days are the same really, that's what make the job so exciting.'

'It's the buzz of getting it right, it's the buzz of outwitting the market,' testifies Trevor Cass. 'A colleague of mine talks about it in the sense of a game of poker. 'There are a number of cards they're dealt out, each individual has a set of cards in front of him. He'll have different suits and some court cards.

And the way he plays those will be partly predicated on his knowledge of what the other hands are – who holds what, where – and that will dictate his play but he will also be playing to what he thinks the characteristics are of the various people: whether he thinks they're risk-averse or risk takers.

'Trading is something in a similar vein. We all know broadly what the issues are, we all essentially know what the figures published by the agencies are – capital flows, trade balance, invisibles, gaps, everything like that, unemployment figures and production stuff – and so what we make of them individually is up to us. We play our cards in the game on a daily basis and those of who are successful get a tremendous kick out of doing it.

'I really believe the money used to be secondary but I think that over the last ten years – when the rewards have become very much higher – clearly the need to earn a lot of money is rather like a snowball effect. It feeds upon itself.

'So there's that driving it as well but really I think that there's a tremendous buzz that comes out of getting it right. And that's feeding an ego and the ego is linked-in to the self-belief issue. If you have self-belief you certainly have an ego. If you have an ego you need to feed that ego. How do you feed it? This is clearly a circular argument.'

And there's the money. It should be enough to satisfy most egos. Even outsize ones, perhaps.

A trainee broker would in early 1994 start at a salary of £8,000 to £10,000 a year which Tony Porter describes as 'barely enough net of tax to cover their rail fares.' Those who stay the course can expect to peak at somewhere in the £100–120,000 range, including performance-related bonus and various allowances. Tony Martin, in charge of Marshall's two teams on $:DM and rated the tops as an active dealer in the spot market, might expect in the region of £200,000 gross.

A senior trader at a bank would gets £50–75,000 a year basic remuneration, a chief dealer £80–120,000 and in each case the bonus can double that.

It looks a lot. It is a lot.

In the parlance of the markets, foreign exchange broking

and dealing is 'a footballer's career.' The analogy is a good one.

These people I'm meeting on the dealing desks are the Premier League players. They've risen above the bank-clerking ranks of part-time professionals in the minor league clubs, fought their way up through the divisions to the top.

There they may earn several times as much as their soccer counterparts and on a par with top international stars but only about one fifth as much as the leading international model who struts her stuff on the catwalks of Paris, Rome, New York.

One important difference is that they are paid on performance. That can be, and is, measured individually and precisely to the last dollar. Stop scoring and you're out.

And like a footballer's career, it is short-lived.

'You put your balls on the line all day long and if you don't perform, if you don't meet your targets, you're out,' says Joe Green. 'You can make a lot of money in a short space of time. It's a bit like a footballer. A footballer's career is over really when he's in his early – mid 30's. There's a saying you're only as good as your last deal. And it's true.'

They call it burn-out.

It happens to brokers. Eugene Quinlan is thirty-one. 'People do burn out, yes definitely,' he told me. 'You have enough of it after ten years' (pause) 'fifteen years.' (He has been in the business eleven years.)

The traders still active on the dealing desks know it happens and accept the fact. 'I should, at twenty-nine, be coming to the peak of my career,' Steve volunteered spontaneously.

Joe Green, his partner, is twenty-four. ('He looks about forty-four, doesn't he?' says Steve.) 'Late twenties, early thirties is probably the time you're at your best,' says Joe. 'Generally people at that stage have been doing the job five, or six or seven years, know the market quite well and at that sort of age can handle the pressure. Particularly on the high-pressure job like $:DM you'll see fewer and fewer people over the age of thirty-three, thirty-four, thirty-five doing the job.'

But while agreeing that it happens, they disagree about the cause. Some accept it as an intrinsic characteristic of the job, others blame lifestyles (with the implication that they can escape it).

'It depends on the individual,' suggests Andre Katz. 'Some people burn the candle at both ends. You start trading at 21 and five years later they've been going out every night and they're still going out. Sure, you're going to burn your body out and you're going to feel tired before your age comes up.

'Ten years ago people would say that a forex dealer wouldn't still be at his best by the time he reached his early thirties.'

Acknowledges Joe Green, 'Aside from the actual dealing there's a fair amount of entertaining going on and I'm twenty-four and it can get you. You know: two or three evenings a week and you soon start to feel the pace.'

For each of them, entertaining the customers and counter-parts is an integral part of the job, often essential to sustaining a relationship constantly under pressure during the day's terse contacts.

'You meet on a regular basis at buffets which brokers put on,' says Andre Katz. 'We put buffets on. When you go into the City and go into a restaurant or a bar for a drink you always bump into someone from the market.

'It's unique. They don't have the set-up in New York, I think. They go to their job and they don't want to know the other guy at the other bank.

'In London you've got to create a relationship so you get information. Like for instance Deutsche Bank called up and said they think the Banque de France is in the DM:Paris. They've given me information hoping that I give them information. I'll take a position and hopefully we'll make some money. It's important to see the business, to see the flows, to make money and the only way to do that is to get out and meet people.'

This aspect of the job, undoubtedly enjoyable, can become demanding. And it can easily become a chore adding to the premature male menopause. 'There's a good social life if you want to get involved,' acknowledges Steve Harris. 'That's probably why you'll find people at thirty to thirty-two looking a lot older than they actually are because they work hard but they also play hard.'

It can also impose strains on family life. Andre Katz's wife found it hard to accept at first that he needed to be out for sometimes several evenings a week of business entertaining. Now, with a two-year-old baby daughter, he makes a lot of effort to see and stay with them at the weekends. 'If my wife wants to go out or if she wants to have the neighbours or friends round, then, although I've been out a reasonable amount, I make an effort.' Somehow, he also manages to squeeze in a morning's golf at the weekend, however.

Whether it is hedonism or the fatigue and nervous stress of the work itself which causes them to burn out, all the dealers can cite you the exceptions, the traders who somehow manage to go on year after year with apparently undiminished energy, enthusiasm and effectiveness.

'We've had traders who've been quoting up to the age of almost forty who were as good a year ago as they were when they were twenty-eight or twenty-nine,' asserts Joe. 'And they're still in the bank and still going ahead. They've been quoting, they've been in the firing line, since they were twenty-one or twenty-two. So it depends on the individual: your mentality and how you cope with it.'

From the assurance that comes from being a managing director with a future beyond the $:DM broking he heads at MW Marshall, thirty-three-year-old Tony Martin accepts that he won't add many more to the thirteen years he has been on the desk but points out his right-hand man: 'Dave's forty, he's still going. He's been doing it twenty years, he's still going. It's a shorter career than most careers but I think that people exaggerate it a bit when they say you're over the hill at thirty-five or whatever. You can prolong your career.'

Nomura Bank International's Tom Elliot affirms that in five years the average age of foreign exchange traders in the London market has risen from twenty-eight to thirty-two. That reflects, however, the effect of banks' having concentrated a wave of redundancies on younger trainees rather than revenue-generating seniors.

'I heard all that stuff when I first came to London at twenty-three,' recalls Tom, 'and I was told that without doubt by the time I was thirty I'd be looking for a domestic branch banking job again with Bank of Scotland and inevitably that would be back in Scotland because you can't last the pace of this business beyond the age of thirty, because you don't have the mental dexterity for that.

'But I do agree that mental dexterity is very much a part of the stress and strains of short-end market making; the guys, the spot traders, who are making all day long. That's a very tiring — an exhausting — area of activity and if you restrict yourself to that area then perhaps your lifespan is going to be fairly limited, a footballer's career.

'There are a lot of casualties, people who are past their sell-by dates, who didn't — may not have had the ability, let's say, or just have not — moved with the times.'

The evidence, however, is unmistakable. Look around any dealing room and you will not find many active dealers beyond their late thirties.

Inherent in the job or simply overpaid young men living foolishly? Trevor Cass, having experienced it and survived into the higher reaches of bank management, suggests that the factors causing burn-out lie deeper in the psyche. 'The ability to trade forex is an ability which, like some others in life, once you light that particular candle it has a finite life,' he suggests. 'You might light that candle at aged thirty or twenty-five or thirty-three.

'If the candle burns for ten years because you are what you are, then it burns for ten years and that's it. It's a temporal ability, it has its life within you and at the end of it, you know it's over. You've either become bored by it, by the game, or you're intellectually curious about other things or you find it doesn't excite you any more.

'What was a very stimulating, exciting business in the end becomes boring. That's a personal view but if it happens to me then I guess that perhaps I'm not totally exceptional and I reckon in a way it happens to a lot of other people.

'And I suppose in a way it's the triviality of it all that becomes very boring. Although we're talking about enormous amounts of money and we're talking about movements that wash across boundaries in terms of capital flows and what have you, in the end God help us if there isn't more to life than buying and selling currencies or commodities.'

While agreeing with Trevor Cass that it is so intensely personal, Tony Porter can afford to affect some equally personal amusement. A newspaper article about the foreign exchange markets years ago referred to burn-out at thirty-five immediately below its picture of Tony Porter in the classic position of holding two phones. When his wife recently came across the newspaper cutting she framed it and put it in Porter's gymnasium where at age forty-seven he works out each morning.

'It depends on the individual. David 'Alice' Cooper has always been a character in the market and he'll always be the Peter Pan of the market and he'll never burn out. It's almost a drug to him. Chris Lewis round the desk. He worked for me and I've been off the desk quite a few years. He's got to be forty-three or forty-four. He will never burn out because he never caught up, but he has this other magnetism. There's an element of the customer base that really trusts in him, believes in him and is prepared to see him do the business on their behalf. He's a survivor and he has that persona that has this element of customer base.'

But those are the exceptions. What of the rest? What happens to foreign exchange brokers and dealers who have burnt out?

As with football, where a club will have perhaps twenty-five or thirty players for its first and reserve teams but only one manager and one coach, the foreign exchange dealers who make it into management are few indeed.

'If you haven't made it into management by thirty-five or forty, what are you going to do with the rest of your life?' observes Peter Maltz. 'You have a working span of less than twenty years, possibly only ten and not all of those are at the top.'

Commercial success and a fast-growing international business have enabled a broking firm such as Marshall to cushion the blow. 'We have sought to bring down the retiring age,' Tony Porter told me. 'The retiring age anyway for the pension scheme is fifty-five but with the ability to take free-standing pension schemes which are geared into fifty – and in an ideal world we'd like to run it down to forty-five – there haven't been too many casualties at the moment.

'They don't stay in the spot forex necessarily but there's the forward areas which are a bit slower. There's public relations. We have a big workforce writing reports, going to see the customer – salesmen if you like.

'There has been a process of job creation but some will say "I've had enough. I've earned my money and I'll ride off into the sunset and do something else".'

But Marshall is known in its markets for being humane to its staff without compromising the quality of its customer service in an almost ruthlessly competitive business. The sustainability of its approach when there are more senior passengers to carry, when the volume of currency trading dips or even just slows in its growth, is questionable.

Barclays, like other banks and many brokers, views burn-out as a fact of life which has to be lived with. 'There's this period when it works and then it stops working,' Trevor Cass told me. 'When it stops working then you find people have to decide what they're going to do with the rest of their lives and there are a whole range of options which people have, predicated essentially on the fact that during the ten, or twenty, or however many years it's worked for them they've been able to amass sufficient wealth to make them relatively independent or at least able to make choices.

'In that case you'll see some people go out of the business altogether, go and open antique shops or something else. Some would go into smaller banks – we've seen that very often – and a minority would progress within the bank, would progress up the ladder within their own institution, or within like institutions, being more managers and less proactive traders, thinking more of strategy and less of day-to-day or minute-by-minute movements.

'A few will fall by the wayside for whatever reason and will fall out of our sight.'

10

INVESTORS

Who Uses the Markets is the Markets

Who moves the foreign exchange markets? Not the people who make markets but the people who use them. Not the foreign exchange brokers at the heart of the market: they cannot speculate or even trade on their own account but can execute only the orders they are given. Not the dealers in the bank dealing rooms: they are limited in the position they can take during and at the end of the day. However much they speculate in one direction during the day, they largely unwind – taking profit or loss – before they close.

Not even the central banks, even though they sometimes try to influence exchange rates and – if they coordinate their intervention and are realistically modest in their aims – may enjoy transient results. 'With exchange markets as large and active as those of the present day, central bank intervention can only have limited effect in influencing exchange rate movements and even then only if tactics and timing are handled skilfully,' says Bank of England associate director Ian Plenderleith. They were powerless to keep sterling in the ERM in September 1992 or the ERM itself together in any meaningful sense in July 1993.

There are, of course, companies which trade internationally and establish manufacturing units in several countries. International trade in 1992 was about $4000 billion and, according to UNCTAD*, companies invested outside their home countries about $150 billion on direct investment (that is, in the tangible means of producing and selling goods, rather than in shares).

* World Investment Report published by United Nations, November 1993

Trade and direct investment would together account for fewer than five days' trading on the foreign exchange markets that year. They are what currency markets are for; it is to service them that currency markets exist. They affect exchange rates in line with economic fundamentals. At the same time, trade and investment are influenced by exchange rates and these diverge from economic fundamentals in response to the behaviour of other players.

These other players include the banks' proprietary traders, less time-sensitive than the dealers on the desks, and investing their banks' capital for weeks, perhaps months, in speculative positions; institutional investors, such as insurance companies and pension funds, which have considerably increased their investment in overseas bonds and shares while separating out the currency element; the so-called hedge funds, often based offshore and thus beyond the control of regulatory authorities, of which Quantum Fund run by Mr George Soros is by far the best known.

One central bank, Malaysia's Bank Negara, is the maverick of the markets. Other central banks, burdened with their awesome national and international responsibilities, act with considerable restraint in the foreign exchange markets. Negara trades the market for what it can scalp.

The Bank of England, the US Fed, the Bundesbank and others, may intervene to influence exchange rates and smooth markets which are becoming disorderly. Negara is often blamed for causing sharp swings in the markets. Its attitude towards the markets appears to be different from the rest.

Other central banks, for national policy reasons, deploy their currency reserves to influence exchange rates and recognize that properly functioning markets are a matter of international interest, part of a central bank's wider responsibilities. Negara makes forays into the markets, trying to turn a profit to boost its reserves, often causing disruption and never seeming to care about its effect on the markets.

'They are probably the most active central bank in the foreign exchange markets globally,' says Tom Elliot, head of foreign exchange dealing at Nomura Bank International.

'Whether they make or lose money, their involvement in the market is always sufficient to massage the price action.'

Rumours that Negara lost $4 billion in the foreign exchange markets by going 'long' in exact contra-position to George Soros gained credence when the bank's 1992 accounts showed a M$10 billion ($3.9 billion) charge against special contingency funds, arising from a loss in its gold and foreign currency reserve holdings. The bank's annual report also admitted to a M$2.7 billion contingent liability on forward foreign exchange transactions. The fall in the reserves was equivalent to the government's yearly spending on development. Yet even after this it remained an aggressive and apparently reckless trader in currencies.

'I wouldn't recognize Bank Negara as a counterparty in the marketplace,' says Tom Elliot, willing to say openly what I found many in the currency markets, feel but few dare express. 'They utilize the illiquid markets to their advantage and contribute nothing in return. They choose when they want to be involved and invariably they want to be involved at highly volatile, generally speaking illiquid, times.

'And you can't specify whether it's going to be mid-morning, lunchtime or late in the afternoon because it can be any of those times. It's not the only time they're involved – that would be unfair – but there's evidence to suggest that the majority of their activity occurs only when liquidity is extremely strained and, therefore, by executing those orders that they've done, the impact on the price will become more pronounced.

'Historically, Negara has raised eyebrows at other central banks when, to use Malaysian government officials' own phrase, they have massaged their reserves through the Deutschmark, dollar or yen.

'The activity of Negara is not supported by the central banks within the G7. It's seen to be maverick and cavalier. There are no other central banks which adopt that type of activity.'

In January 1994 Bank Negara declared war on 'currency speculators' in the Malaysian dollar. Then, at the end of March, it admitted to having incurred further foreign exchange losses, of M\$5.7 billion (\$2.1 billion), in 1993. These might have been greater but for the bank's ploy in driving down the Malaysian dollar in December 1993, thereby raising the value of its foreign currency reserves so that they appeared less depleted than in fact they had been.

The bank governor, Jaffar Hussein resigned; fittingly perhaps, on 1 April. He was quickly followed by the head of Negara's foreign exchange operations, Mohamed Yakcop. Many locals saw them as scapegoats. Finance minister Anwar Ibrahim rejected opposition calls for an official investigation on the basis that the facts were known and the culprits had resigned.

'There was neither any fraudulent practice nor were there any individuals benefiting from the losses incurred,' he said. 'Errors were committed and this entailed huge losses.' The term 'to run amok' is of Malay origin.

Ordinary commercial banks make considerable profits out of foreign exchange trading. One of America's four banking regulators, the Comptroller of the Currency, says that in the four years 1990–3 inclusive, New York moneycentre banks – the nearest equivalent to high street banks in Britain – made half their profits from foreign exchange business. At one of them, Citicorp, foreign exchange profits have averaged \$500 million a year. In Britain, Barclays' trading income from foreign exchange was £220 million in 1991, £288 million in 1992 and £302 million in 1993. Wall Street investment bank Salomon Brothers tripped up in the markets during 1993 but still made \$416 million from proprietary trading. The previous year it had made \$1.4 billion.

The banks are restricted in the gambles they can take. Talk to a bank dealer on the desks or a trader taking longer-term positions in currencies and the subject of their limits quickly surfaces. These they regard as the maximum exposure they are allowed to incur – the most they may have outstanding – in any currency during and (a lower figure) at the end of the day; limits which for reasons of prudence the Bank of England imposes.

The Bank of England, however, sees them slightly differently. 'We don't like to call them limits,' banking supervision manager Richard Allen told me. 'We like to call them guidelines.

'The difference is a subtle one. It's a soft limit. It's designed in such a way that we don't mind if people exceed it, within reason, and it's set at such a level that it will be exceeded at times and when it is exceeded that gives us an indication that the level of business or the manner of business has changed.'

Then, within a trading room itself, the chief trader or foreign exchange manager will give out certain limits to his traders, depending on how good they are, how experienced they are, what sort of currency they trade and what level of trading relates to corporate activity.

The limit may be larger in a currency which does not move very much because the risk is smaller but the dealer would also need to take a larger position to make worthwhile profits. That would apply to anyone trading in the DM:Netherlands guilder. Limits will be tighter for anyone dealing with erratic currencies such as, recently, the Scandinavian currencies.

Other factors can make vital differences between theory and practice. Guy Hurley, proprietary trader at Barclays Bank, told me, 'I try and stay away from things like dollar to Deutschmarks because everyone in the world's trading them.

'What I'm looking at actually is weird crosses no one else is looking at: Finmarks against Stockie (Swedish krona), pound to lira, that kind of stuff. I try and trade in things no one else is trading because if no one else is trading them then no one else is looking at them. Therefore it's easier to make money out of them.'

As a proprietary trader Guy runs his own book for the bank, never quoting prices and never dealing with customers. 'It's just me and my computers – I've got three of them – and the longest I've ever run a position is three months. The shortest is about two seconds. It just depends how the position holds.'

Compared with colleagues on the dealing desks who must make prices to customers, he has, he says, much more flexible exposure limits. 'I'm not officially marked to market every night [his positions are revalued at closing market prices to show the overall profit or loss at that moment] because if you are, psychologically you know you've got a position and it's quite a big position and you might have sold at the end of the day and the revalue might be much higher.

'You're going home with a £50,000 loss on your book. Now it's not really a loss but that's just because of the way you've been revalued. But it makes life pretty difficult if you're going home with a big loss on the book like that. So they don't officially revalue us although you know – and they have a good idea of – whether the book is looking good or bad.'

More critically, the size of position he will take must, he insists, be considered in the context of the market.

'I had a big position last night, given the liquidity of the market, given the way the market was moving and the volatility of the market and given the time of the year and liquidity involved. It was DM50:lira. The way to work out whether that's a big position or not, it's not about absolute numbers, is to take the standard deviation of that and work out how much you could lose given a two standard deviation move overnight based on the last ... I don't know – month. I haven't actually done the numbers on that, I could do it very easily.'

Because banking is an international business, governments have been concerned about the possible domino effect around the world of a major bank going down. But they have also been concerned that if banking regulations in one country are lax, its banks may have an unfair competitive advantage.

Capital adequacy is the name of the issue. A bank's own capital acts as a financial buffer to ensure that even when some borrowers default on their loans, the bank is able fully to repay its depositors and other lenders. A bank which is under-capitalized and sailing very close to the wind, however, has a competitive advantage over one which has the burden of meeting out of its fees the costs of servicing a heavier share capital.

International rules being introduced to create fair competition and avert the risk of an international banking collapse differentiate between various types of risk a bank may run. It need not worry about money lent to its own government for instance, as much as about a loan covering the whole cost of a speculative shopping development in London Docklands. The rules about how much capital banks should set aside to cover their foreign exchange exposures and how risks should be measured have stirred considerable technical controversy.

However enlightened the regulatory regime of the Bank of England, there is some restraint on the banks. There is none on the big investors, the institutions. Most notable of late have been the US pension funds. UK pension funds and insurance companies, wearily aware of Britain's economic under performance over the decades, needed no urging to spread their investments worldwide. As soon as exchange controls became ineffective in late 1979 they began investing abroad. US pension funds discovered the joys of global diversification more recently and they are bigger than their UK counterparts. Much bigger. The amount of capital they export each year to investments around the rest of the world doubled between in 1993 to $46 billion. Earlier years' outflows, and the growth of the investments they bought, meant that the pension funds had $260 billion of securities in their portfolios outside the USA.

Their liabilities – to pay pensions – are in dollars. So that is $260 billion of currency risk to be covered, together with however much they add each year. Today, they manage that currency risk separately from the underlying investment in bonds or shares. The popular technique is called currency overlay.

'Technology, innovation, free capital mobility and investors' desire for international portfolio diversification have by now all combined to increase vastly the potential for shifting large amounts of capital around the world, and across currencies, at great speed,' observes the Bank for International Settlements.

'For, even leaving aside outright speculation and also the relatively new highly leveraged 'hedge funds', far more investors now have an interest in exchange rate developments than formerly. In other words, even the managers of the traditionally conservative institutions such as pension and insurance funds, as well as retail investors, must now necessarily take account of perceived exchange rate prospects – and they doubtless do.'*

Connecticut consultancy firm Rogers, Casey found in a survey of US funds that more than half of them expected active currency management of their international investments to increase and 71 per cent expected currency overlay to reduce the volatility of these investments. Howard Flight, joint managing director of fund management group Guinness Flight, claims they pioneered the use of various financial instruments and derivatives and what he calls 'efficient portfolio management techniques' to manage currency exposure separately. But he insists it remains an integral part of the fund management.

'We don't believe that separate currency overlay as a service makes any sense at all,' he told me, 'because unless you know what has been factored into the initial investment strategy and decisions you don't know how far you should go and you may in a sense be over-egging the cake.

'So our position is that it is natural and appropriate – particularly for international bond portfolios – to manage the two separately but really it is better done by the same manager.'

The firepower behind this whole movement is growing apace. No longer is international investment, with or without separate currency management (or speculation?) the sole preserve of big investors.

As US interest rates dropped, Americans searching to maintain the return on their savings withdrew money from bank deposits and put them into mutual funds (the US equivalent of Britain's unit trusts), largely those investing in fixed interest bonds rather than ordinary shares. At the end of 1993 US mutual funds deployed a sum equivalent to 85 per cent of the amount banks held in deposits, compared with only 10 per cent ten years earlier.

And this popularization is growing more widespread. British savers are now subjected to the blandishments of US stock-

* BIS 63rd annual report to 31.3.93

broking firm Charles Schwab which offers them the chance to invest in any of fifty bond, share or currency money funds without any transaction charges. You can buy or sell twenty-four hours a day, seven days a week.

This, after a fashion, is bringing to the masses what the very rich have been able to get from hedge funds such as those run by George Soros.

Who's afraid of the big bad wolf?

A great deal has been said about hedge funds, with the misleading implication that a great deal is known about them. Fears about hedge funds may prove to have been more misdirected than exaggerated. First of all, what are they?

'There is no precise legal definition of leveraged or hedge funds and they come in a variety of forms,' comments Bank of England associate director, Ian Plenderleith. 'The term is loosely used to refer to investment vehicles structured so as to be exempt from a number of regulatory requirements and therefore able to enjoy flexible investment strategies and objectives.

'One feature that many hedge funds do have in common is that they do not just run hedged positions. Their strategy typically involves taking both long and short positions, leveraging and using derivatives.

'Typically, such funds seek high minimum levels of investment from high-worth individuals. Most have their origins in the United States, where they can be based onshore, in which case they tend to be structured as private partnerships, or offshore, where they can be incorporated as closed or open-ended investment funds, and they may be listed on an exchange as well. The number of these funds and the amount they have under management have multiplied rapidly in the last few years.'

Because of difficulties of definition, the number of what may qualify as hedge funds is unknown. A Swiss bank offering private banking services to HNWIs – High Net Worth Individuals – may pool some of each client's funds into a collective international portfolio of currencies and manage these very actively. Few would call it a hedge fund and in the banking parlours along the Bahnhofstrasse from Zurich station to the lake they would bridle at such a description. But in essence the operation is the same. An unknown number of secretive hedge funds are registered offshore in tax havens around the world, secluded from prying eyes.

What differentiates Soros from his peers and imitators, apart from the success and scale of his operation, is his overtness. Michael Steinhardt of Steinhardt Partners, Julia Robertson Junior of Tiger Management, Bruce Kovner of Caxton Corporation and Paul Tudor Jones II of Tudor Investment are just the larger and better known hedge-fund managers. Unlike Soros they do not court public attention and are secretive, sometimes to extremes.

'Our knowledge of what hedge funds are doing and how they're doing it is still probably a bit sketchy,' Richard Allen told me at the Bank of England. 'They're really not operating from the UK. They're operating from the USA or offshore and we're still finding out about what they're doing but I would say that the main risk – the main concern that we would have – is if they were organizations or institutions setting up which were making markets in the underlying assets – that is actually making two-way prices.'

For as long as they are simply big investors roaming free, in other words, they are part of the markets and interference would probably do more harm than good. Deregulation of pension fund and insurance fund investment has been, after all, a worldwide trend – alongside freedom of capital movements – with benign effects. It is if the hedge funds stood alongside the banks and started being market-makers rather than market users that the Old Lady of Threadneedle Street might feel concern.

'They would then become the people that we would regard as needing to be supervised,' says Richard Allen. 'The need for supervision is where you have someone making a two-way market in something and where they are large enough to have a major market impact. It's difficult to justify supervising a corporate because it will usually be an end-user, and whether customers should be supervised is an interesting question, but in my view the supervision should be of the market-maker, not of the end-user.'

The House of Representatives banking committee held Congressional hearings on the possible dangers of hedge funds in early to mid-April 1994. The USA's own regulatory authorities testified that hedge funds pose no potential risks calling for fresh legislation. 'Hedge funds do not pose a significant risk to the national banking system,' advised Eugene Ludwig, who as Comptroller of the Currency monitors a large part of the US banking system.

'It is important to recognize that hedge funds are not fundamentally different from other institutions,' argued one of the Federal governors, John Laware.

George Soros himself argued persuasively that it was not the hedge funds but mutual funds (unit trusts) the committee should be looking at because these were by definition trend followers. However, Securities & Exchange Commission chairman Arthur Levitt said he was 'concerned about the risks that could be posed to our markets by the activities of some of these large, very active and aggressive hedge funds'.

Hedge funds have their origins back in the 1920s when investment professionals on Wall Street put together moneyed people into 'market pools'. These operated very aggressively going long or short of a limited selection of stocks the professional tracked closely. Often they would focus on just one stock such as, for instance the Radio Corporation of America pool of which Joseph Kennedy, US Ambassador to Britain and father of John F., was a member.

The immediate successor to that concept came from the Wall Street firm of AW Jones which in the 1950s and 1960s organized investment partnerships – which are not so tightly regulated – and said they did not know which way the market was going so would always have a neutral position overall against the market. They would do so, however, by being 50 per cent short of the stocks they thought most overvalued and 50 per cent long of the stocks they saw as cheapest. As the long and short positions balanced, the fund would be neutral in its overall market stance but be backing its views on individual stocks.

It was managers of such funds and their imitators who set up their own aggressive investment vehicles which would seek out opportunities in non-US securities – a daring concept to Americans at the time – in commodities and currencies. 'They have moved from fifty/fifty to enormous leverage,' comments Michael Lipper of Lipper Analytical, long regarded in the US securities industry as the most authoritative research firm on the securities and fund management companies. 'It is not unusual to see assets ten or even twenty times their equity base.'

Tom Elliot of Nomura Bank endorses the lower of those figures. In his experience, hedge funds put up capital in cash or near-cash – in Treasury bills, cash bunds or gilts – as security with the bank for their margin and may leverage ten times, depending on the types of currency risk they are undertaking. They must then transact the business through the bank which is giving them the facility.

'When the position in the market starts losing money we can make a margin call – require the client to put up more cash to restore his percentage margin – and we have the right if he doesn't meet it to close him out,' Tom explains. Thus, should the market fall 10 per cent and the client fail to put up any fresh funds, the bank would sell the entire position, wiping out the client's money but incurring no loss itself.

'These speculative funds run their ship pretty close to home really,' comments Tom Elliot. 'They sail close to the wind but if the investment they have made goes offside by 1–1.5 per cent then they're all running for cover.'

Leveraging up on a ten-to-one basis would mean that the known hedge funds may in March 1994 – when their losses in bond markets were causing concern to central banks – have had the capacity to run total exposure of $1,000 billion, twice what was then estimated. Michael Lipper endorses the higher figure. 'Individual big players are as big as the central banks themselves,' he notes. Moreover, that $1,000 billion of gross assets which he and others estimate hedge funds may control, is roughly equal to the sum total of official reserves in the world's central banks.

The two are not equal, however. Central banks have much greater potential to borrow further foreign currency if the need should ever arise. An even slight adverse movement in the markets, on the other hand, can maim a hedge fund.

Subject to that qualification, however, they have considerable firepower, are outside the control of any regulatory authority and because they are not subject to limits, can keep open their positions for weeks on end, perhaps able by that greater stamina sometimes to move the markets at will.

Does it matter? Markets allocate resources. When you go down your local high street and study the savings market – banks and building society windows and the like – you probably would not leave much money in a bank deposit paying only 3 per cent if the building society were offering 8 per cent. The resources of your savings will be allocated to housing because that offers a better return than the banks can earn on lending to their customers.

But markets also provide signals. My neighbour judges from market prices whether it is more profitable to grow courgettes or cauliflower. Hedge funds may not cause misallocation of resources but they may distort the signal markets are giving.

'For policymakers the challenge is therefore to adapt to the consequences of the flows these funds can generate, which are large enough at times to amplify substantially the messages the market is seeking to deliver,' says Ian Plenderleith. 'For regulators, the challenge is not one of investor protection – since the investors have deliberately chosen not to be protected – but rather to seek so far as possible to ensure that the risks which the main, supervised market participants are running are reasonable, that management understand those risks and that sufficient capital is held against them.'

The concern, in other words, is not that the people who invest in hedge funds might lose their money. They've brought that on their own heads – arguably through their greed – and deserve no sympathy. But the danger worrying central banks is of hedge funds losing on a scale which hits the banks as well.

*   *   *

'Everyone who's seen their interest rates come down by 6 per cent should go up to George Soros and shake his hand,' declares Michael Northeast, treasurer of the Dixons electrical retailing group. He was referring to the way Soros supposedly bet $10 billion against sterling staying in the ERM and made nearly $1 billion profit helping to force it out on Wednesday, 16 September 1992. Did this one man force events, thwarting the will of the elected British Government? The overwhelming consensus is that he just recognized the inevitable – was not alone in doing so – and moved both nimbly and daringly.

'Had George Soros not been there then maybe the market would have staggered on until the result of the French referendum and then the pound would have got some support at that stage,' concludes Roger Bootle, chief economist at Midland Bank. 'But the fundamentals were so much against the pound when you look back now.

'What state would we have been in had we stayed in the ERM? It's pretty clear we had to come out or at least devalue substantially.'

The limitations to his power have been well demonstrated. Soros wrote in the French newspaper, *Le Figaro*, on Monday 26 July 1993 that he would not join the attack on the French franc. The so-called 'franc fort' policy he described as having popular support.

Within days – after the Bundesbank had on Thursday 29 July decided against an interest rate cut – he sent a fax to Reuters to say that he was no longer bound by that previous statement. He later told the *New York Times* that he had not sold francs ahead of Friday noon, New York time (which would be six o'clock Paris time).

Moreover, when in February 1994 the Fed raised US interest rates by a mere 0.25 per cent, that triggered a collapse in bond markets because hedge funds had quickly to limit their losses. Quantum Fund, which is just the largest in the Soros stable, lost $600 million in a single day.

Quantum has suffered such misjudgements before, most notably in the 1987 crash of stock markets around the world

when Soros bet that Tokyo would fall furthest and pulled his
money back into Wall Street. He got it wrong. Wall Street fell
but Tokyo was comparatively resilient. Nevertheless, Quantum
came out ahead on that year as a whole. Its average return,
income and capital combined, has been about 30 per cent – a
year.

If you had put $100,000 into Quantum in 1969 it would by
the end of 1993 have grown to $80 million. But you couldn't
have put in $10,000 instead, Quantum does not accept petty
sums. The fund is officially based offshore, registered in the
island of Curacao in the Netherlands Antilles. Forget any idea
of Mr Soros luxuriating in the sun-soaked Caribbean, picking
investments from the poolside, however.

First, Curacao is a dump. A massive oil refinery makes the
place the equivalent of Canvey Island but hotter and more
uncomfortable. When reporting on the Eurocurrency markets
took me there in the mid 1970s the only sightseeing 'attraction'
any taxi driver could suggest was a brothel – provided for
tanker crews – consisting of rows of wooden huts behind a
high wall and looking at best like a barracks, at worst a concentration camp.

George Soros lives on Fifth Avenue, New York City. Quantum Fund and most of the rest of his fund management empire
operates out of the 33rd floor of a midtown Manhattan sky-
scraper overlooking Central Park. They can stay there so long
as they do not sell investments directly and knowingly to US
citizens. The Curacao registration means that the funds are
legally offshore from the USA so the rich Europeans who are
its investors pay no US taxes on their further accretions of
wealth. It also means that Quantum is exempt from the US
Securities & Exchange Commission's reporting requirements.
And everyone else's.

Most unit trusts or mutual funds – which, like Quantum,
are open-ended – sell to new investors at a premium over their
net asset value and redeem – buy shares back – from existing
investors at a discount to asset value. For Quantum, however,
the management sets the premium with no obvious relationship to asset value at the time. Soros and a close circle seem

to benefit from this arrangement considerably more than the client investors.

George Soros describes himself as a philosopher manqué. His first book, *The Burden of Consciousness*, written as a student, has not been published. Born in Budapest in 1930, he achieved the considerable feat of surviving as a Jew throughout the Nazi era by living under assumed names. He left Hungary in 1947 and, two years later, became a student at the London School of Economics before moving on to New York.

One of his two published books, *The Alchemy of Finance* published in 1987 – just as he was misjudging the stock markets he was offering the public an insight into his thinking – argues the importance of imperfect understanding in investment. What he terms the 'theory of reflexivity' can be simplified as the argument (beloved of many chartists) that it is irrational psychology rather than theoretical models, which drives markets.

With a modest rather than opulent lifestyle – socializing with intellectuals rather than plutocrats – he is a philanthropist on an unstinting scale, particularly in the countries of the former Soviet bloc – his other published work is called *Underwriting Democracy* – and makes no effort to conceal the extent of his benefaction.

While other offshore hedge-fund managers can make Trappists seem like blabbermouths, Soros has in recent years taken to announcing publicly some of his major strategic decisions. There was the incident with the French franc but also his forays into gold and property. It was not always so, recalls Tom Elliot of Nomura Bank, 'Quantum has in a short period gone from being very protective of its activity to being very visual and open to the media, comfortable talking about its position. If we go back as recently as 1990 then very few people knew the activities of Quantum Fund and they were very protective.'

What is the value of this exhibitionism? It would appear to move the market against him. Unless he were to make public decisions only after he has taken that stance in the market, at which point he might benefit from the announcement effect: of followers moving the price in what is now his favour.

As hedge funds, bank proprietary traders and other specu-lators pour ever increasing amounts into the foreign exchange markets, chasing a turn to be made from anomalies, the sheer weight of money chasing the slightest disparity must reduce their profit margins. It then takes ever larger sums to earn ever smaller turns in the market.

'The hedge funds need high leverage to make worthwhile profits out of small movements in the currency markets,' remarks Michael Lipper of Lipper Analytical. 'But it means that when they lose, they lose big.'

Howard Flight is dismissive of the idea that big speculators can force market movements which will then give them a profit. 'It's a false thesis to think that that's what drives exchange rates.

'Those sort of operations are only successful when all the other odds are stacked in their favour and moreover, people naturally tend to want only to do them when the arguments are staring at you as to what ought to happen.

'Therefore you can turn it entirely on its head and say the governments and central banks are endeavouring to maintain something which is economically not really sustain-able and the speed and aggressiveness with which markets get round to unwinding it varies but inevitably includes crescendos.'

Richard Noble, currency and fixed income investment strat-egist at Wall Street investment bankers Salomon Bros, built quantitative models and would look for relationships which diverged. 'Then you get in and as they converge you get out.

'If you continuously buy all the way up in a rising market and then sell all the way down you end up not making any money. You have to take a risk – a divergence position. Wait for something to get cheap and then you buy it. Wait for it to get expensive again and sell it.'

Mr Soros and his kind have to do that for diminishing returns. 'Over time, speculation eventually wipes out capital,' pronounces Michael Lipper.

Meantime, if the speculators who move the markets are chasing and correcting ever smaller moves then the wilder swings which have so troubled exporters and other international traders in the past, should be less frequent and less severe.

11

CORPORATE TREASURY
The Fountain-spring of Foreign Exchange

The Crown is according to the saying the
'fountain of honour'; but the Treasury is
the spring of business.

Walter Bagehot

Allied-Lyons, the food and drinks group, admitted in April
1991 that it had lost £150 million on speculation in the
currency markets. Out went the finance director, Cliff Hatch.
Chairman, Sir Derrick Holden-Brown, and chief executive,
Richard Martin, soon followed as the full facts of the débâcle
came to light.

In the previous July, the Bank of England had discreetly
warned the top management at this pillar of the British
business establishment that Allied-Lyons seemed to be overtrading in foreign exchange and had become the biggest player
in the foreign exchange market. Sir Derrick Holden-Brown,
one of the last bastions of 'the Beerage' – the wealthy families
which for centuries held Britain's breweries as their fiefdoms
– replied that Allied-Lyons was a big company.

Allied-Lyons had been a writer of currency options. Those
options which it sold gave the holders the right – but no obligation – to buy dollars from it at a fixed exchange rate. If the
dollar fell or failed to rise then the right to buy dollars cheaply
would be worthless and Allied-Lyons could simply book as
profit the money it had received in selling those options. But
the dollar did rise, sharply. The holders exercised their rights
to buy at the fixed exchange rate dollars which Allied-Lyons
had to buy at the ever-rising rate.

Showa Shell Sekiyu, the Japanese affiliate of the Royal Dutch/Shell oil giant, revealed in February 1993 that it had unrealized losses of about $1 billion from foreign exchange dealing. A secret group in Showa Shell's treasury had gambled that the dollar would rise against the yen. They were wrong. Exactly how big a loss they have incurred from a $6.4 billion forward exposure will depend on the movement of exchange rates for several years after the cupboard yielded up this skeleton, but President Bill Clinton's threat in February 1994 to drive the yen even higher against the dollar would not help matters.

Another Japanese oil company, Kashima Oil, admitted in early April 1994 to cumulative losses of Y153 billion ($1.5 billion) from guessing wrongly about the dollar.

Hanwa, the Japanese steel company, had in January 1994 to write off Y120 billion (then about £720 million) because its speculation in financial markets had gone wrong. A slide in Tokyo share prices didn't help but Mr Shigeru Kita, Hanwa's president, had given the company a formidable reputation as a currency speculator. It was one of the leading exponents of the speculative financial trading – *zaitech* – to which many Japanese companies became addicted, and from which some earned the greater part of their profits, before the speculative bubble burst.

'Of course everything was going their way,' comments Dr Brendan Brown, head of research at Mitsubishi Finance International. 'You could never discriminate in a bull market [when there is a general upward trend in prices] whether the treasurer is making his money because he is clever or just because the market is going up and you give him, maybe, the benefit of the doubt. That tends to feed activity.'

Corporate treasury is the fountain-head of foreign exchange trading. Foreign currency dealing between banks and between other speculators has today reached a level many times the volume of world trade and international capital investment, but it is from this source that all dealing springs. Without real movements of goods and investment, giving rise to payments with an underlying purpose, the speculators would as soon trade in rainfall as in currency.

'Of course there is a speculative element in the market but the great bulk of activity, we think, is geared to making sure you don't make losses from what you're doing,' says Terry Smeeton, head of the Bank of England's foreign exchange division, 'and behind that is the actual business of buying and selling goods between one country and another in trade. A lot of activity is by way of insurance to ensure you don't incur a loss for which you could be held responsible. Unless you took prudent hedging decisions to protect yourself against potential movements, then people would be vulnerable but that can so easily be characterized as speculation. That is what happens on the Continent where there are tremendous hang-ups about Anglo-Saxon speculation against the French franc, or Belgian franc, or whatever. That is quite misguided.

'There is now tremendous activity coming from French companies and Belgian companies who realize that they have a risk which they thought no longer existed.

'To undertake what appear to be quite simple transactions in foreign exchange – for instance the pound against French francs for a week tomorrow – you actually need to undertake several deals, so that all gets added into the total. That is easily the most important cause of the high turnover in foreign exchange markets. As I say, a lot of people are insuring themselves and taking prudent, protective action.'

I have cited some of the more egregious examples of corporate treasury going wrong. The scope is there for it to drive the entire fortunes of companies making anything from cars to cosmetics.

The textbook example is simple enough: a British company is selling goods abroad for foreign currencies but has to pay in pounds its wages and other costs of making those goods. The risk is that the foreign currency it is to receive will fall in value against sterling so that it does not cover cost or, at least, the profit diminishes significantly. The company treasurer, through the banks, undertakes financial operations to cover against that risk.

Come into the real world. First, manufacturing accounts for about 20 per cent of the British economy today. We import more manufactured goods than we export. (Sales of services to overseas customers make up the difference.) Second, treasurers not only have to deal with the immediate foreign currency risks of buying imports from abroad or selling overseas but also have to try to secure the company's competitive position for the future. And some may be more concerned not with real transactions but with how loans raised in foreign currencies or factories and other investments around the world will translate in the balance sheet. That can seem – and sometimes is – cosmetic. Not always, however. Ironically, it was getting that aspect of its affairs wrong which pushed J Lyons into the arms of what was then Allied Breweries nearly twenty years ago.

Redland, the building components group, operates in thirty-five countries, yet – because its products are bulky relative to their value – engages in almost negligible international trade. Apart from the occasional piece of aggregate crushing machinery or brick-making plant to be imported as capital equipment from Germany, group treasurer Stephen East is concerned not with international trade but with the consequences of Redland earning some 85 per cent of its profits, and having an appropriately large proportion of its assets, overseas.

For example, Redland's standing in the USA is such that it enjoys good access there to the commercial paper market – where companies borrow short-term funds for a few months by issuing IOUs which are tradable as securities. It also has large businesses in France. 'The cheapest way to fund them is to borrow dollars and use the foreign exchange market to buy French francs spot, sell them forward,' he told me. 'From a foreign exchange point of view that's all hedged out but we have borrowed our French francs cheaper than from a bank in France.

'We use the foreign exchange markets a great deal for generating the funding in the currency we actually want it in from the cheapest underlying source.'

Corporate treasury has been one of the UK's fastest-growing occupations. The professional body – the Association of Corporate Treasurers (ACT) - started with fewer than 400 members in 1979 and today has more than 1,800 together with about 1,000 students for what have become rigorous examinations.

Some companies have had someone with the title of treasurer since the 1920s but the role has been transformed. Sir David Lees, chief executive of GKN and previously its finance director, once told me how the role of their treasurer had been 'to lunch with the banks' keeping on good terms with them.

'It was the breakdown of the Bretton Woods system which meant that for the first time companies recognized that floating exchange rates could actually affect their profits,' recalls Gerald Leahy, former treasurer of Unilever and now director-general of the ACT. 'Chairmen were getting a bit fed up with standing up and explaining why the very good figures they'd expected, suddenly, when translated into the domestic currency, didn't look so good.'

Another major event was the lifting of exchange controls in 1979 which freed companies to invest abroad. Briefly, the role of the corporate treasurer appeared likely to diminish, as Britain joined the ERM. With fluctuations between EMS currencies so restricted, many had thought it no longer worth the transaction cost to hedge against such small risks. Some companies – and their treasurers – got a rude shock when the ERM fell apart and the risks rematerialized.

The predilection of companies to take foreign exchange management in-house rather than delegating it to the banks has been fortified by the trend – augmented by mergers and by the propensity of banks to throw money at uncreditworthy propositions – for companies to become larger and stronger relative to their banks.

This has meant they have been more creditworthy than the banks and so able to borrow in the money markets sometimes more cheaply than the banks can raise money, let alone what they charge for lending it. It has also meant that companies can command direct access to the foreign exchange markets, on a par with their banks.

'When I first got involved in foreign exchange twenty years ago,' recounts James Wrangham, treasurer of Courtaulds, 'you went to the account officer, who didn't know very much about foreign exchange, asked what you really wanted, rang the dealer (who was probably in a different building), got a rate from him. He rang you back and asked if it was okay. And you were probably doing the same thing with someone else. That was fairly inefficient.'

Banks tried plugging company treasurers straight through to their traders but that didn't work. The small size of each transaction was an encumbrance to the bank's trader almost as much as the treasurer's frequent wish to chat first about what was going on in the market. Today, all banks provide within their dealing room a dedicated dealer for customers, who transacts at the same rates as those the traders in his room are using.

Corporate treasurers stand shoulder to shoulder with the banks in the inter-bank market, getting exactly the same exchange rates (but not committed to the reciprocal obligation to quote a price). And their reach within their own companies can sometimes be deep. Legitimately so.

'We were dealing with fifty-odd companies in the UK,' recalls Gerald Leahy. 'Seventy-four countries, because Unilever was that kind of business. As in all large companies you had two streams of information. One was the official accounting stream which would give you your cash projection twelve months forward to the last place of decimals which was pretty useless; but what was much more important was that the chief buyer of van den Bergh's would ring up and say, "Gerry, I want to buy this parcel of oil. It's going to be $20 million. Is that going to worry cash?"

'You had to develop a relationship with the operating companies so that they would tell you what was really happening out there. Ships were late, there were parcels of oil being bought or you decided you were going to plunge into the market or "I don't want to buy soya beans yet but I'd like to take cover". All these were issues where the treasury was the buffer between the operating companies to reduce their level of risk in the financial area so that they could concentrate on the job of what they were making and selling. So one of the most valuable meetings I used to go to in Unilever was the three-monthly sales office managers meeting of all the big Unilever companies, van den Bergh's, Wall's, Lever, Bird's Eye.'

In some cases, the treasurer has an unseen role in the negotiation of contracts. Thus when Michael Northeast arrived as treasurer of Rover he found that it had taken a position on the Netherlands guilder which seemed inconsistent with every car being fitted with a radio from Philips of Eindhoven. He discovered that in its days of full state-ownership Rover (then BL) had an edict against foreign exchange exposure and required all contracts for supplies to be in sterling. 'So they had negotiated sterling prices and all that it was was a guilder invoice that at date of invoice was translated into sterling and then invoiced in sterling to the company. So the underlying exposure was still to the Netherlands guilder.

'Now we were doing a hedging policy based on having a long guilder exposure whereas in fact we were very very short guilder if you really took account of this supply contract coming in.'

It was a lesson he took with him to his present role as treasurer of Dixons, the electrical goods retailer. Walk round any Dixons store and you will quickly realize that most of the £2 billion a year of goods which pass through its shops have come from the Far East's newly industrializing countries – South Korea, Taiwan, Hong Kong, Malaysia, Singapore and the Philippines – the so-called 'tiger' economies.

'We are purchasing from suppliers in the tigers who prefer to invoice in dollars. That in its own right means that I have to be very very certain of the contractual terms of the agreements under which these are negotiated. And again this is the group treasurer getting down into the buying decision. I have to be there at the buyer's right arm – in spirit if not in body – so that he's certain when those contracts are being negotiated that he's not just creating some sort of exposure in hiding by means of a functional currency for payment.

'If he fixes it to pay dollars in three months' time then he's exposed to the dollar against whatever he's going to buy those dollars for during those three months. In terms of future transactions that are placed on that order then if there is a linkage between the Taiwanese dollar and the US dollar you've got to be certain of that parity or you've got to be certain that your contract is actually in fixed-price dollars and not just using the dollar as a surrogate for the Taiwan dollar to the extent that the supplier is passing his little bit of foreign exchange exposure over to you.

'You need to get into that purchasing contract basis. My team are very involved in that, which is hard because you have to break down barriers with people who regard this as part of their bailiwick. Their job is to negotiate contracts and that includes the price of the contract. It is not welcome if somebody comes along and says, "Do you really mean that as a price?" but that has to be done by consensus.'

As the aspects of the job have grown more varied and more complex, the Association of Corporate Treasurers has become more ambitious about its standards for qualification. It started off modestly enough. As Gerry Leahy admits, 'If you could put steam on glass you were in, as it were.

'But we very soon decided that we wanted to have examinations. So with immediate effect we set out to produce the first educational material, which we found you couldn't buy in. So we wrote our own. Four people wrote four manuals and we had the first examinations in 1985.

'We started off with the feeling that we needed to educate young people coming into treasury. In those days if you said, "I want someone to do corporate dealing", no one understood what the hell you were talking about. So we said let's set up our stall to train people to do that; but we then went on to make the examination of an MBA standard which effectively stopped a lot of those sort of people getting through Part II.'

Many, especially those from banks and building societies, settle for just the partial qualification of the first stage.

'We have a joint venture on Part I with the Institute of Chartered Accountants of Scotland because you've got to give people a foundation in accountancy, law, taxation and monetary economics before you can understand the balance sheet

and understand the effect of what you're doing on it. It's a
jolly good overview of the whole of the finance function. And
that satisfies a lot of people.

'Our typical student is still about thirty years old and a graduate chartered accountant, often still in the accountancy profession. So it's a tertiary qualification.'

The danger of this is that it impresses the commonsense out
of the board. There is an insidious progression to which a
treasurer might succumb. At first the operation is merely to
insure the group against the risks of adverse movements in
exchange rates. That's called hedging the risk.

Hedging can sometimes be expensive. There are two choices.
First is to decide whether it is worth incurring such an expense
when the risk seems remote and it would not hurt much even
if it materialized. Many people take a similar decision when
their motor insurance comes up for renewal at an exorbitant
premium and they decide to move from fully comprehensive
to third-party-only cover. But bankers are constantly
extending the range of financial instruments by innovation.
The treasurer faces the opportunity to use financial engineering which will cost less, cover most of the risk and might even
produce a small profit. From there, it seems a small progression
to taking on a small risk in return for a potential profit if
exchange rates move in the particular direction you expect.
You've slid from hedging into trading. Your company is no
longer just in the business of baking cakes. It's also in financial
market speculation. The board may not, and the shareholders
certainly do not, know this is the business they're in now.

'In foreign exchange the possibilities of moving from a hedging to trading position are numerous,' affirms Gerry Leahy.
'You take out a futures position which starts off as a hedge
and you decide that the underlying cash position matures but
the hedge position is going quite well, so let that run. Then
you've got a trading position.

'The temptation to do that is enormous. A lot of companies
run what they call a net trading position, in other words they
net off the assets and liabilities in particular currencies in the
centre and just run the net position. Others will run both

sides and will move actively. There is a tremendous spread of possibilities.

'The biggest problem in the treasury area is that the board of directors has often not kept pace with what's been happening in the development of treasury operations.

'One of the biggest dangers is where a corporate treasurer is appointed to a company from outside. Rather like a star footballer – the £1 million transfer who feels he's got to score a goal in his first game – there's something like that for the treasurer who comes in. He's got to trip the light fantastic and do amazing things. That is hugely dangerous.'

Anthony Stern, treasurer of the brewery and hotels group Bass, tells of a corporate treasury which wanted to borrow in dollars and decided instead to borrow in Kuwaiti dinars, because they would get a better rate and if the currency depreciated it would be cheaper for them. 'Then the Gulf War happened and they repaid their loan. It cost them almost nothing. They go around saying that they're brilliant. I think they're stupid. To me, the risk that this was going to go wrong – another oil find in Kuwait, the value of the dinar goes up – you might find yourself in the position where you've done something too clever and it just doesn't work.'

For Courtaulds' James Wrangham the most common mistake of corporate treasurers is 'being prepared to move away from the risk-averse position without being rigorous on the degree of group resource available to be used for that risk, not just in terms of attributing capital to it but making sure that the board understand that instead of selling dollars today I've, voluntarily for potential profit, not sold them.'

The key, all agree, is ensuring the board understands, approves and takes responsibility for what is being done and for the consequences. That, asserts James Wrangham, does not mean the board has to understand all the details. 'If I can come up with a scheme, if I can say what the Doomsday is, the cosmic worst is, put a probability on it, then okay. Then you're putting your return against your worst case. No board is going to decide to manufacture viscose rayon only by knowing every detail of the chemical process. It's no different from that.'

Cost centre or profit centre? The great debate is about whether corporate treasury exists as a necessary overhead, trying to minimize the cost of reducing the risk of adverse movements in the financial markets, or whether it should be a profit centre, seeing the flows of currencies in its business as creating opportunities to make money from operating in the financial markets. The profit centre approach was much in vogue among the more aggressive entrepreneurial companies of the 1980s. Their talk then was that it was a derogation of duty to let assets lie under-utilized, the treasurer should 'make assets sweat' in the words of Paul Buchanan-Barrow, then of headhunters, Goddard Kay Rogers.

Even BP espoused the argument that it could make money make money and, looking at its considerable flows of funds, it embarked on plans to turn its corporate treasury into an autonomous bank which would also seek outside customers. That idea the Bank of England vetoed on the grounds that for a bank to be owned by an industrial or commercial entity was wrong in principle.

A 1994 survey by Record Treasury Management found that, even among companies which rank on the stock market as mid-size, 9 per cent expected to operate their corporate treasuries as profit centres. 'That is enough to give you all the disasters you need for the next twenty years,' says RTM's chief executive, Les Halpin.

'Dixons has a history of being profit-centre oriented in its treasury department,' vouchsafes Michael Northeast. 'Previous incarnations of the group treasurer have been very active as traders to the extent where, in the mid-1980s, financial services in terms of treasury transactions within Dixons Group could almost be regarded as a bank in terms of volumes. The volumes being transacted through the trading floor here had absolutely no relation to the underlying cash flow. So one could argue that was pure profit-centre trading.'

That was an attitude which changed before Michael Northeast's arrival. Catharsis came in the takeover tussle with Kingfisher, the retail group which owns Woolworth, B&Q and Comet. One of Michael Northeast's predecessors at Dixons –

reputedly uncomfortable with its hyperactive transactional approach – had been Anthony Stern, now of Bass. There he happily embraces a more cautious approach: 'We believe that the real objective of our treasury is to demonstrate savings to the group from more efficient use of the markets, from the fact that we are a wholesaler and have the expertise in our central treasury to do foreign exchange deals in a way that our divisions haven't. We can go direct into the London market or wherever else it is and get the best rates. We are more sensitive to exchange rate movements and therefore our timings are marginally better.

'There are times in which we will take a different view – because let's say that all of the divisions want to cover Deutschmarks because they're required to do so and we believe that as a group we should not be exposed to the Deutschmark quite as much as that – then we should as part of a deliberate policy say that we don't want to be 100 per cent covered on Deutschmarks as a group, we only want to be 50 per cent covered and therefore we will not cover everything.'

However oriented the approach, groups such as Bass, Courtaulds and Redland, which have large numbers of subsidiaries trading overseas, operate their treasuries much on the line of in-house banks. At Bass, for instance, all divisions must cover their exposures for six months ahead with the group's treasury. They can decide for themselves whether to cover a further six months ahead but can only use outside banks if exchange controls or similar anomalies mean that would give them a better rate.

Courtaulds' principle is that all the transactions that the centre does with the businesses should be priced and managed as much at arm's length as is practicable, so as not to blur the decisions which the operating managers make.

'Those businesses,' notes James Wrangham, 'should be as risk-averse as they sensibly can in dealing with foreign currency arising from imports or exports. But in the end it is their decision as to what the most risk-averse stance is.

'If a particular business is selling regularly in dollars to a particular country or customers and experience say that 80 per cent of those orders get fulfilled but regularly 20 per cent are cancelled, then it wouldn't be risk-averse for that business to sell forwards 100 per cent of its nominal export ledger to us. It would actually be overselling if it did that.

'It would probably sell forward to Courtaulds' treasury 70 per cent of its order book and then top it up to the tune of about 10 per cent a bit closer to delivery. But that's something on which we in treasury don't feel we can second-guess the businesses. We can say to them that they're not there to speculate in currency and that they should not speculate on their margin but should try and transact with us in a way which is least view-taking, least speculative, least risky in relation to the margin on their business.

'We will help them in working out what that is but the transaction they actually do with treasury is as arm's length and as documented as those Courtaulds does with the bank.'

As a retailer, Dixons works on tighter margins in turnover than would most manufacturing companies. Turnover is in the region of £2 billion a year and, as Michael Northeast puts it, 'Retail profits in the UK are around £100 million or we hope they will be over the coming years.'

With such a high proportion of turnover imported and a margin of only 5 per cent, this is transaction risk in a pure and critical form. Currency rates can make all the difference to the bottom line.

'Therefore, the risk criteria that must be adopted are fairly tight in terms of producing what in the end is a good price for the consumer when he walks into our shop and wants to buy a piece of kit,' expounds Michael Northeast. 'There is a quite interesting tightrope to walk between making certain you can get the best price, so that there is the best possible achievement of margin in the goods, but at the same time not taking too much risk in achieving that price. You could create on the bottom line effects through your treasury department which can more than outweigh the effect that's going through the retail chain.'

If only life were as simple as this: make sure the contract has no hidden currency traps, cover each transaction as soon as it's agreed and so make sure there is no currency risk. Unfortunately for Dixons, though fortunately for its customers, competitors complicate considerations of currency.

'When I was working for Dixons we were covering our currency on the importing of goods into the UK in an absolutely standard way,' relates Anthony Stern. 'As Christmas got nearer the pound got stronger and the prices at which we imported our goods turned out to be bad prices. They were good at the time because we had fixed our currency rates. But we suddenly found that our competition were selling the goods in the shops at prices which clearly meant that they hadn't covered their currency at all.'

By taking that risk the competitor had the advantage of benefiting from sterling's strength making the imports cheaper, unburdened by the extra costs which Dixons had incurred in its currency transactions to obviate the risk of the pound weakening. This would enable them to undercut Dixons' prices without any loss of profit, perhaps while still enjoying an enhanced profit margin if the pound strengthened enough. Dixons, having taken on the extra cost of currency insurance, now faced the risk of either having unsold stock – because its prices were higher than the competitor's – or matching the competitor's price and forsaking its profit margin, perhaps even incurring a loss. There is no risk-free decision available.

'The question you have to try and anticipate is not only what are you doing but also what is your competition doing,' concludes Anthony Stern. 'There is no way, I think, that we could have anticipated at the beginning of the year that they wouldn't cover their currency. We anticipated that they would have done the same as us, which was to cover a reasonable proportion of their currency and lock in prices, just in case the pound went the other way. They were taking a much bigger risk than us but it paid off for them.'

Today's treasurer at Dixons, Michael Northeast, knows they will be buying from the tiger economies of Asia for the foreseeable future. The problem is that there are not speculators willing to take on risks for the indefinite future and therefore there is no long-term currency instrument available in the markets. 'So on a transactional basis you're fairly limited to what you can do in the markets. The markets are a lot better than they used to be but they're still the most active in up to one year forward. Up to one year forward, though, is a good time as it happens to be a business cycle as well. Therefore we tend to look at our exposure one year forward. So, at any particular time I know that I have a risk which is what I identify as my core economic exposure going forward.'

Because of competition, he must assess the severity of each risk and whether to insure against it or whether there is a greater danger that such insurance will make the company uncompetitive. That means judging how likely is the risk of one currency moving sharply against another, which brings in currency forecasting. In such circumstances, the treasurer cannot avoid taking a view on currency prospects.

'The treasurer is a risk manager and my job for Dixons is that we have a significant risk involved in fluctuating currency markets,' says Michael Northeast. 'The risk is what we have to translate our goods at, which affects eventually our margin and our bottom line. My job is to try and manage that risk. Having identified with it I can't just take a *laissez-faire* approach and say that I don't want to do anything with it.

'It is therefore important that I know the commercial realities of what we're doing. It's not just an ivory tower. What I'm not doing is speculating on where currencies are going, that's why I don't get involved outside the currencies in which we are actually transacting business. I'm not interested in making money out of money. What I am interested in doing is maximizing or optimizing the freedom that I have over gaining margin out of selling goods in the UK that are imported from abroad.'

Hyacinth Bucket, living in suburbia and desperately keeping up appearances, has a kindred spirit in corporate treasuries, according to some. Translation exposure, they suggest, is just a matter of cosmetics and only in exceptional circumstances has any underlying reality.

A British company produces its accounts in sterling, naturally. If it owns factories overseas – in the USA, perhaps – then those factories, valued in dollars, will appear in the balance sheet at a sterling value which will depend on the £:$ exchange rate on the date of the balance sheet. As that exchange rate fluctuates so a factory which appears almost worthless one year seems to be a prized asset the next, vitiating the whole purpose of a company's accounts in showing how it has performed.

Worse, if the company borrows foreign currency – say dollars – and uses them to invest in sterling assets, then a change in the exchange rate can suddenly make its liabilities – the debt incurred – greater than its assets.

Moreover, even though its US subsidiary may have traded very successfully and increased its profits (in dollars), if the dollar has weakened against sterling, the British parent business may show it to have declined.

'I would regard translation exposure as the danger that at the end of the financial year when you report to shareholders you will look a chump as the chairman of an organization when you stand up and say "Profits are half what I said they were going to be because exchange rates have moved," or "My borrowings are twice what I said they would be because exchange rates have moved",' argues Anthony Stern.

'I have a very simple philosophy which is that if chairmen of companies could stand up in front of shareholders and say, "Well of course they've moved because exchange rates have moved, what do you expect? You shouldn't expect otherwise," then translation exposure wouldn't be an issue. It is, because there is some requirement in the City for profits and balance sheets to be reasonably predictable. For the reason, in my view, that stockbrokers don't want to look stupid to their customers, there is the need to finesse the balance sheet in terms of currency.

'To an extent, some of these problems are of presentation but not entirely. There is one company which I know has bought and sold options to protect the sterling value of its French franc profits and it's done it because it is an advertising agency and they say that in advertising agencies it's all about confidence. "If we produce profits which are outside the range of expectations of the City then confidence will be dented and our share price hit so this is a small price to pay to ensure that our profits are maintained.''

'My view as a treasurer is that you should never spend cash in order to create, if you like, a balance sheet profit or loss result when there is no economic reality.'

One classic way for a company to hedge its currency risks is to finance an overseas investment by borrowing in the local currency, so that if an exchange rate change makes the dollar asset fall in sterling value, so too will it lower the sterling amount of the liability to repay the dollar loan. It is a practice which Courtaulds, for instance, follows in general principle but is difficult to implement consistently because of a host of other variables demanding consideration: tax rules, interest rates, exchange controls in some countries and very often the wishes of a joint-venture partner. Moreover, it may not suit the investment intentions of the company's own shareholders.

Treasurer James Wrangham avows, 'It's very difficult to be dogmatic, so we try to be pragmatic within an overall policy of essentially not wanting to go to either extreme, taking the view that someone who invests in Courtaulds is investing in a company which they know has the bulk of its turnover outside the UK and therefore expects to be taking on non-UK risk in some form.

'If people are investing in us they are investing in a portfolio of overseas investments, UK-controlled but with a relatively small UK component. Why then should we try and switch off one part of the overseas risk, which is the foreign currency risk? I don't think that our investors, if they think about it, would really expect that and we wouldn't be thanked if we tried to switch all that off.

'Therefore one rejects the extreme of saying we should borrow every dollar, finance every investment overseas. We think that shipping some of the group's equity into the foreign currency is probably a sensible thing to do.'

This then becomes an issue not for the corporate treasurer to deal with by trading in the foreign exchange markets but for the whole board to decide in its long-term strategy and consideration of the group's balance sheet.

Even for conservatively managed groups such as Courtaulds and Bass, currency mismatch may be an integral part of overall strategy.

'We believed, when we bought Holiday Inns, that we were buying a business that was going to generate cash,' recounts Anthony Stern of Bass. 'We thought, as a sideline, that the dollar would tend to strengthen against the pound over time. So we took a foreign exchange view that we would not borrow the whole of our foreign exchange liability in dollars but just 60 per cent in dollars. This will have two advantages. If the dollar strengthens as we expect it to do, half of that benefit would come to our shareholders in higher profits, and half would be matched because the interest on the dollar borrowings matches out the interest on the dollar profits. So what you get is a certain smoothing of dollar profitability in sterling terms but not too much, a reasonable balance between the two.'

Tax and accounting rules have the incidental effect of encouraging such a practice. Under UK accounting regulations, if a company has more foreign currency borrowings than foreign currency assets the foreign exchange movements on the excess have to go through its profit and loss account. If, on the other hand, it borrows in foreign currencies no more than it invests abroad, the foreign exchange movements basically net out and go to reserves in the balance sheet, bypassing the profit and loss account.

It was the translation aspect of exchange rates which caused Japanese banks suddenly to clam up on their property loans in the USA. Suddenly, they refused to renew loans on which borrowers had depended and, with devastating economic effect, began remitting funds back to their home country. The dollar's gyrations against the yen hurt at both extremes. A fall in the dollar meant that the banks showed nasty losses on their holdings of US bonds; but a rise in dollar assets and liabilities swelled the banks' balance sheets and made the banks appear undercapitalized.

Under international agreements banks must maintain their equity – share – capital above a certain minimum as a percentage of their total borrowing and lending to act as a safety buffer so that the banks can still repay deposits even when customers default on loans. The Japanese banks' equity capital is in yen and, although they had balanced their lending in the USA with loans raised in dollars, the whole balance sheet grew out of proportion to the capital. Insurance companies, which must likewise maintain adequate capital to secure their ability to meet claims, face a similar translation hazard.

For ordinary industrial and commercial companies the concern will normally be a minor one of ensuring they do not break their loan and banking covenants. When a company borrows money it usually undertakes that its assets will be enough to cover the debt and its profits enough to cover the interest payments a specified number of times. In theory at least, if either falls below those covenanted levels, the loan will become immediately repayable. A company which borrows heavily and invests largely overseas must monitor closely the effects of translation exposure.

A British company with overseas interests can opt to protect its overall ratio of borrowing to capital – its gearing – or to protect the sterling value of its share capital. But it cannot do both at the same time. Suppose you have a 50 per cent mortgage on your home in Britain and buy a second home in Spain. If you borrow in pesetas to cover half the cost of your second home then you have secured your gearing ratio at 50 per cent all round. But, if you were to draw up a personal balance sheet, whereas the sterling value of your 'unmortgaged' half of the UK home would not be influenced by exchange rates, a movement in the value of the peseta against the pound would affect the sterling value in your personal balance sheet of the 'unmortgaged' half of your Spanish home.

While Anthony Stern of Bass talks of translation exposure almost dismissively, for Redland's Stephen East – with negligible international trade but operating in thirty-five countries – it is a major concern. When UK interest rates were high and those in the USA low, it was 7 per cent cheaper to borrow in dollars than in sterling. Of course, against that reward for borrowing in dollars there was the exchange rate risk that the dollar might rise against the pound, thereby increasing the sterling equivalent of any borrowing; or fall and lower the value of profits earned in dollars.

'We concluded that with the pound's exchange rate at that stage about $1.60 and it having moved up from $1.50 and looking as if it might go higher, the bigger risk to Redland was actually that the pound went to $2 and therefore reduced the value in sterling terms of our US dollar assets and the sterling value of dollar profits,' recalls Stephen East. 'Therefore we decided to fully hedge our dollar assets at that stage and to use the interest cost on that dollar borrowing to offset the profits.

'So if the pound went to $2 you got reduced sterling value of profits but you were also getting reduced sterling cost of dollar interest. The two covered each other. We use the interest payable on our overseas currency debt to hedge the profits. We always make sure that we never have in any single currency excess debt over assets or excess interest over profits, because we don't want to go out and create a risk, we want to manage the risk down cost-effectively.

'That doesn't obviate the need to manage the balance sheet risks because, for instance, if you don't manage them, you could end up with what would be classic economic theory – you have $100 of assets, you have $100 of debt and you therefore have no exchange risk. However, if you have just that one investment overseas and your equity in the UK, then if the exchange rate moves your gearing can change hugely, with no real change in the underlying economics.

'That could have real economic consequences because it can make the City worry about a rights issue, it can raise worries about the dividend; all those sorts of issues all then come out. So while it's classic economic theory to fully hedge, that might not be the right thing to do.'

You might be struck by both Anthony Stern of Bass and Stephen East of Redland acknowledging the need to take so much account of how an event will be perceived by the City investment analysts, as distinct from the real economic effects on the company. So was I.

But what should a company do when, for instance, it is bidding for an overseas contract and must offer a firm price? Months may pass before it knows whether its bid has been successful and in that time the foreign currency in which it is bidding may fall against the pound, lowering the sterling amount it is to receive and out of which it must pay wages and other costs in pounds.

Were it simply to engage in a forward or futures deal the company would be committing itself to exchange at a fixed rate into sterling foreign currency, which it might later discover that – because it has failed to win the contract – it is not to receive. It has merely substituted one exchange rate risk for another as large.

This is where options come into their own. Because an option is a right but not an obligation to buy one currency for another at a fixed rate, the company can secure itself against untoward currency movements without entering into any commitment.

'We started dealing in currency options about eight years ago – quite early among corporates – because we identified, and still do, quite a lot of transactions where both courses of action create a risk,' says James Wrangham of Courtaulds. 'What we've done, by educating the businesses, is to say that if you use options in a sensible way, with the help of treasury, then the business will gain competitive advantage on its transactions compared with others. You are dedicating a small part of your margin to give yourself the flexibility to put out a price list in Finmarks when you don't know what orders are going to be taken; to change your cover policy if you find that your main competitor is doing something different from you and therefore has a flexibility you haven't; to put out a tender and not know whether you're going to get it and cover yourself.

'We've been doing that for quite a long time. We don't say to the business involved that they are to do an option and we're not saying that we're taking options to protect our own central position.

'We say, "Think through your risk. You're in a position now where actually it would be good business for you if you could quote a firm price in that particular product for the next year but you don't know whether you're going to get fifty orders or a hundred orders. This is the pricing we can get for you on an option which will enable you for a finite amount of money – an insurance premium – to give yourself a competitive advantage as compared with someone else who's not prepared to do that." We do that pretty symmetrically.

'When you do that there will be a period during the life of the option when the business, which has either lost the contract and wants to sell the option or has got the contract and wants to turn the option into an outright forward, will then sell the option back to us. There have been occasions when instead of then selling the option back to the market we have kept it, because the price didn't look realistic for selling it back and so have a small position, but usually the option we buy in the market is a mirror image of the one we've written for our business.'

Corporate treasurers rely almost exclusively on OTC – Over The Counter – options. These now have the lion's share of foreign exchange option business. Traded options, with standardized exchange rates, amounts of currency and expiry dates are quoted on various exchanges around the world and find favour with some large international investors who want either to insure their portfolios against exchange-rate risk or to speculate on currency rates. Banks create and sell OTC options bespoke to their corporate customers' needs on size, exchange rate and expiry date. But for someone such as Stephen East at Redland an option – which lasts for only an agreed limited period and then expires worthless if it has not been exercised – is just too expensive as a form of insurance when he is covering translation effects on his company rather than actual transactions.

Michael Northeast at Dixons, forever watching for opportunities to save on costs and steal a march on competitors, claims to use a method of 'synthetic' option strategies which is only half the cost of an option provided by the bank. It relies on using the forward market, in which the two parties agree to exchange currencies at a rate agreed from the outset on a specified date. That rate will reflect the current spot exchange rate together with the difference in interest rates between the two currencies.

The other popular instrument is a currency swap. The simplest way to explain it is to think of that home in Spain mentioned earlier and imagine that you have a fixed outgoing to pay in pesetas on it, perhaps the premium on the insurance you took out to secure the mortgage. The sterling equivalent of that will naturally fluctuate with the exchange rate and present a fearful uncertainty in your domestic budgeting. Alonso, the waiter in San Pedro d'Alcantara, has got himself stuck with making regular payments in sterling to the English girl who got pregnant when she met him there on holiday. He cannot plan sensibly without knowing the peseta cost of those payments. *Olé!* You undertake his payments and he yours.

That's the simplest example of a swap and a gross over-simplification to show the principle. Investment bankers and financiers never keep things simple if they can squeeze 0.0001 per cent more by adding refinements and complications ostensibly to meet better the customer's needs.

'These instruments are enormously useful,' enthuses James Wrangham. 'Swaps enable you to unbundle a decision on borrowing money between a number of separate components. The interest rate you can manage one way; the commitment to provide it for a long period you manage somewhere else, the actual getting hold of the money day by day somewhere else.

'You're taking out the different components and managing them separately. If you do it properly and you're quite clear what your risks are you can get a greater degree of flexibility than by saying that the only way of getting ten-year dollars is to go to JP Morgan and borrow $10 million from them for ten years.

'Short-term currency swaps we're using all the time as a means of managing our book. If our exposure on a minute-by-minute basis rises by $5 million because a particular business has just got a contract and covers forward those dollars for three months ahead, we would immediately sell those dollars spot and then, later in the day or the following day, do a currency swap deal for three months out with a different bank as a way of managing the forward part of the book separately from the spot. That's a forward currency swap, a relatively standard bargain, day-by-day dealing the banks do all the time.'

And if you were wondering what, if that's fairly standard, the complicated ploys are like, try wrapping your mind round a swaption. That's an option to make a swap.

The problems, however, don't always present themselves to the corporate treasurer in nice, clean, clear-cut form. They can be nebulous as, for instance, Redland's Stephen East finds himself juggling with decisions: 'judging when the other business risks start or cease to justify moving away from whatever one believes is the status quo.

'If you make the assumption that the status quo is that the group has 30 per cent gearing overall, then your mainland Europe basket of currency assets and liabilities should be 30 per cent geared, sterling should be 30 per cent geared, your North American block should be 30 per cent geared and so on. At which point do the other business issues – in terms of interest rates, likely movement in the economy and offset in the economy, the risk to the group as a whole in terms of its profit profile – justify being more heavily borrowed in dollars compared with the average?

'Those are the decisions which one spends longest on. US aggregates and roof tiles will have slightly different though similar cycles, for instance. What risks are inherent in our various businesses which give a natural offset to the currency and interest rate risks? It's a constantly changing judgement.'

Even relatively simple transactions, points out James Wrangham, throw up teasers. 'Buying woodpulp to make rayon, what's the group's exposure? Is it at the very short end, the moment we've actually decided we're going to call off another twenty tonnes from the plant in South Africa or wherever? That is an absolutely clear exposure and we need to cover that. Is it the period of three months in which we've been in overall discussion with the supplier on our likely requirements? Is it one year, when you have your annual negotiations and change the price? Is it five years, because you'd know probably in that period whether you were going to be changing supplier.

'Essentially you could make a case for almost any time. And what we're doing is more and more trying to think through the businesses, what is their real economic exposure and whether doing it rather mechanistically as we do at the moment is the right way to do it. We're trying to tackle that with some outside help at the moment. What is the most sensible way to manage that sort of situation? It applies on selling as well as on buying and it's not particularly easy. It's one of the areas that, as one has more sophisticated instruments, more derivatives, one may perhaps find the mix of those that matches that particular risk profile. That is quite challenging.'

Anyone who ventures even into the periphery, let alone the darker recesses of corporate treasury, quickly comes to appreciate how facile can be judgements about appropriate prudence and irresponsible speculation. The translation Anthony Stern disregards is something to which Stephen East must rightly give priority. Instruments eschewed by Michael Northeast are espoused by the certainly no less conservative James Wrangham.

'It is totally ridiculous to think that you can formulate best practice for treasury,' Northeast says, 'given the whole range of different corporates, different businesses and different risk criteria that can be taken by that corporate at any time, let alone on a continuing basis where the environment is changing all the time anyway. What was a good idea yesterday will not be good today.'

Meanwhile, at the sharpest end of hour-to-hour dealing with the bank traders, a corporate treasury's several dealers are each calling a different bank simultaneously. Whichever is calling the best price to the chief dealer tells the bank trader, 'Done!', while the others tell their respondents, 'No thanks'. They keep – and must keep, all treasurers agree – a freedom to exercise their own discretion whether to deal immediately a subsidiary deals with them or several hours later, running the position.

'I've got a dealer and her boss who also deals when she's busy doing something else,' comments Michael Northeast. 'They have to be very professional so that when our button lights up on the bank dealer's screen we get service. He picks it up and doesn't think of our people as that bunch of hicks from Mayfair. To be very professional they have to have the knowledge, they have to have confidence and they have to be able to make their own minds up.

'If the dealer at the other end thought they were just a cypher for a medium-term strategy they'd get ripped off something rotten because he'd see them coming a mile away. You have to give them freedom and responsibility to take their own short-term positions – as long as you're happy with the risks that they're taking – so they have fairly strong stop-loss position that they have to adhere to. And they have overnight and intra-day open-position limits. And I can monitor them. Within that and within the general framework of the strategy I want to develop they can go off and try and add value to that which we've had as orders from our commercial guys. That's where we try and add value.'

The Allied-Lyons affair made boardrooms throughout Britain's major companies wonder what corporate treasurers got up to. And worry.

'What's now happened is that everyone's rushed round,' recounts Gerald Leahy. 'Accounting firms must have made lots more money from special audits of the treasury function. Could we have an Allied-Lyons here?

'There's been a lot more control put in but that is equally dangerous in my view because auditors often don't understand how derivatives and financial instruments work and the danger is that you pile control on control so that there you have lots of controls and underneath you can't see what's happening. The name of the game on controls is the old one, KISS – Keep It Simple, Stupid.'

But the future for treasury may lie in the ultimate complication, according to Swiss Bank Corporation chief currency economist, Dr Jim O'Neill:

'There are some US corporations for which we have devised such a complex programme and because we run such a global book we can offer a range of risk management advice which others can't. We do all their foreign exchange risk management for them: by options, basket options.

'We take all the assets and liabilities in their balance sheet and we've devised a very complicated option structure so that, depending on various market developments, there's continuous protective action taking place.

'The fee they give us for that is less than the cost of running a lot of people in corporate treasury. They still have a treasury but for other purposes and they don't have a lot of dealers who think they're running a bank and saying that the dollar's going up or whatever.

'You still have in the UK corporate treasury dealers who are trying to do the same job as our spot $/DM dealer.'

They are not confined to the largest British companies, the constituents of the FTSE 100-share index and others of like size. In effect confirming the findings of Record Treasury Management, Nomura's Tom Elliot told me:

'You sometimes find that the punchier customers are well outside the FTSE 100 and they need to generate the speculative revenue.

'All that business grew from client efforts to make treasury cost-efficient. Having done that and done a few things on a very timely basis and made money, then many of them have grown to anticipate and expect their treasury staff to perform the function of a bank without being a bank.

'And whereas a bank has limits imposed by the Bank of England, they have none.'

On that basis, there may be another Allied-Lyons (or worse) out there, just waiting to happen.

12

SQUARING THE CIRCLE

Are foreign exchange speculators damaging the economy and costing jobs? To defend its currency a government must sometimes raise interest rates, holding back growth or perhaps even tipping the economy into recession. Statistically it is indisputable that the amount of foreign exchange dealing is many times the volume of international trade and investment. Most of it, therefore, can have no underlying purpose other than speculation.

The speculators are largely the foreign exchange traders like Andre Katz at Barclays with whom we began. They may also be the hedge fund and other investment funds, or even corporate, treasurers. Do they impose a hidden tax on trade?

Exchange rate risks add extra costs. A manufacturer must build an extra margin into prices either to cover currency fluctuations or the costs of financial instruments to hedge – insure against – that risk.

Academic economists suggest there is another hidden cost, an inefficiency resulting from exchange rate uncertainty. This occurs when a company tends to locate its activities in a spread of countries to match the currencies of its costs with the currencies of its revenues, eliminating or reducing exchange rate risk. A strategy based on such criteria rather than locations which offer the highest comparative advantage produces inefficiency. It does not optimise resources.

However, it is trade which creates risk, speculators just accept it. If we did not buy video recorders from the Far East, oil from the Middle East or did not sell anything from whisky to worsted in the USA, there would no need to exchange currencies and therefore no risk from the rate of exchange varying.

A business can decide to accept the risk it has created or if that is unacceptable, can pass the risk on to someone else willing to take that risk. The person or entity taking risks we call a speculator, often applying as a pejorative a term which describes a useful role.

We could try to eliminate or at least reduce significantly the risk: a return to the days of greater certainty and the fixed but flexible exchange rate system the world enjoyed for a quarter of this century under the Bretton Woods agreement. Manufacturers would be fairly sure how much they would be getting for what they sold abroad and customers could know how much they had to pay. With less risk to worry about, business would flourish, and goods could be made wherever was most efficient, holding down prices and improving the prospects for jobs.

Naturally, the fiftieth anniversary, in July 1994, of the original meeting in that New Hampshire hotel engendered voluminous debate about the future of the IMF and World Bank, together with discussion of whether and how a system of fixed but flexible exchange rates could be reinstated. Led by former Federal Reserve Board chairman Paul Volcker, the Bretton Woods Commission (an independent group of former ministers, central bankers, academics and leading financial experts from private sector banks and companies) suggested as a long-term goal the creation of 'flexible exchange rate bands' – or target ranges – for the dollar, Deutschmark and yen. They acknowledged this could not be achieved immediately. A necessary precondition is that the leading countries strengthen their economic policies – by, for instance, cutting their budget deficits – and achieve greater economic convergence of key variables such as inflation.

There is the inconsistent trio. You cannot have fixed exchange rates, differing economic policies and free movement of capital.

Often overlooked is that the Bretton Woods arrangement for exchange rates held force in an era when there were considerable restrictions on movements of capital. When capital moves freely, a country with high inflation must offer returns adequate to match those available in a low inflation economy. Real interest rates will thus converge, negating the benefits of exchange rate depreciation which is inflationary. Controls on the movement of capital, imposed in an endeavour to stabilize exchange rates, would thus have the opposite effect to that intended.

If capital – the resources of savers such as yourself, perhaps, who buy life assurance or subscribe to a pension scheme – moves freely it will seek out the best returns. The most deserving – potentially most rewarding – project will not be thwarted for want of resources. Savers will not suffer their thrift being committed to futile ventures. Moreover, free movement has made capital markets so efficient they have significantly reduced the amount nations must hold unfruitfully through their central banks in foreign exchange reserves.

Capital controls would impose greater costs than those created by the currency fluctuations they set out to prevent. An attempt to reimpose capital controls would in any case almost certainly fail, being frustrated by the Euromarkets. Any imbalance in trade between two countries leads to the deficit country's currency being held overseas and used as capital.

Another palliative put forward is a tax on capital movements set at a level low enough not to encumber genuine capital investment but high enough to restrain speculation. However, when currency rates become unrealistic the rewards for speculation are, on a per year basis, high. Sweden, after all, could not deter speculators against the krona even with overnight interest rates at 500 per cent.

Could we square the circle: have exchange rates fixed enough that industry would not have to worry but flexible enough to reflect the differences in the underlying economies? This would mean accepting the need for currency adjustment but steadying the process.

To achieve greater stability of exchange rates when capital flows freely, attention has focused on that third member of the inconsistent trio: economic performance. Currencies cannot stay pegged together indefinitely if their inflation rates differ and goods still move freely across borders. If Germany gives priority to keeping inflation down while Spain has other priorities, tolerating higher inflation, something has to give. Either as prices in Spain rise people will buy from Germany instead and Spaniards will, ultimately, be thrown out of work; or the peseta must fall in value against the Deutschmark. To avoid currency adjustments, the actual economy must be made to comply. Thus the managing director of the IMF, Michel Camdessus, wants to promote policy coordination between the major countries so that their economies diverge less.

Likewise, beneath the ERM and the Maastricht treaty plans for a single currency lay the idea of fixing the currencies and making the economies converge. Many member currencies joined and clung to the European Exchange Rate Mechanism so that they would be anchored to the Deutschmark and Germany's low inflation rate.

However, even if two economies converge in the long run, their inflation rates, interest rates and economic growth rates will at any moment differ – and their currencies fluctuate in relative value – unless their economic cycles exactly coincide. Capital will move between them until currencies adjust to reflect the interest rate and inflation rate differentials of the moment.

Then there are extraneous factors. A sharp rise or fall in oil prices will affect Denmark and Italy differently. Japan has an ageing population and therefore its savings behaviour differs from that of the USA, which is still demographically a young country. Such variable factors make the relative value of currencies unstable.

A system of forced economic convergence and fixed exchange rates means that if one country became less competitive then, instead of its relative prices adjusting through the exchange rate, it could either cut prices and wages – with all the political and social disruption that would bring – or factories would close and jobs be lost. The ERM fell apart when the speculators bet – and were right – that people would not put up with it and would decide the gain was not worth the pain. The speculators in effect sided with the populace against the politicians.

Michel Camdessus has proposed the IMF create a new lending facility so that it could defend against speculation any currency the exchange rate of which it considered to be basically right. This would require the IMF to have a better understanding of the country's economic fundamentals than the net judgement of the international markets. It would also mean the world's politicians and central bankers ganging up to prevent the speculators rescuing the people again.

If the factors which decide currency values are in line then political arrangements become superfluous. If economies are diverging in their performance then continuing fluctuations in exchange rates, day by day, hour by hour, are a less disruptive and less painful adjustment than measures imposed by governments in an endeavour to bring economies into line. To let business insure itself through the markets is certainly cheaper than to incur the inefficiency of imposing a rigid economic framework.

The benefits of exchange rate stability may be much exaggerated, certainly more theoretical than real.

Depending on how its costs are structured – which fixed, which variable and how they vary – a company may be able to gain more on the swings of extra sales when the exchange rate is favourable than it loses on the roundabouts when the exchange rate is disadvantageous. But managements – reflecting the wishes of investors – would rather settle for consistency but a lower overall return through the economic cycle than a more variable but, in aggregate, greater return. Should they?

If companies wish to hedge the currency risk of their manufacturing operations then they can – and usually do – by the structure of their borrowing in different currencies. The key to avoiding the inefficiency of mislocation is to leave the financial markets free to provide what companies need to obviate exchange rate risk.

*   *   *

Do speculators impel exchange rates, with derivatives giving them extra firepower so that they dictate economic events? There is no evidence to suggest that speculation or the greater volume of dealing generally, have made exchange rates more volatile. Commonsense suggests the opposite: that the more money there is chasing after each such deviation, the smaller will the departure from fundamentals become. The more speculators there are, the less influence any one has.

The sheer scale of speculation, apparently a threat, is itself a safeguard. Speculation so dominates the foreign exchange markets that it must be, on balance, a zero-sum game, with the profit or loss Tom Elliot makes at Nomura, for instance, being balanced by loss or profit collectively elsewhere in the market. Thus, just to stay even they must compete fiercely one with another. With no overall profit to be divided, they have nothing to gain from collusion even if that were practicable among such a dispersed multitude.

When an exporter or importer incurs an exchange rate risk of, say, the dollar value for £100 million in three months' time, the speculators and foreign exchange dealers disburse it not only into smaller sums but also into shorter periods, so that one dealer may hold a dollar risk in perhaps £10 million for an hour before passing it on. For each dealer the size – and, as important, the short duration – makes the risk tolerable. And as transactions pass that risk on throughout the days and weeks, the total amount of dealing will be many times the value of the underlying trade with which it began.

Derivatives do not create risk nor do they increase it. For each futures contract, option or swap there is both a party taking risk in one direction and the counter-party taking the exact opposite risk. It is again a zero-sum game. Derivatives may, however, concentrate and conceal risk.

Whereas the buyers of derivatives may be numerous, a high proportion of the risk on the other side appears to lie with a small number of banks who have often devised sophisticated derivatives. If a bank were to default on its derivative contracts, that would cause considerable damage.

The first safeguard is that the companies trading in swaps and options with that bank should be able to see the danger. Every company publishes a balance sheet so that those who might do business with it can see whether it may be overtrading and would not have enough capital to absorb any loss in the event of a mishap. Bank balance sheets show depositors that their money is safe. It is a solecism that banks should be able to conceal off balance sheet the almost unquantifiable risks they incur in providing exotic derivative instruments over the counter. Banks must be made to show what they are up to.

Allied Lyons and Procter & Gamble suffered severe losses in derivatives not in the normal course of their business but because they diversified from their business of beer and soap into financial trading. Any company should be as free to shed a few hundred million of shareholders' funds like this, as it is in the other misguided diversifications and acquisitions with which corporate history is littered. However, the extra danger from corporate treasurers dabbling in derivatives can arise when they don't know what they're playing with. If a corporate treasurer takes on cocktails of financial instruments, the full effects of which either she or her board do not fully understand, they might accumulate potential losses which would threaten not only the company but the counter-parties to whom it would default.

We do not allow companies to deal negligently with chemicals the mishandling of which would endanger the community. Company law is devised to prevent, or at least deter from, overtrading. There is no reason why we should allow companies to accumulate hidden liabilities which would harm more than themselves. Disclosure is needed here, too.

Disclosure should be enough. The danger here is that over-regulation might reduce the fundamental benefit foreign exchange markets offer: diffusion of risk.

The customers of an insurance company collectively pay premiums which, more or less, are equal to the total amount paid in claims. That's a zero-sum game, too. But each policy-holder thereby secures themselves against what would otherwise be the intolerable cost of an accident, illness or loss. The risks of those mishaps are diffused.

Whether it is a George Soros hedge fund, a corporate treasurer such as James Wrangham of Courtaulds or André Katz in Barclays' dealing room taking positions by the tens of millions for perhaps only a minute or two, the foreign exchange markets are making it easier for the rest of the world to get on with its business.

Index

Serious Creativity

Using the Power of Lateral Thinking to Create New Ideas

Edward de Bono

The lack of fresh, constructive thinking is the vital missing ingredient in the way many businesses and people tackle the problem of the 1990s. With *Serious Creativity*, world-renowned Edward de Bono brings right up to date his landmark concept of lateral thinking, drawing on twenty-five years of practical experience on the deliberate use of creativity.

Creativity is becoming increasingly important for all businesses as competition intensifies, because it is the best and cheapest way to get added value out of existing resources and assets. New concepts are essential for the 'Sur/Petition' that is coming to replace traditional competition. Edward de Bono's *Serious Creativity* has undoubtedly become *the* standard textbook of creativity around the world, demonstrating that his techniques of lateral thinking do work for individuals *and* corporations.

With this step-by-step approach to creativity on demand, creative thinking at last becomes a usable skill instead of a matter of talent, temperament – or just luck.

ISBN 0 00 637958 3

'My Style of Government'
The Thatcher Years

Nicholas Ridley

'The best inside job on the Thatcher years so far'   *Financial Times*

'I always admired her, but it was some time before I really understood the force of her character. It was her immense conviction about the rightness of certain basic ideas which carried through. She had at the same time an acute political understanding of the prides and prejudices of her fellow countrymen, many of which she shared. This combination of knowing instinctively how millions of people in the country would react, together with her iron determination to achieve something, or to stop something, but never to fudge, was all-powerful.'

Enlivened with revealing anecdotes, inside stories and considerable humour, Nicholas Ridley's book is nevertheless hard-hitting on the central issues on which Mrs Thatcher eventually foundered, and assesses candidly those whom she entrusted to carry out her aims, making an important contribution not only to the political history of the past twelve years but also to the debate on future Conservative Party policy.

'Ridley writes with passion and clarity'   *Independent*

'An important contribution to the story of Mrs Thatcher's rise and fall and a magnificent assessment of the Thatcher years'
Norman Tebbit, *Evening Standard*

ISBN 0 00 637822 6

The Official Guide to Success

Tom Hopkins's Own Personal Success Programme

Tom Hopkins

In *The Official Guide to Success*, Tom Hopkins, who made his first million at the age of twenty-seven, makes public his tried and tested motivational and inspirational techniques to help you achieve your goals. Whether you seek money, fame, personal happiness or another kind of success, you can use Tom's practical success formulas to become one of life's winners.

Learn how to:
- Overcome worry and use stress positively
- Increase your image and self-esteem
- Break out of the chains of the past
- Function creatively without a need for the approval of others
- Change negative behaviour patterns and create new success-orientated habits
- Unleash untapped mental and physical energies
- Set priorites and use self-discipline for quality time management
- Get happy and stay happy

ISBN 0 586 06315 3

Harold Wilson

Ben Pimlott

'One of the great political biographies of the century.'
A. N. Wilson, *Evening Standard*

'The rehabilitation of Wilson has begun – and Ben Pimlott, the best British political biographer now writing, has made a hugely impressive job of it . . . His narrative of the young Wilson, from sickly boy scout to academic pupil of the formidable William Beveridge, and then to chirpy junior minister is quite outstanding – clear, thoughtful and gripping. This early part of the book is central to its larger achievement, since Pimlott shocks the reader out of basic anti-Wilson prejudice by demanding a human sympathy for him. The little, blinking, stubborn boy, hiding his hurt with cocky self-confidence, lives on as a permanent presence within the powerful politician . . . Some biographies enter the political discourse at once, thanks to their innate qualities and lucky timing. There are so many echoes of the Wilson years in the politics of today that this happy fate must surely belong to Pimlott's book. Wilson's soured relationship with the press (and the terrible problems it caused for him) – the conflict within him between national leadership and good party management – even the growing debate about national decline – are all suggestive and worth lingering over. As, indeed, are almost all of these 734 well-researched and finely written pages.'   Andrew Marr, *Independent*

'A masterly piece of political writing.'
Bernard Crick, *New Statesman*

'The narrative gallops along, sweeping the reader with it in a rush of excitement. A mass of complex detail is marshalled with the art that conceals art.'   David Marquand, *Times Literary Supplement*

'Fascinating . . . Pimlott the X-ray has produced another work of formidable penetration.'   Roy Jenkins, *Observer*

ISBN 0 00 637955 9

Manage Your Time

Sally Garratt

The Successful Manager series
Edited by Bob Garratt

'The working day just isn't long enough . . . I never have enough time'

This, the distress call of so many managers, is something that can be cured. Solving your time management problems will not only make you more efficient day to day, but it will enable you to plan more effectively for your company's future, and spend more time enjoying your personal life.

Sounds impossible? Sally Garratt, who has run numerous personal-effectiveness courses for managers, shows that it can be done. She examines every area of time management – from the telephone and the 'open door', to the diary and setting priorities. She looks at how you cope with meetings, organize your office, the way you plan ahead and how you give work to your staff (if you give work to your staff!) There is an invaluable section on delegation, with advice on when you should and when you shouldn't delegate.

Practical, realistic, and packed with real-life examples, this book will open the door to more effective management of your time.

'It reminds managers of the things they know they should be doing and rarely do. I recommend it for all managers'
        Michael Bett, President, Institute of Personnel Management

ISBN 0 00 638411 0

Cultures and Organizations

Software of the Mind

Geert Hofstede

The Successful Strategist series

Edited by Bob Garratt

People of other countries, of another generation, social class, job or organization, often think and act in ways that puzzle us. To these people, of course, we are the ones who behave in a surprising manner. What separates them from us is the culture in which either of us grew up. 'Culture' in this sense is not the same as 'civilization'; it encompasses much more. Deeply-rooted and, therefore, often unconscious values lead us to consider as normal what others think abnormal, as polite what to others is rude, and as rational what others find irrational.

Geert Hofstede shows that national cultures differ along five dimensions:

- The degree of integration of individuals within groups
- Differences in the social roles of women versus men
- Ways of dealing with inequality
- The degree of tolerance for the unknown
- The trade-off between long-term and short-term gratification of needs

Organizational cultures, however, are a different phenomenon; they do not follow the same dimensions, are more manageable, and in fact offer an opportunity to bridge national cultures. Following twenty-five years of research into multinational companies, Geert Hofstede reveals the circumstances in which organizational cultures can be managed effectively, and outlines ways of learning intercultural communication which are essential to success in the 1990s and beyond.

'An understanding of our cultures is essential if we are to develop a more stable world and at the same time create national wealth'
Brian Burrows, *Futures Information Associates*

ISBN 0 00 637740 8

☐ MAKING IT HAPPEN: REFLECTIONS ON LEADERSHIP
  John Harvey-Jones   0-00-638341-6 £6.99
☐ MADE IN JAPAN: AKIO MORITA AND SONY Akio Morita 0-00-638342-4 £6.99
☐ ODYSSEY: PEPSI TO APPLE
  John Sculley with John A. Byrne   0-00-638343-2 £6.99

These books are available from your local bookseller or can be ordered direct from the publishers.

To order direct just tick the titles you want and fill in the form below:

Name: _____

Address: _____

_____

_____

Postcode: _____

Send to: HarperCollins Mail Order, Dept 8, HarperCollins*Publishers*, Westerhill Road, Bishopbriggs, Glasgow G64 2QT.

Please enclose a cheque or postal order or your authority to debit your Visa/Access account –

Credit card no: _____

Expiry date: _____

Signature: _____

– to the value of the cover price plus:

UK & BFPO: Add £1.00 for the first and 25p for each additional book ordered.

Overseas orders including Eire, please add £2.95 service charge.

Books will be sent by surface mail but quotes for airmail despatches will be given on request.

24 HOUR TELEPHONE ORDERING SERVICE FOR
ACCESS/VISA CARDHOLDERS –
TEL: GLASGOW 041-772 2281 or LONDON 081-307 4052